Recession, Recovery, and Renewal: Long-Term Nonprofit Strategies for Rapid Economic Change

SUSAN U. RAYMOND, PhD

WILEY

For general information on our other products and services or for technical support, please contact our Customer Care Department within the United States at (800) 762-2974, outside the United States at (317) 572-3993, or fax (317) 572-4002.

Wiley publishes in a variety of print and electronic formats and by print-on-demand. Some material included with standard print versions of this book may not be included in e-books or in print-on-demand. If this book refers to media such as a CD or DVD that is not included in the version you purchased, you may download this material at http://booksupport.wiley.com. For more information about Wiley products, visit www.wiley.com.

Library of Congress Cataloging-in-Publication Data:

Raymond, Susan Ueber.
  Recession, recovery, and renewal : long-term nonprofit strategies for rapid economic change / Susan U. Raymond, PhD.
    pages cm. – (Wiley nonprofit authority)
    Includes index.
    ISBN 978-1-118-38198-4 (hbk.) – ISBN 978-1-118-42072-0 (ePDF) – ISBN 978-1-118-62403-6 (Mobi) – ISBN 978-1-118-41773-7 (ePub) 1. Nonprofit organizations–Planning. 2. Global Financial Crisis, 2008-2009. 3. Strategic planning. I. Title.
    HD2769.15.R396 2013
    658.4'012–dc23

                                                                                                    2012049071

Printed in the United States of America.

10 9 8 7 6 5 4 3 2 1

For Rich and his encouragement, support, patience, and love

Contents

List of Cases

Acknowledgments

The author would like to acknowledge and thank a number of people whose assistance was irreplaceable in developing this book:

- Katherine Becker, Allison Duignan, Nicolas Picard, and Sally Park for their research support.
- Kathleen Sullivan and Kieran Wilson for assistance with case materials and editing.
- My colleagues at various Omnicom agencies for their willingness to participate in the case-writing process.
- Violet Aldaia of LLNS for assistance in developing brand indicators.
- Marjorie Laryea and Albert Insogno for their administrative support.
- Finally and especially, Marie Molese for assistance with all of the myriad details that go into a manuscript.

CHAPTER 1

Introduction

The speed with which the economy unraveled from December 2007 through June 2009 was heart stopping. The lack of speed with which it recovered into 2012 was heart wrenching. It seemed for many months that Samuel Taylor Coleridge's Ancient Mariner had once again returned to tell his tale, with an economy that, like his ship, was becalmed, "as idle as a painted ship/upon a painted ocean."[1]

Virtually no institutions, and precious few individuals, were spared either experience. The 2007–2009 downturn was a recession, not a depression. But the human memory often recalls trauma in Technicolor. For many, therefore, there remains a "depression memory" of a recession. It is likely that the memories of the Great Recession and the certainly-not-so-great recovery will last for a generation. One does not lose 40 percent of one's lifetime savings in six weeks and quickly forget. One does not lose a job and remain unemployed for a year and not remember how fragile life can be.

Looking Back and Its Dangers

This "depression-memory" of a recession, will likely guide the behavior of both institutions and individuals for years to come. For many, that will be a necessity. Having depleted financial resources over 24 or 36 months, a long period of recouping losses lies ahead. Individuals will look forward with great financial caution, aware that any future security will rest with savings and with careful and cautious views about investing. This return to tight purse strings is meritorious in some senses. Savings rates provide important sources of capital to fuel investment.

In some senses, however, this lesson about caution itself provides a self-fulfilling prophecy for weak economic recovery. In the United States, consumption fuels 70 percent of gross domestic product (GDP). Without the propensity of the consumer to buy, the sell side of the table reduces production, delays investment, and cuts back on jobs. The slow cycle of recovery, therefore, can be fed as much by continued memories of the past as by unfolding realities and expectations about the future.

But it is not just individuals with memories of the Great Recession who will shape the future in the near term. Nonprofit and philanthropic institutions that drew down fund balances to cope with unprecedented losses in revenue from asset earnings, governments grants, and individual philanthropy will need years to restore their balance sheets. There will be a natural tendency to look back, to recall the recent past, and to fear extrapolation of that past into the future. Caution can be a good thing. However, just as Federal Reserve Board Chairman Alan Greenspan opined in the midst of the dot-com bubble of the mid-1990s, "irrational exuberance" can most definitely be a bad thing.[2] Learning from the past is a critical element of informed management and effective institutional strategy.

But caution based on the past does not necessarily equate to prosperity in the future, either for individuals or for institutions. Looking back has its own risks. Indeed, in this memory of the past lies the potential for real danger.

Looking Forward and Its Challenges

For the nonprofit sector the lesson that needs to be learned is not how to look back. It is how to look forward.

As will be seen in Chapter 2, a core element that intensified the speed and depth of the Great Recession—highly integrated global markets and economic systems—will drive future decisions. And that integration is going to become even more tightly bound, not simply in terms of markets and commercial institutions, but in terms of global demographics themselves.

Two billion new members of the middle class in emerging economies will drive new types of consumption and alter the geographic focus of commerce. Today's rapid-growth economies will set the pace for change, and that pace will be at lightning speed fueled not by yesterday's Internet, but by new generations of handheld devices that will enable not just information sharing but *content creation* for all types of information sources by all types of people at all social and economic levels—and, equally importantly, in real time.

The economic race will be won by those who innovate first and constantly. Wealth will accumulate for innovators more quickly, and spread more rapidly geographically. Yesterday's backwaters will be tomorrow's economic engines. New generations of corporate leaders will bring new conceptions of relationships to social problem solving. In turn, the line between the commercial and the social, between profit and not-for-profit, between enterprise and social mission will disappear.

The problem for nonprofits, and the philanthropies that support them, is twofold.

First, unlike private commercial institutions, nonprofits and philanthropies have historically operated without the discipline of a market view, without a consequently constant pulse-taking of what people want, and without the taskmaster of price-to-value as an indicator of worth. Without such barometers, how can nonprofits put in place capacities to continually measure and understand change, let alone sort through all the elements of change to identify the parts that matter? How can they choose and assess indicators that will anticipate rapid twists in the road?

Commercial organizations adapt to change because they are actually looking for it, always and everywhere. The business of business is to capitalize on change. Because they are created to meet (and lead) the desires of the market, they build into their very essence the desire to know and understand not just change as it happens, but what change will happen (or what change they could make happen) in the immediate future. Those who are successful at mastering and leading change grow and prosper. Those who are not successful die (or are bought, dismembered, and rebuilt). The nonprofit sector lacks this market orientation, and hence most nonprofit institutions (and the philanthropies that support them) do not have (and do not build) this constant orientation to change.

This first problem promises to become one of the most significant barriers to nonprofit growth and stability in the future, and adapting to it will be one of the most important adjustments that philanthropies and philanthropists must make. It is philanthropy that provides important financial incentives to nonprofits, and hence it is philanthropy that must begin to place a premium value on understanding and mastering constant change. In turn, nonprofits will need to internalize a culture of constant change, looking not inward to what they have done or what an economy has done to them, but rather outward to what the independent forces of change are creating relative to the problems they address, the people they serve, or the issues that form the core of their mission.

The pace and direction of global change documented in Chapters 2 and 3 of this book will wait for no individual, nor will it mark time for any institution.

Second, however, even if nonprofits can access and process the intelligence that predicts change, how can they adapt management, programs, skills, leadership, and governance to take advantage of, rather than suffer through, rapid and constant change? Nonprofits, and the philanthropies that fund them, are focused on being true to mission. Management systems, programs, and technical capacities are all geared to that end. Upheaval in organizational design, skills, programs, human capacity, technology, and governance can all be required to move an institution (funder or nonprofit) from a static view of its operating environment to a view that values constant change. This structural need will prove a challenge for the nonprofit sector at a level of significance that it will be hard to overestimate.

The problems will come together in the most acute way for nonprofit partnerships with private corporations and high-net-worth individuals. It is here that the rapid change in economics, markets, and wealth will create entirely new and constantly changing dictates, expectations, challenges, and, if correctly anticipated, opportunities.

Organization of This Work

The intersection of these two challenges—being constantly oriented to know and anticipate change and building an organization that can manage the consequences—will confront the nonprofit sector as never before.

But one cannot design for situations whose dimensions are unknown. There is much literature about the importance of flexibility and adaptability in this new world. There is also much literature about the challenges posed. However, the nonprofit literature is devoid of quantitative evidence, of the disciplined evidence needed to actually measure the pace of change or provide clarity as to its dimensions. This is certainly true of economics, a subject rarely found in nonprofit literature, but it is also true of such areas as diverse as demographics on the social side and industrial structure on the financing side of the coin. Yet these are fundamental parts of the nonprofit operating environment. There are few concrete facts that provide the strategist or manager with a sense of the depth or breadth of the realities of economic, demographic, and social change; a sense of what indicators actually matter in charting and tracking change; and a sense of what, in fact, those who provide the funds to philanthropies—philanthropists, corporations, and foundations— are likely to do about it. Without evidence, it is impossible to judge the scope or implications of change, or determine appropriate actions, or even to assess the need for action at all.

The purpose of this book is to actually document the nature and levels of current and future economic change, and to derive strategy from facts not from speculation.

Part I sets the stage with an examination of the Great Recession and its effect on government finance, the loci of economic growth, and the likely economic policy path forward.

Part II documents economic and industrial structure and performance over the next two decades, domestically and globally. This section also documents future changes in the loci of wealth, in terms of individuals and institutions. Finally, it quantitatively documents implications of generational change, especially as regards the differing ways in which the next generation of corporate leaders will have been educated, and hence will view their leadership.

Part III looks at the implications for nonprofits of these changes in terms of engagement, governance, partnership expectations, and leadership, with special attention to implications for corporate partnerships and their content and objectives, as well as to the growing value placed on entirely new innovative hybrids that serve social ends with variations on market and commercial metrics and indicators.

Part IV provides a practical guidance for how to establish a system of indicators, and an associated culture of evidence, that can provide the intelligence needed at a rapid enough pace for constantly adjusting to change. This approach, called *fluid discipline,* includes illustrations of critical indicators that can provide managers with an initial dashboard of how to determine when and where organizational adjustment is needed to keep up with (or overtake) the pace of change in the operating environment. Appendix 2 of the book contains a self-administered questionnaire that managers and boards can use to assess the adequacy of their own systems for recognizing and adapting to change.

Throughout the book, a series of concrete, real-life case studies illustrate the ways in which nonprofits and philanthropies have attempted—with and without success—to adapt to and capitalize on change. The "solutions" to these cases are contained in Appendix 1. Authored by agencies of the Omnicom Group, these cases illustrate the use of new skills and new techniques for adapting to change.

Notes

1. Samuel Taylor Coleridge, "The Rime of the Ancient Mariner." First published in *Lyrical Ballads,* 1798.
2. Alan Greenspan, "The Challenge of Central Banking in a Democratic Society." Speech to the American Enterprise Institute, Washington, DC, December 5, 1996.

Recession and Recovery

P rivate philanthropy and the nonprofit organizations through which it acts are expressions of the commitments of individuals to the common good. As such, both philanthropic and nonprofit institutions are extensions of culture and values. But they are not immune to economics. Good times are infinitely easier to navigate than bad times. The Great Recession of 2007–2009 represented bad times indeed. But it also represented a fundamental change in the global economy. Part I traces the origins and consequences of the Great Recession, and sets out the general directions, shifts in economic power, and changing nature of economic leadership that will set the operating environment for nonprofits and the nature of philanthropy for the coming decade.

CHAPTER 2

Cascading Crisis
The Great Recession of 2007–2009

It would not be technically accurate to say that no one saw the crisis coming. In fact, Nouriel Roubini of New York University's Stern School of Business saw in 2005 that housing was approaching speculative levels that could bring the economy down. That same year, Raghuram Rajan of the University of Chicago wrote that the financial system itself was swimming in the deep end of the risk pool and that the system was in danger of collapse. In 2006, *Barron's* magazine warned of an approaching collapse of the housing market.

Overall, however, economists and policy makers continued to mistake exuberance for truth. Sages often portend the future in isolation. The fact is, for most Americans, the 2007–2009 recessionary freight train appeared out of the ether. And it fueled its head of steam from the felled dreams of millions of households.

In September 2007, unemployment was 4.7 percent. In October 2008 it was 6.6 percent, and by December 2008 it was 7.4 percent. A year later, in December 2009, unemployment had risen to 10 percent, the highest rate since the Great Depression, and the percentage of people underemployed, furloughed, involuntarily working part time, or having withdrawn from the labor force approached 20 percent in some states (see Exhibit 2.1).

What made the recession so devastating and persistent was the fact that, because its origins were in the credit and financing system, elements of the economy that normally would have balanced one another in a recession all went into simultaneous free fall. Rather than compensating for weaknesses with strengths, as happened in the 1980–1981 and 2001 recessions, the stock, housing, and labor markets all sank at once.[1]

Between December 2007 and June 2009, real gross domestic product (GDP) fell 3.6 percent. Between November 2008 and April 2010, 39 percent of households in America—nearly two of every five—either experienced a wage

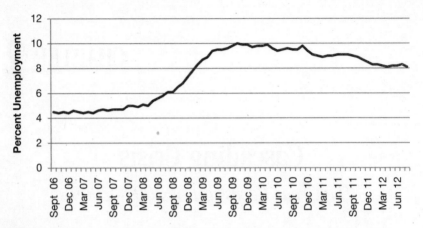

EXHIBIT 2.1 Unemployment Rates September 2006 through September 2012
Source: Bureau of Labor Statistics, Current Population Survey

earner unemployed, had negative equity in their home, or had been in arrears on a home payment.[2]

The Near-Term Roots

Books have been and will continue to be written about the causes and consequences of the Great Recession. This will not be one of them. However, because of its long-term effects, and because it has set the scene for, and indeed is somewhat a product of, the changes to which the world will adjust over the next decade, the event bears a review. It is equally important to understand its nonprofit consequences.

What has come to be called the Great Recession resulted from two immediate causes and a myriad of longer-term conditions.

As the United States emerged from the high-tech bubble and its bursting that led to the 2000–2001 recession, the Federal Reserve Bank lowered interest rates to push money into the economy. The result, in part, was a surge of housing construction and the first breath of wealth surging into a new bubble, this time in housing. The economic adrenaline rush of 2002–2006 was on.

In the immediate term, the 2007 burst of the housing bubble led to the collapse of the real estate market. In turn, this resulted in a collapse of several financial instruments that had been the means for the housing market expansion in the first place. From a deeper and longer perspective, however, the severity of the recession was tied to aggressive innovation in the way in which collateral for loans was "counted" in the mortgage and banking system.

Mortgages are collateralized loans. A loan is made on the basis of the value of the property and the ability to pay the mortgage at the interest rate offered. In 2001, low-income households represented 40 percent of all households but 12.2 percent of total incomes.[3] The average income was $21,639. With policy urging, mortgage requirements were loosened and home buying expanded. The market consequences were predictable. With demand increasing faster than supply, home prices doubled between 1995 and 2005.

The resulting mortgage loosening did not just benefit low-income households. Middle-income families were able to purchase second and vacation homes or refinance to obtain larger mortgages at lower rates and use the capital for home improvements, tuitions, or vacations. That new heated swimming pool was just a few pages of documents away. The tripartite gap between income, housing prices, and mortgage size began to yawn.

With all of the home buying going on, the finance system came up with new ways to move even more money in "affordable" ways. Subprime mortgages, jumbo mortgages, interest-only mortgages—the homeowner had multiple choices for how to cash in on home equity. As prices increased the value of homes, more and more lending could be built on that increased equity, creating spendable cash for consumers through increased borrowing on that equity.

Banks then bundled these mortgages and resold them as collateralized debt obligations (CDOs). These CDOs were then traded (known as credit default swaps, or CDSs) as insurance on the underlying value of the CDOs. The CDSs were insurance contracts to protect against a credit event (e.g., a default). Since the purchaser of the CDS did not have to have a stake in the underlying entity, CDSs became speculative instruments about housing, not insurance mechanisms.[4]

The value of CDOs was based on the presumed value of the properties covered by the mortgages, and the CDSs were valued based on the presumed value of the properties in the bundled mortgages. CDSs were then backed by the value of other CDSs, which were backed by the value of CDOs. So long as property values kept rising, and people paid their mortgages, all would be well with this particular approach to the world.

But all was not to be so well. Debt levels of individual households rose and savings fell. The housing market bubble burst in 2007, and housing prices began to fall. As values fell, homeowners could no longer refinance to access lower interest rates and make mortgages affordable. Variable rate mortgages, with gradually rising rates, pushed mortgage payments up. With falling equity and no savings, homeowners could not pay mortgages.

Moreover, as property values fell, the equity behind CDOs and CDSs also lost value, meaning that these instruments could no longer be traded. Indeed, it meant that it was difficult to even tell how much these financial instruments were worth. Many—though not all—financial institutions in many countries held large numbers of these instruments, which now appeared to have little equity behind them.

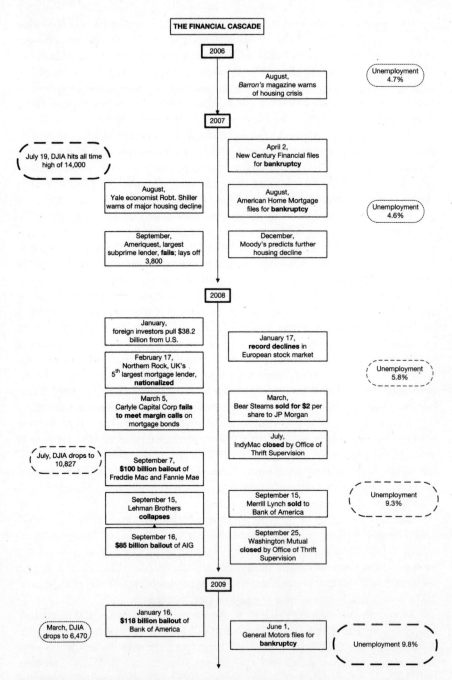

THE FINANCIAL CASCADE

2006

August,
Barron's magazine warns
of housing crisis

Unemployment
4.7%

2007

July 19, DJIA hits all time
high of 14,000

April 2,
New Century Financial files
for **bankruptcy**

August,
Yale economist Robt. Shiller
warns of major housing decline

August,
American Home Mortgage
files for **bankruptcy**

Unemployment
4.6%

September,
Ameriquest, largest
subprime lender, **fails**; lays off
3,800

December,
Moody's predicts further
housing decline

2008

January,
foreign investors pull $38.2
billion from U.S.

January 17,
record declines in
European stock market

February 17,
Northern Rock, UK's
5th largest mortgage lender,
nationalized

Unemployment
5.8%

March 5,
Carlyle Capital Corp **fails
to meet margin calls** on
mortgage bonds

March,
Bear Stearns **sold for $2** per
share to JP Morgan

July,
IndyMac **closed** by Office of
Thrift Supervision

July, DJIA drops to
10,827

September 7,
$100 billion bailout of
Freddie Mac and Fannie Mae

September 15,
Lehman Brothers
collapses

September 15,
Merrill Lynch **sold** to
Bank of America

Unemployment
9.3%

September 16,
$85 billion bailout of AIG

September 25,
Washington Mutual
closed by Office of Thrift
Supervision

2009

January 16,
$118 billion bailout of
Bank of America

March, DJIA
drops to 6,470

June 1,
General Motors files for
bankruptcy

Unemployment 9.8%

EXHIBIT 2.2 Timeline of Critical Events in the Great Recession

The recession actually began in December 2007, fed by the clearly strained housing market and its impact on the overall economy through reduced consumer purchasing and therefore reduced production throughout the economy. But it gathered breathtaking speed because of the deeply compromised value behind the financial assets held by many, many storied financial institutions. As Exhibit 2.2 shows, between March and October 2008, some of the oldest and most respected financial institutions closed their doors, merged, or were bought for pennies on the dollar. Bear Stearns, founded in 1923 and one of the most renowned—and some would say, feared—investment firms in the world was sold for $2.00 a share, and then only with the strong guarantees of the Federal Reserve system, in part because the "toxic" assets on its books could not be valued.

When Lehman Brothers, another global investment bank founded in 1850, collapsed on March 16, 2008, the market was in free fall. More important, credit markets began to freeze. Banks would not lend to one another—let alone to consumers—because no one knew what anything was worth, and no one trusted book values. Trust is at the heart of the financial system, and trust had been tarnished. Once trust had eroded, consumer and financial confidence plunged.

The Length and Depth and Breadth

Since the Second World War, the average recession in the United States has been 10 months. The Great Recession of 2007–2009 lasted 18 months and was the longest and deepest in the United States since 1947. (See Exhibit 2.3.)

In total, $10 trillion in assets were lost in the United States in a matter of months. Globally, that number was $25 trillion. The federal budget deficit soared as the federal government poured resources into rescuing financial institutions. Moreover, the federal government also had to ride to the rescue of

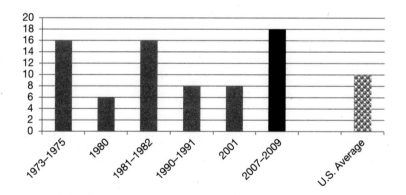

EXHIBIT 2.3 Historical Precedents: Average Months in a Recession

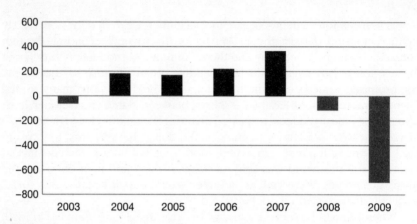

EXHIBIT 2.4 U.S. State Budget Balances, 2003 through 2009 ($Billion)

Source: S. Raymond, S. Park, and J. Simons. *The Public Finance Crisis: Can Philanthropy Shoulder the Burden?* (New York: Changing Our World, Inc., 2011)

the states. In 2006, only four states (South Carolina, Alaska, Mississippi, and Michigan) had unemployment of 6 percent or higher. In May 2011, nearly two years after the end of the recession, 42 states had unemployment of 6 percent or higher—over 10 times as many. As the crisis had unfolded, the bottom had fallen out of state and local budgets as income, sales, and property taxes disappeared. As noted in Exhibit 2.4, three years of budget surpluses were wiped out in just one fiscal year. Because the states are major employers, as well as funders of critical social programs such as Medicaid, federal resources flowed to support of the states.

In January 2007, the federal budget deficit was less than $200 billion. By January 2012, the deficit was $1.48 trillion, and the Congressional Budget Office predicted it would not return to $200 billion before 2020.

The Federal Reserve estimates that from December 2007 to May 2011, with the recession officially over for more than two years but the echoes still reverberating across the economy, consumption forgone in the United States totaled $7,300 per person.[5] In the 1990–1991 recession, it took 23 months for per-capita consumption to return to levels seen prior to the recession. In the 2007–2009 recession, even 42 months after the beginning of the Great Recession, per-capita consumption was still 1.6 percent below prior levels.

The economic effects were exceedingly deep and the recovery exceedingly long. Unemployment in the United States was 4.7 percent in November 2007, the month before the recession hit. Unemployment hit its peak in October 2009 (four months after the end of the recession), topping off at 10.1 percent. The deeper definition of unemployment, which includes all people looking for work, people involuntarily working part time, and people who have given up looking for work, topped 17 percent. Over 8.5 million jobs were lost, and the average duration of unemployment reached levels never before seen in the United States in any previous recession. This is a stunning statement, not simply for its economic importance; it is stunning because the personal and family toll on hopes and aspirations will last, and trust in the stability of the future is put at risk.

Moreover, even as unemployment rates began to fall, the ratio of employment to population did not rise. Growth in population exceeded growth in jobs at the beginning of employment recovery, and hence the fall in unemployment was often difficult to discern at the household level.

The effects were also exceedingly broad. European banks had been deeply involved in the securitization process, and hence the consequences of the disappearance of equity value often were as serious for European banks as they were for U.S. banks. The global financial system was deeply tied together in risk. Financial markets, governments, and households and social structures throughout Europe were part of, and were therefore pulled into, the vortex of the plunge. Levels of debt—private, institutional, and public—exceeded values of assets and levels of income.

But even where that was not true, where banks remained strong, the recessionary repercussions extended into nearly every economy. India's story provides an example of how the errors in one large economy can endanger economies that, in the past world of less globally interconnected trade and finance, might have escaped. That was not the case in the Great Recession. It will not be the case ever again. In this sense, the Great Recession really was different.

The Indian banking system was not at all tied to the subprime mortgage market or to the securitization process that created such an erosion of asset value in Western institutions.[6] Domestic growth had been primarily a result of domestic investment and consumption. But with the integration of trade and investment and the globalization of consumer markets, distance and discipline no longer provide economic immunity. India's merchandise exports plus imports rose from 21.2 percent of gross domestic product (GDP) in 1997–1998 to 34.7 percent in 2007–2008. Capital inflows were over 9 percent of GDP, well in excess of the current account deficit. The Great Recession caused a reduction in the demand for exports, a reduction in foreign investment, a slowing of remittances from migrant workers, and a decline in confidence of India's banking system in the stability of enterprise.

Even though India had been a rapid growth country, even though its economy was large and largely internally driven, even though it was not exposed to the securitization crisis, the recession in the United States and Europe flowed into the Indian economy through trade, foreign exchange volatility, and the global credit freeze.

The Costs in Human and Economic Terms

The costs in human terms were stunning. In the United States, over 8 million jobs were lost. At the height of job loss, 1 in every 10 adults wishing to work could not find a job. Moreover, jobs that were available (and would likely grow with recovery) were not the jobs that many unemployed could win. Construction and manufacturing jobs were lost. Technology, science-based, and engineering jobs were also lost, but these recovered rapidly, as noted in Exhibit 2.5. Indeed, science and engineering unemployment have been as low as 2.5 percent while overall national unemployment was above 9 percent.

Time was a critical factor to the human toll in the Great Recession. The average length of unemployment rose to levels never seen before. On average, those who lost their jobs were out of work for 10 months. The longer a person was jobless, the worse the prospects for getting a job. Moreover, as the recession persisted for an unprecedented period of time, the ranks of those seeking work included not only those who lost their jobs, but three years of young people just entering the job market from high school or college. These new entrants competed with older workers, and the game often when to the young. But even the young felt the pinch. Teenage unemployment exceeded 26 percent in 2009. Not until the spring of 2012, nearly five years after the onset of the recession, did new college graduates face a receptive job market.

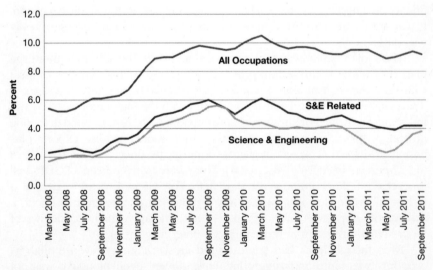

EXHIBIT 2.5 STEM and Overall U3 Unemployment March 2008 through September 2011

Source: 2012 National Science and Engineering Indicators

As jobs were lost and incomes fell, whole neighborhoods were compromised. By the end of 2011, foreclosures represented 28 percent of the entire housing market, a level six times that normally seen. In early 2011, at the prevailing rates of home sales, it would take three years just to clear the market of the 1.9 million properties in some form of foreclosure. Even by the summer of 2012, a third of all mortgage holders owed more than their homes were worth. Neighborhoods with concentrated pockets of foreclosed homes found overall home prices depressed by the presence of foreclosures, further weakening the financial position of even those who managed to stay solvent. Moreover, the effect was often greatest in those neighborhoods where housing prices were weak from the start.[7]

Without the value of an asset, and with compromised credit ratings, people who had once been in the middle class began to fall into the social safety net. And with compromised state funding, that net began to fray. As noted in Exhibit 2.6, for example, enrollment in the Supplemental Nutrition Assistance Program (SNAP), formerly known as food stamps, shot up between 2008 and 2010. In the five-year period 2003 to 2008, approximately 7 million new participants were enrolled in SNAP. In the three-year period 2008 to 2010, that enrollment increase was 12.1 million new participants.

As serious as the Great Recession was in the United States, and as slow and painful as the recovery has been, Europe's woes have been worse in many ways, and indeed have represented an added weight on global recovery. By May 2009, international trade had contracted by 20 percent, a level unprecedented in previous global economic downturns. Because European companies are more export-dependent than their U.S. counterparts, the trade

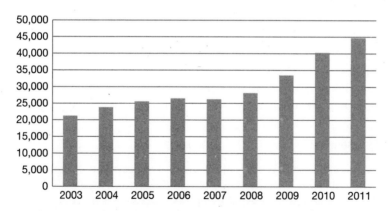

EXHIBIT 2.6 Total SNAP Enrollment 2003 through 2011 (in thousands)
Sources: S. Raymond, S. Park, and J. Simons. *The Public Finance Crisis: Can Philanthropy Shoulder the Burden?* (New York: Changing Our World, Inc., 2011); USDA Food and Nutrition Service Data, www.fns.usda.gov/pd/snapmain.htm

effect was more pronounced. Unemployment rose to near 20 percent in southern-tier countries in Europe. By 2012, 50 percent of young people were without jobs in some European nations. Construction and associated industry jobs fell by 30 to 50 percent in the space of two years. Banks and government sovereign funds had been highly leveraged in the subprime and securitization markets, and the disappearance of those asset values plunged Spain, Italy, Greece, Portugal, and Ireland into financial free fall. By the summer of 2012, the United Kingdom and Spain had fallen back into a double-dip recession.

The European crisis extended into questions about the viability of the euro itself, and weakening of European financial and monetary unity, illustrating the degree to which the tight bonds of global investment, finance, and trade have created a web of economic dependencies in which weaknesses are transmitted across the web and societal consequences are felt far beyond the origins of crisis.

Globalization is not otherness. It is not a matter of foreign markets and foreign policy. It is not "over there." Globalization is, in fact, the reality of the corner of Main and Elm in Anytown, U.S.A.

The Nonprofit and Philanthropic Sector

In the United States, the rate of formation of nonprofits continued even as the economy and giving fell. But the lens of organizational proliferation provides a poor optic of reality. The nonprofit sector would not escape the consequences and was vulnerable on a number of levels.

As previously noted, demand for the programs and services of nonprofits rose markedly. Nonprofit job training programs, food pantries, emergency heating programs, and programs for the aged all saw rapid and significant increase in demand. A national survey of hunger relief organizations in 2008 found that over 90 percent had an increase in demand for food, and 50 percent had actually run out of food. However, resources could not keep up with demand, and private philanthropy could not keep up with the erosion of the public resources that are key to social service provision in many areas.

Private Resources

Despite the extraordinary free fall of the global economy, American philanthropy held its own. Declines occurred, but they were a pale shadow of the overall economic crisis. Overall giving declined by 3.5 percent in 2008 and 6.5 percent in 2009, but in percentage terms, these declines were in keeping with declines in other periods of severe economic challenge. (See Exhibit 2.7.)

As the stock market plunged, the assets of most foundations followed suit. Many foundations pursue the "Yale model" of investing, focusing on very

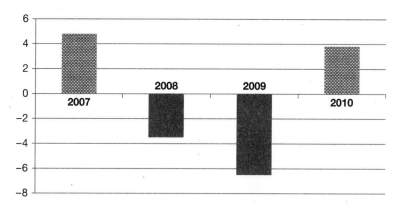

EXHIBIT 2.7 Percent Change in U.S. Giving 2007 through 2010
Source: Giving USA Foundation, Giving USA, 2011

long-term returns. This kept foundation asset losses at levels less than the market average. Still, foundation assets fell by 28 percent in 2008. By the end of 2010, those assets had recovered and were only about 9 percent off their 2007 high of $682 billion.[8]

Foundations reacted differently to the decline. Over a quarter (28 percent) reduced grant budgets, but an equivalent percentage decided to maintain grant-making levels, and 15 percent responded by actually increasing to meet rising needs.[9] Indeed, despite the marked decline in assets, foundation giving in 2008–2009 declined by only 2.7 percent, and by only another 0.2 percent in 2009–2010.[10]

Corporations, whose pretax profits fell by over 10 percent in the third quarter of 2008 alone, focused heavily on demanding clear and measurable impact from donations. Overall, and despite being in the vortex of the economic crisis, corporate giving rose by 11.4 percent in 2008–2009 and by another 10.6 percent in 2009–2010.[11]

In the total period of 2008 through 2010, individual giving, the largest portion of American philanthropy, only decreased by 1 percent. More people were donating because of the economic crisis, digging deep and reaching out to their communities. Large gifts declined (33 percent for gifts over $1 million in the second half of 2009), but more philanthropic engagement by more people helped to compensate.[12]

This resilience of giving can be seen internationally as well. Overall, giving to charity declined by 11 percent, a larger fall than in the United States; 54 percent of adults continued to give, nearly equal to the portion giving to charity in 2006. Indeed, the mean amount per donor in 2008–2009 was larger than in 2006–2007 (£31 versus £29,) while the median remained the same (£10).[13]

Private Resources and the Public Resource Crisis

The real crisis for nonprofits in the Great Recession came not simply from the decline in philanthropy, but also from the decline in government funding. On average, private philanthropy accounts for only about 26 percent of nonprofit revenue. The dependence on private dollars is greater for arts organizations, for example, than for health care, education, and social services because these latter sectors involve more service- or program-related revenue and more funds from the public social safety net.

In a 2011 original study of public funding in the nonprofit sector,[14] Changing Our World, Inc. examined detailed budget data for states that had been severely affected by the recession. That study found that for social, health, and education sectors funded by the state and dominated by nonprofit institutions, philanthropic giving is highly unlikely to be able to compensate for reductions in state funding. In the sample of states examined, public budgets for social services, higher education, public education, and Medicaid fell by a total of $38.5 billion. The question was whether philanthropy in those states could pick up the burden. An examination of giving at the state level, assuming distribution of sector recipients that approximated national proportions, indicated that, in fact, there would need to be as much as a 60 percent increase in philanthropy for the four examined sectors in a single year to make up the difference. (See Exhibit 2.8.)

Looking at the 20-year historical record in those states, there had never been more than a 50 percent increase in household giving in any five-year period (let alone in a single year), and there had been a 22 percent decrease in the 2005 to 2010 period. Hence, significant and lengthy state cutbacks would necessarily have nonprofit funding implications that no reasonable model of philanthropic growth could accommodate.

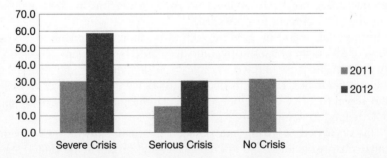

EXHIBIT 2.8 Percent Required Change in Household Giving to Accommodate State Budget Decline

Source: S. Raymond, S. Park, and J. Simons. *The Public Finance Crisis: Can Philanthropy Shoulder the Burden?* (New York: Changing Our World, Inc., 2011)

The Resulting Effects: Emerging Changes in Competition for Nonprofits

Overall, nonprofit organizations lost $3 billion in the value of their assets during the Great Recession.[15] Nevertheless, these assets represented $2.53 trillion in 2009, and had grown 33 percent since 1999.[16] The combination of declines in funds and eroded assets meant that nonprofits, even as they cut expenses, had to reach into dwindling net balances to balance budgets and meet needs. As a result, many nonprofits find themselves in weaker financial condition than before the recession began. The future holds the promise not only of increased demand for services, but the necessity to rebuild the financial base will be critical for many nonprofits.

That being said, the fact is that nonprofit employment grew 2.1 percent in the 2000 to 2010 period, compared to −0.6 percent in the commercial sector, which represented nonprofit job growth in every year of the period, including during recessions.[17] Indeed, in 2008–2009, when jobs in the commercial sector fell by 6.2 percent, nonprofit jobs increased by 1.2 percent.

The resilience of the nonprofit sector is good news for service provision, but it is also good news for the economy. In the future, however, that may say more about the demand for services than it says about any unique role for nonprofits in providing those services. An aging population demands health care services. And a prosperous population demands education. In the period 2007, the increase in employment in for-profit organizations providing those services was actually larger than in nonprofits providing those services.[18] Even within subsectors of those broad rubrics, for-profit service providers grew faster than their nonprofit counterparts. The rate of increase in employment in for-profits was more than twice that of nonprofits in nursing homes (2.9 percent versus 1.3 percent) and nearly twice as high in education (4.5 percent versus 2.3 percent).

As the United States and Europe age and economies become premised on services, commerce will become a counterpart to traditional nonprofits in meeting those service needs, creating a complex, competitive arena for nonprofits as economic growth returns.

Case A: Plunging Resources and Community-Wide Crisis

Author: Ann Davidson, Managing Director, VOX Global

Partner: Crisis Assistance Ministry

CRISIS
ASSISTANCE
MINISTRY

(continued)

(continued)

Situation

For more than 25 years, Crisis Assistance Ministry has served as a safety net for residents around Charlotte, North Carolina, who are facing eviction or loss of utility services due to financial hardship. By providing temporary financial relief for these monthly expenses, thousands of families have been kept from becoming homeless during a time of struggle with employment, health care, or other costly personal challenges. In 2005, under CEO Carol Hardison, the organization undertook a long-term strategic planning process in anticipation of continued pressures on the nonprofit's ability to meet local needs given the growing population trends in the region. The goal was to be able to grow the organization's financial base and cadre of both paid staff and volunteers to serve twice as many clients by 2015.

Stakes

In the winter of 2007, front-line caseworkers reported some unusual patterns. In this once prosperous banking center of the South, people were coming for help because the properties they rented were being put into foreclosure and they did not have money to make the deposit on another apartment or rented home. Members of the community who had worked for years with consistent employment as housekeepers or groundskeepers and in food service were showing up with empty pockets. Before long, families considered "middle class" were arriving, unable to scrape together funds to cover their monthly electric bill.

Similar stories began circulating among other local social service agencies in town. By late 2008, the banking industry that had once been a vital job-growth engine for Charlotte was now at the center of the economic recession, making traditional fundraising challenging. Hardison and her leadership team knew that the execution of the long-term plan to increase funding to meet anticipated demand was going to have to be accelerated. "We didn't want people sleeping in cars, and we didn't want to add to the community's anxiety by suggesting that our own organization could not live up to the promise in our name of assisting those in crisis," Hardison said.

Strengths

While Crisis Assistance had been well respected for its fiscal management and customer-service operation (which also includes a high-quality free store containing furniture and clothing managed largely by volunteers), the rapid and far-reaching economic strains brought heightened visibility to the agency—an opportunity and a risk. Media were regularly arriving at the door looking to report on the growing need.

Crisis Assistance Ministry had worked hard during more prosperous times to build collaborative partnerships with other nonprofits, the business and faith communities, civic organizations, and government leaders. But with all sectors of the economy facing strain, a leadership vacuum impacting the local United Way's ability to serve as a fundraising beacon for social service agencies, and some nonprofits forced to sharply reduce services or even close their doors, could Crisis Assistance survive and thrive? Where would money come from to meet the doubling in daily demand, not to mention the staff to handle the caseload? And how would they compete for scarce dollars with the other social service agencies?

Strategy

By late 2008, as the recession heightened, Crisis Assistance Ministry CEO Carol Hardison appreciated that rushing to the media, government, or corporate leaders crying for help would not lead to solutions but rather pit them against other social service agencies facing similar risks. Instead, she worked with peer organizations to create a complete picture of the wide range of needs including housing, food, health care, and employment. She shared the data with the county manager, who controls the government flow of dollars to nonprofits, and the Foundation for the Carolinas, a philanthropic organization largely supported by higher-income community leaders from diverse sectors of the local economy. Providing these leaders with a comprehensive picture of need would more likely create a comprehensive approach.

"Once we presented our city leaders with the data, we had to have the patience and trust to put the situation in the hands of those who had the resources to collectively address the totality of crisis facing Mecklenburg County, while we figured out how we could handle long lines and packed lobbies," Hardison said. "By early 2009 many of us in the nonprofit sector were at the point of having 'women and children first' days when it came to disbursing aid, which we know was not the way to get families back on their feet permanently." To make matters worse, the city itself was also beginning to suffer a shortfall in project funding available for social services.

With the fundraising responsibility temporarily shifted to the community leaders, Crisis Assistance Ministry focused on preparing team members to take on new tasks. Those who had typically worked in the furniture bank, for example, also learned to be intake managers. The caseworkers implemented a short form to speed the process of data collection, allowing them to see more clients in a day. "We had to sacrifice some of the detailed information we typically collect and even begin conducting group interviews," Hardison explained. While there

(continued)

(continued)

was actually a surge in volunteerism, this also created management challenges, as those new to the agency and its operations had to be trained, organized, and deployed responsibly. Partnerships with other agencies bore fruit as the nonprofit leaders worked to ensure they were not duplicating services and instead coordinating aid to those with multiple needs.

Solution

See Appendix 1.

Notes

1. M. Hurd and S. Rohwedder, "Effects of the Financial Crisis and Great Recession on American Households," RAND Working Paper, WR-810, November 2010, p. 2.
2. Ibid., p. 1.
3. A. Katlov, "The Great Recession of 2008–2009 and Government's Role," *Proceedings of ASBBS,* 18(1) (February 2011): 898–906.
4. D. K. Nanto, "The Global Financial Crisis: Analysis and Policy Implications," Congressional Research Service, CRS Report for Congress, 7-7500, October 2, 2009, pp. 33–34.
5. K. J. Lansing, "Gauging the Impact of the Great Recession," Federal Reserve Bank of San Francisco Economic Letter, July 11, 2011, p. 1.
6. Data for the Indian illustration are taken from "Impact of the Global Financial Crisis on India: Collateral Damage and Response," a speech delivered by Duvvuri Subbarao, Governor of the Reserve Bank of India, at the symposium on "The Global Economic Crisis and Economic Challenges for the Asian Economy in a Changing World," organized by the Institute for International Monetary Affairs in Tokyo, February 18, 2009.
7. J. Schuetz, V. Been, and I. G. Ellen, "Neighboring Effects of Concentrated Mortgage Foreclosures," Working Paper 08-03, Furman Center for Real Estate and Urban Policy, New York University, September 2008, p. 5.
8. *Foundation Growth and Giving Estimates: Current Outlook 2011 Edition* (New York: The Foundation Center, 2011), 5.
9. "Smart Funding in Tough Times: Philanthropic Funding in an Economic Downturn," Credit Suisse White Paper, June 2009, p. 14.
10. Giving USA Foundation, Giving USA, 2011.
11. Ibid.
12. "Smart Funding in Tough Times," p. 16.

13. The Impact of the Recession on Charitable Giving in the UK. Charities Aid Foundation and National Council for Voluntary Organizations, November 2009. 1–2.
14. S. Raymond, S. Park, and J. Simons. *The Public Finance Crisis: Can Philanthropy Shoulder the Burden?* (New York: Changing Our World, Inc., 2011).
15. K. L. Roeger, A. Blackwood, and S. L. Pettijohn. *The Nonprofit Sector in Brief: Public Charities, Giving and Volunteering, 2011* (Washington, DC: The Urban Institute, 2012), 3.
16. Ibid., p. 2.
17. L. M. Salamon, S. W. Sokolowski, and S. L. Geller. "Holding the Fort: Nonprofit Employment during a Decade of Turmoil." Nonprofit Employment Bulletin No. 39, The Johns Hopkins Nonprofit Economic Data Project, Center for Civil Society Institute, Johns Hopkins University, January 2012, p. 5.
18. Ibid., p. 12.

CHAPTER 3

Recovery and Near-Term Economic Prospects

G iven the economic complexity of the upcoming years and the implications of that complexity, not simply for nonprofits but for the dimensions
of the social issues that nonprofit strategy will need to accommodate, it is
important to understand the scope of the problems that still lie before us. One
must first admit that the United States is not the Scythian Empire; we do not
face imminent collapse into the mists of history from a position of global
power. The recovery will take hold, and growth and job creation will pick
up speed. The fundamental assets remain, both human and financial. But, as
this chapter points out—and as will be seen repeatedly in Part III—the
changes that are under way and the challenges that remain will make
the process formidable.

Overall Growth

As noted in Exhibit 3.1, the recovery in the United States has been weak and
erratic. The economy is, as Federal Reserve Chairman Ben Bernanke
described to Congress, "stuck in the mud."[1]

After a relatively strong performance in 2010, growth fell off markedly in
2011 and 2012. Most important, gross domestic product (GDP) growth rarely
exceeded 2.5–3 percent, the necessary level for net job creation. Without that
level of economic growth, persistently high unemployment rates cannot
be addressed.

A weak economy over long periods of time exacts a heavy ultimate
toll. An economy of $15 trillion—such as the United States'—growing at
1.7 percent annually, will be $5 trillion smaller than if it had grown at just over 3
percent. For perspective, $5 trillion is about the current size of the Australian

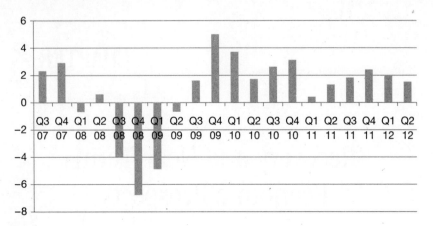

EXHIBIT 3.1 U.S. Quarter-Over-Quarter GDP Growth Rate (Percent)
Source: Bureau of Economic Analysis, U.S. Department of Commerce

economy. So losing that capacity would be like losing the productivity of Australia.

The recovery has been uniquely slow in modern American economic history. The average course of a recession sees the economy growing 12 to 15 percent over its indexed low within 18 quarters of the recession's peak. Within that time period, the U.S. economy has grown by about 2 percent.

The critical issues facing the recovery as of this writing are consumer and business confidence and employment. A weak labor market, high unemployment, and uncertain job prospects suppress consumer spending, which is 70 percent of the economy. That weakness dissuades business. Low incomes and business hesitancy together reduce tax receipts and the cycle continues.

There are, however, signs that the road back, although long, will be traveled in the next two or three years. U.S. equity markets have recovered, and corporate profits are near all-time highs. Housing prices are rising and sales are increasing.[2] The economy is growing, although slowly, and, as measured by the Conference Board Leading Economic Index, producing one step back for every two or three steps forward. Job creation is recovering, although the sheer level of unemployment and underemployment leaves a persistently high unemployment rate.

The critical issue is time. It will likely be 2014 at least before Main Street broadly experiences a stable economic and reliable path forward, assuming there is no further major global economic shock (see the discussion of Europe later in this chapter).

Public Finance

The federal stimulus spending that underpinned the economic rescue of 2008–2009 left behind one of the largest budget deficits in history. The federal budget deficit in 2007, before the recession, was $200 billion. By 2009, just two years later, it was $1.2 trillion, a sixfold increase. Depending on whose projections one wishes to consult, by 2019, that deficit will still be between $800 billion and $1 trillion. The economic and political debates about the consequences of that deficit are intense and divisive, which in and of itself does not help the recovery.

The federal deficit that is running on a parallel track with the recovery is important to the nonprofit sector both because it results in budget reductions that contract payments to nonprofits for service provision, and also because reductions in general social support structures increase, at least temporarily, the demands for privately funded social services. For some nonprofits working in areas directly federally funded (e.g., health care), the prospects of at least a decade of federal belt-tightening within the context of a weak recovery promises to create significant revenue stress.

But for much of the nonprofit sector, the public finance crisis that matters even more is that of state governments and budgets. As noted in Exhibit 3.2 and emphasized in Chapter 2 as well, it took only two years of the recession to wipe out the previous four years of budget surpluses at the state level.

While several states have recovered, especially those with economies strong in natural resources and extractive industries, overall state finances remain fragile and are likely to stay that way for the next several years. By the end of fiscal 2012 (June 30, 2012), 31 states had to address total fiscal 2013

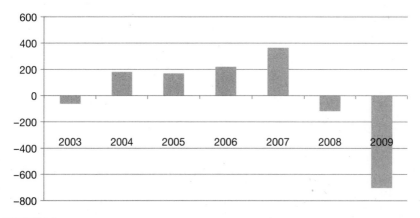

EXHIBIT 3.2 Total Budget Status among U.S. States ($ billions)
Source: S. Raymond, S. Park, and J. Simons. *The Public Finance Crisis: Can Philanthropy Shoulder the Burden?* (New York: Changing Our World, Inc., 2011)

budget gaps of $55 billion, the deficits largely due to continued declines in tax revenues.[3] While this is only half the level of the 2012 deficits, it is larger than the deficits among states prior to the recession.

The prospects for public finance at the state level over the next several years are problematic. Weak revenues will confront increased spending demands in such areas as education, but also in such new areas as health care, where demand for subsidized health insurance through Medicaid will increase as employers cut back benefits to stay afloat and as health care reform places more demands on state management capacity to create insurance exchanges.

At the depths of the recession, the federal government poured money into state budgets to support programs and payrolls as tax receipts plummeted. That money is now spent, and it will likely not be replaced given the size of the federal deficit itself.

Hence, it is almost certainly true that, for most states and hence for many nonprofits (including educational institutions) that rely on state-financed service payments, the recovery is at least two years away and perhaps farther. The Center for Budget and Policy Priorities calculates that the extent of the recession's impact on state budgets has been such that even if state tax revenues grew at the 8.3 percent level experienced in 2011, it would take until fiscal 2019, or a full decade from the beginning of the recovery, to restore the losses from the recession.[4]

Employment and Jobs

As of this writing in the summer 2012, U.S. unemployment remains at 8.3 percent. The deeper unemployment rate, reflecting those who are working part time involuntarily and those who have stopped looking for work, approaches 16 percent. For minorities, the numbers are worse: 10.3 percent for Hispanics and 14.1 percent for blacks. Nearly a quarter of teenagers seeking work are unemployed. Although jobs are being created, the entry of new job seekers into the market (e.g., new college graduates) as well as the inability of older workers to retire given the erosion of pensions, means that unemployment remains persistently high. In January 2012, the U.S. Conference of Mayors predicted that in 80 metropolitan areas across the United States, employment would not recover to its pre-recession peak until at least 2017.[5] That is a jobs recovery that will be eight years after the technical end of the recession.

Moreover, one of the most persistent problems is one of gender. Men were more likely to lose their jobs in the recession and remain less likely to find employment. As a result and as noted in Exhibit 3.3, three years into the recovery, in nearly 40 percent of married households, women earn more than men, nearly double the rate before the recession, and 10 times the rate of 1970.

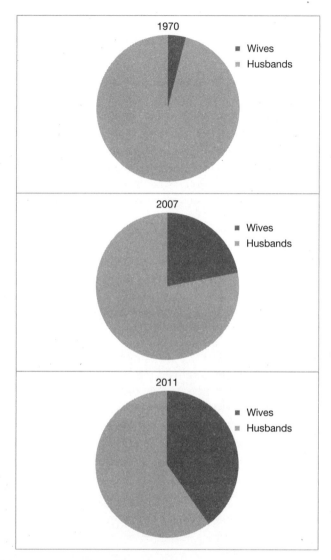

EXHIBIT 3.3 Percentage of Households Where Wives Earn More Than Husbands, 1970, 2007, and 2011
Source: Internal Revenue Service

A detailed study of Massachusetts in 2011 found that the unemployment rate for men remained at 9.2 percent, while the rate for women was 5.9 percent. To get men back to their full-time employment level of 2000 would take the creation of 215,000 jobs for men alone.[6] This employment precipitate from the Great Recession is unlike any experienced in previous recessions. Moreover, it has family and social consequences for which most communities and nonprofit programs are ill prepared. Services for women and children are common. Services focused on men—and especially on men in their prime earning years—are much less common.

This is not to say that women are faring universally well. A 2010 survey of laid-off workers, presented to the American Sociological Association but unpublished as of this writing, indicated that the Great Recession, in addition to being a "he-cession" could also be called a "mom-cession." Separating the data by marital status and parenthood, co-authors Maroto and Serafini found that married mothers, once laid off, had the poorest record of finding new jobs.[7]

The second critically different element of the employment and jobs problem in the recovery is the concentration of long-term unemployment. Since 1992, both in and out of recessions, long-term unemployment (more than 27 weeks—more than 6 months—without work) has never represented more than 23 percent of the ranks of the unemployed. As seen in Exhibit 3.4, by July 2012, these long-term unemployed represented 41 percent of the total number of people seeking jobs.

Those unemployed more than four months represent more than half of the unemployed. This represents three to four million adults whose chances of finding work are exceedingly poor. Furthermore, these are not simply the unskilled. Indeed, those with a college degree are more likely to be found in the ranks of the long-term unemployed. They are not from the manufacturing sector, but from finance, advertising, and the media. These are adults who are increasingly disconnected from the workforce and from the formal working sector.

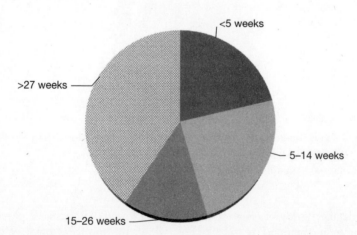

EXHIBIT 3.4 Percent Unemployed by Length of Unemployment, July 2012
Source: Bureau of Labor Statistics

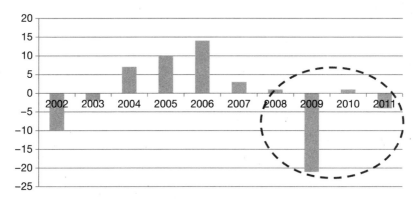

EXHIBIT 3.5 Year-Over-Year Percent Change in Corporate Capital Expenditures
Source: Bureau of the Census

Hence, the recovery increasingly faces a structural rather than a cyclical unemployment problem. Jobs are not lost due to business downturn and return when business improves. Jobs lost during the recession may never return, leaving those unemployed with the need to transition to whole new industries or geographies. Even at its best, this structural unemployment is difficult to absorb. When skills are mismatched and when the housing crisis limits geographic mobility, the result can be arthritic for recovery.

The unemployment aspects of the recovery, then, may take much more than time. And, indeed, for many—especially older men—there may be no employment recovery in the formal economic sector at all. The question of job creation is certainly one of the most central crises for the coming two years.

The other side of the employment problem is, of course, corporate investment. As noted in Exhibit 3.5, capital expenditures remain exceedingly low.

Suppressed consumer spending and uncertainty over federal economic policy have combined to make business hesitant about expansion. At the same time, corporations hold extraordinary levels of cash. In 2009, nonfinancial corporations held $5.13 trillion in liquid assets, equal to the entire U.S. economic output from January through May of that year.

Hence, the longer-term prospects for the recovery are actually good. Some industries, such as the technology sector, have begun to grow robustly. Private investment needed to boost employment has stayed on the sidelines, one of the core reasons for the slowness of the recovery.

Household Incomes

Between 2007 and 2010, the mean American family's net worth dropped 38.8 percent. The collapse of the housing market, described in Chapter 2, was at the

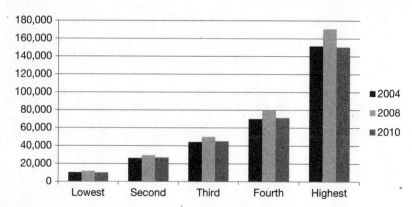

EXHIBIT 3.6 Disposable Median Household Income
Source: Bureau of the Census

core of that loss, along with the sharp decline in the stock market. Family net worth is now at the level of the 1990s, representing two decades of missed asset growth, and boding ill for the disposable income of those nearing retirement as well as for the ability of younger families to purchase illiquid assets such as housing.

Median household income also fell and has yet to recover. Indeed, by 2010, families of all income levels had experienced reduced after-tax income with median disposable income back to their 2004 levels, as noted in Exhibit 3.6.

Indeed, incomes have fallen more during the recovery than during the recession. From December 2007 to June 2009 (the end of the recession), median household income fell 3.2 percent. From June 2009 to June 2011, incomes fell another 6.7 percent.[8]

The story for men is much worse still. In line with the disproportionate unemployment rates experienced by men, male median income in the United States in 2010 was lower than it was in 1968 on an inflation-adjusted basis. This is an extraordinary hollowing out of the labor force and of family earning capacity. Extended periods of unemployment, and the cessation of unemployment benefits for many of the long-term unemployed, will only compound this problem for the recovery.

An additional recession and recovery phenomenon also poses a challenge. Faced with unemployment and poor job prospects, and having gone through savings, many of the Baby Boomer generation decided to opt into their social security benefits. Only 17 percent of Baby Boomers have a traditional pension, compared to 39 percent in 1980. During the recession, 25 percent of Boomers depleted their savings, and a full three quarters of those opting to retire did so at the earliest time allowed by Social Security eligibility. This means, in turn, that those three quarters have locked themselves into the

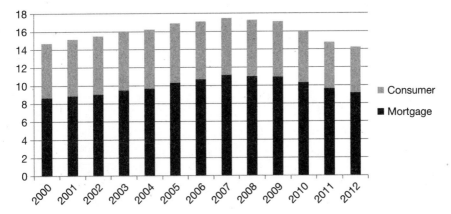

EXHIBIT 3.7 Household Debt Service Payments as a Percentage of Personal Disposable Income (Q1 for each year 2000 through 2012)

Source: Federal Reserve System, 2012

lowest income support bracket of the Social Security system, seriously affecting their long-term household income potential.

There is, however, at least one piece of household income good news. American households have begun to reduce their debt. As noted in Exhibit 3.7, after reaching nearly 18 percent of personal disposable income in 2007, household debt is now at its lowest levels since 2000.

In part, the debt reduction is a function of mortgage payment contraction, as fewer and fewer Americans own their own home. But it appears also to be a concerted effort to learn from the pre-recession consumption binge—a fact that could help the recovery over the long term.

Europe and Asia

The extraordinary events in the Eurozone have been, and may continue to be, a significant drag on the U.S. recovery. It is hard to know where to begin. Greece's flirtation with default and exit from the euro; Ireland's economic collapse; Spain's crushing debt levels, even though it is the fourth-largest economy in the 17-nation Eurozone; murmurings about Italy's economic stability; and Britain's entry into a double-dip recession all served to further contract Europe's economy, taken as a whole the largest in the world. As noted in Exhibit 3.8, the euro area came sharply out of the deep recession, but faltered and returned to just over 1 percent growth in 2011.

At no time in the recovery did GDP growth approach 3 percent, the level needed for job creation, and thus unemployment remained at 10.9 percent in the region, up from 10.1 percent in 2010. By mid-2012, nearly 25 percent of

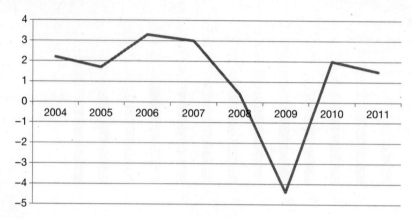

EXHIBIT 3.8 Euro Area Year-Over-Year GDP Growth (Percent)
Source: Central Bank of the Eurosystem

Spaniards were unemployed, as were 22 percent of Greeks. And nearly 50 percent of young people in those two nations were unemployed. The prospects for Europe-wide recovery in the next several years are hence sobering. By mid-2012, even Germany was beginning to feel the pinch as its export-driven economy stuttered with declining foreign demand.

The result of crisis management of the deficits in the southern part of the euro area has resulted in rising debt-to-GDP ratios. As noted in Exhibit 3.9, the total area has nearly a 90 percent ratio of debt to its economic production.

Portugal, Greece, Ireland, Spain, and Italy were all underwater three years after the global recovery from the Great Recession had begun.

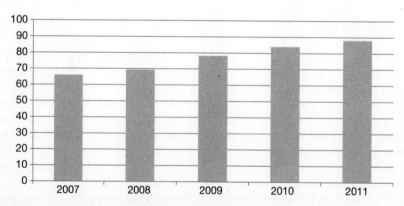

EXHIBIT 3.9 Euro Area Debt as a Percentage of GDP
Source: Central Bank of the Eurosystem

The euro is an irrevocable currency by treaty. Unlike membership in the European Union, which allows for a two-year exit for those wishing to leave the political structure, euro area nations signed a permanent treaty with no escape clause. Individual nations gave up control of their currency, but not of their budgets. Managing the fiscal (budget) problems of member nations (a matter not subject to treaty) using joint monetary tools has proved nearly impossible. Europe is at an inflection point at which some agreement on fiscal policy within the monetary union will be needed if deficit crises of individual nations are to be put to rest and Europe is to return to economic growth. But that will not happen in the near term.

And as the world's largest unified economy faltered, and the U.S. recovery sputtered in neutral gear, China and India began to feel the effects. By mid-2012, both continued to grow at more than a healthy 6 to 7 percent rate, but investment was flat and foreigners were pulling money from the stock market. In the 2012 fiscal year, only $16 billion flowed to Indian stocks and bonds compared to $30 billion the year before.[9]

Similarly, by mid-2012, China's economy had slowed to 7 percent growth for the second quarter, the slowest growth since early 2009. In part a result of Chinese policy tapping the economic brakes, the slowing was also a result of the softness in China's largest markets: North America and Europe. As will be noted in Chapter 6, both China and India are increasingly tied to markets outside of the traditional industrial economies, but the latter still represent the majority of their export markets and are the source of the majority of their foreign investors.

The prolonged recovery has taken its toll not just in the United States and Europe but across the globe.

Summary and Implications

The recovery from the Great Recession has been the nonprofit sector's perfect storm.

Three years into the recovery, most economic indicators are registering sluggish progress at best. Uncertainty reigns.

Some nonprofits have seen fundraising return to pre-recession levels. Yet while giving overall is once again growing, the typical and historical post-recession bounce-back has been soft, with 2011 showing only a bit over 1 percent in growth over 2010. Endowment and fund balances have recovered thanks to a rebounding stock market, but even that market displays tremendous volatility. Indeed, the ability to diversify those investments is highly compromised by a global financial system that lacks stability and the inability to trust that the United States would be able to come to the rescue of financial markets in another crisis.[10]

Public budgets remain under extreme stress. The ability of governments at all levels to fund nonprofit services of all types remains compromised. State tax receipts are down, costs are up, and budget balancing means further cutbacks without the likelihood of federal relief. Furthermore, the unfunded pension commitments of state governments approached $1 trillion across the United States, with only four states having fully funded pension systems.[11] Program funding from public sources in all nonprofit sectors remains under pressure.

Unemployment remains at historic highs, and discretionary household incomes are not growing. The ability of people to allocate smaller and smaller discretionary incomes to charitable giving is also under stress. The prospects for rapid employment recovery are dim, and the new generation of retirees has less of an asset base and less income flow that the generation before.

Corporate profits are up, and many companies are awash in cash. But those resources exist not because their markets for goods and services are robust. They exist because uncertainty about future economic growth and policy directions results in a consequent unwillingness to invest. During the Great Recession, corporate giving held up better than virtually any other category, but the willingness to expand those commitments is deeply affected by the caution associated with compromised consumer spending.

For internationally oriented nonprofits, and those in Europe itself, the story in Europe could not be more disturbing. The Great Recession has led to a recovery (of sorts and in some places) that is akin to a second recession. Public funding sources are shrinking, and high (nearly unprecedented) levels of unemployment are eroding the numbers of people donating to charity and the levels of that giving.

There is good news in Asia, where wealth continues to build and formal philanthropy as well as more informal individual giving is growing. Time will be the issue. If the United States and Europe do not rebound more strongly, even Asia's strength will be compromised.

In many parts of the United States, and for many individuals and industries, the recovery does not feel like a recovery at all. Where that is a fact, there is a deep weakening of the capacity to give. Where that may not be a fact, but it is an abiding perception, there is deep uncertainty and an willingness to commit resources in the near term of charitable or social undertakings.

For the nonprofit and philanthropic sectors, therefore, the critical challenge for the coming five years is revenue strategy. That strategy must be based on:

- A clear-eyed understanding of the nature of changes (economic, social, demographic) in the operating environment that are material, or could be material, to the organization.
- A frank assessment of vulnerabilities within an organization based on those changes.

- The creative design of options to take advantage of emerging opportunities, or to transform change and vulnerability into opportunity.
- Purposeful business planning to convert that understanding into concrete action.
- The correct management skills to execute the plan.

Nonprofits can no longer simply sail into the future with fixed charts and assumptions about the promise of fair winds tomorrow. The Great Recession, its root causes, and the fundamentally changed economic prospects of the next several years will exact a dear price from those who do not proactively take regular soundings of the sea level, keenly study new maritime charts, and keep a lookout in the crow's nest day and night to warn of emerging problems or identify new opportunities on the horizon.

Part II, which follows, examines the fundamental changes in the operating environment of the global nonprofit sector; Part III discusses the specific implications of those changes for nonprofits in terms of both challenges and opportunities.

Case B: Private Resource Strategies for the Long Haul

Author: maslansky+partners

Partner: National Head Start Association

NATIONAL HEAD START ASSOCIATION

Situation

In 2010, demand for Head Start's early childhood education already outstripped available spots. Without a budget increase, more children would have been at risk of falling behind. But ever since the financial collapse of 2008 forced a national scrutiny of federal spending, public programs have been under constant pressure to cut costs and prove their worth.

(continued)

(continued)

In July 2010, *USA Today* published a scathing editorial questioning Head Start's efficacy and demanding that the federal government "fix Head Start before throwing more money at it." And as 2010—with its midterm election upheaval—ticked over into 2011, a new wave of cost cutters swept into Washington with a public mandate to strike billions from federal budgets. President Obama's proposed budget included a $989 million increase for Head Start, but it was coming under much fire, with Head Start named by Republicans as a program in line for a cut, not an increase.

If it wanted to thrive, Head Start needed an argument that would work with the right-wing tax cutter as well as the well-meaning liberal.

Stakes

Congress needed to find programs to cut. Head Start communicators naturally spoke from the heart to convey the mission of their organization. But language from the heart wasn't working across party lines. Objections to Head Start were never about its mission but about its effectiveness. Those eager to cut Head Start funding believed the money was being wasted. To them, the problem was real, but Head Start's solution wasn't.

Strengths

The cause has a number of strengths historically helping it to secure funding. No one believes Head Start employees signed on to get rich. Everyone knows they genuinely want to help kids. And what's more, everyone—Republican or Democrat—understands the importance of education, both to individuals and to the nation.

Strategy

In 2010, Head Start called on maslansky+partners (m+p) to examine the language of the education debate and craft a new lexicon that could circumvent the political posturing going on in Washington.

m+p believed Head Start needed language to explain the program and its goals and achievements that appealed not just to the left or the right, but to everyone regardless of their political leaning. Head Start's arguments had always inspired internal audiences and a supportive base, but they'd previously been able to ignore conservatives and moderates who had now become so crucial.

Using Instant Response dials, m+p and Head Start explored the gut reactions of people from across the political spectrum to find out which words, phrases, and arguments about education really resonated.

Solution

See Appendix 1.

Notes

1. Testimony of Ben Bernanke, chairman of the Federal Reserve Bank, to the Senate Banking Committee, July 17, 2012.
2. B. Appelbaum, "Housing Market Sending Signals It Is Recovering," *New York Times,* June 28, 2012, p. A1.
3. P. Oliff, C. Mai, and V. Palacios, "States Continue to Feel Recession's Impact." Center on Budget and Policy Priorities, June 2012, p. 2.
4. Ibid., p. 10.
5. *U.S. Metro Economics: 2012 Employment Forecast* (Washington, DC: U.S. Conference of Mayors, January 2012), 4.
6. A. M. Sum, I. Khatiwada, J. McLaughlin, M. Trubskyy, and S. Palma, *Recapturing the American Dream: Meeting the Challenges of the Bay State's Lost Decade* (Boston: MassINC., 2011), 14.
7. M. Maroto and B. Serafini, Unpublished paper presented to the American Sociological Association, August 2012.
8. G. Green and J. Code, "Household Income Trends during the Recession and Recovery." Report from Sentier Research, October 10, 2011.
9. J. Yardley and V. Bajaj, "India's Economy Slows with Global Implications," *New York Times,* May 30, 2012, pp. A1, A3.
10. For a sobering review of market alternatives in 2012, see the views of Vanguard founder John C. Bogle, in J. Sommer, "A Mutual Fund Master, Too Worried to Rest," *New York Times,* August 12, 2012, p. B1.
11. "The Widening Gap," Pew Center on the States, 2010, p. 10.

Global Economic Change

U nderpinning and flowing from economic change, fundamental changes in the nature of philanthropy are also under way. The locus of wealth is changing. The coming decades will see major changes in demography, communications, and organizational leadership. A generational shift will take place, and the next generation will come to the fore with entirely different experiences and ideas than the Baby Boomers. These changes will result, indeed are already resulting, in entirely new definitions of "philanthropy," which is becoming akin to social finance. An arc of innovation is emerging that does not displace charity but actually evolves charity into an approach to finance that ties social problem solving to new sources of capital in ways that create sustainability, but also the need for financial accountability. This change creates huge opportunities for nonprofits.

CHAPTER 4

A Multipolar Global Economy

The economic changes that preceded the Great Recession, and that have intensified since 2009, reflect and have reinforced a number of deeper structural adjustments that will determine the future directions of the global economy. In turn, these will set the context within which current nonprofit and philanthropic efforts will take place and will provide the fuel for the growth of philanthropy and for the emergence of new nonprofit and blended commercial-nonprofit institutions in the future.

A single chapter cannot detail every dimension of this change. The central point to be conveyed is that the adjustments within the global economy are irreversible. The pace may speed up or slacken. There may be one step backward for every two forward. There will be cycles and switchback curves. But the direction is clear. The global economy is now multipolar, with centers of comparable economic capacity scattered around the globe and with greater capacity now building in places that once were subjects of humanitarian relief. There is a convergence afoot between the "developed" nations and the "developing" or "emerging" nations. Indeed, these terms increasingly have little meaning except at the extremes of war and poverty.

This is not to say that poverty has disappeared from life, nor that the Alfa Romeo market has decided that market growth is on Main Street. It is to say that, as will be noted in later chapters, the emergence of a multipolar global economy has changed the foci of economic growth and altered the nature and dimensions of social problems as well as the capacity to address them.

To illustrate the breadth and depth of these changes, but certainly not to exhaust their dimensions, this chapter will examine five elements of change:

- Overall economic performance
- The rising middle class
- Industrial structure change
- Capital integration
- Trade patterns

Economic Performance

The most striking element of projections for the global economy for the next decade is the degree to which overall economic growth will be led by Asia and Latin America. Indeed, the nations of Asia, Latin America, and Africa went into the recession later, experienced shallower downturns, and came out earlier than the United States and Europe. As noted in Chapter 2, it is true that no nation was able to erect a perfect buffer to the financial crisis. Even nations with limited exposure to the global credit crisis were weakened. But the return to economic performance has been faster in the emerging and rapidly developing economies.

The International Monetary Fund estimates that between 2010 and 2011, the nations that grew at or below 3 percent (the level needed to create new jobs) were nearly all in Europe and North America. The nations that grew above 5 percent in that period were all in Africa, Asia, and (in part) South America. Indeed, Goldman Sachs no longer uses the term *emerging markets,* believing that the likes of China, Brazil, and Russia have, in fact, emerged. Rather, they are termed *growth markets.*[1] (See Exhibit 4.1.)

This is not to say the United States will not grow and that, as seen in Chapter 3, the economy will not continue to create jobs and wealth. It is to say

Non-OECD country	Global Competitiveness Rankings (Rank 11–30)		
2004	**2006**	**2008**	**2011**
Rank 11 United Kingdom	Hong Kong SAR	Hong Kong SAR	Hong Kong SAR
Netherlands	Norway	United Kingdom	Canada
Germany	Taiwan	South Korea	Taiwan
Australia	Iceland	Austria	Qatar
Canada	Israel	Norway	Belgium
United Arab Emirates	Canada	France	Norway
Austria	Austria	Taiwan	Saudi Arabia
New Zealand	France	Australia	France
Israel	Australia	Belgium	Austria
Estonia	Belgium	Iceland	Australia
Hong Kong SAR	Ireland	Malaysia	Malaysia
Chile	Luxembourg	Ireland	Israel
Spain	New Zealand	Israel	Luxembourg
Portugal	South Korea	New Zealand	South Korea
Belgium	Estonia	Luxembourg	New Zealand
Luxembourg	Malaysia	Qatar	China
France	Chile	Saudi Arabia	United Arab Emirates
Bahrain	Spain	Chile	Brunei Darussalam
South Korea	Czech Republic	Spain	Ireland
Rank 30 Ireland	Tunisia	China	Iceland

EXHIBIT 4.1 Relative Levels of Economic Growth around the World

that, unlike in the past, it is not simply Europe and the United States that will fuel growth; it is not simply Western capital that will power the global economic machine.

As will be noted throughout this and later chapters, the multipolar nature of the economy will have great implications for the nonprofit and philanthropic sectors. This is not simply a matter of where wealth will be and how problems will change, although, as we will see, these are critical elements of global realignment. It is also a matter of the line of sight of economic leaders in communities. All lines of sight will be global, just as the lines of sight of economic leaders in other nations will be global.

In turn, this will mean that the priorities and cultures that will influence problem solving, including philanthropy, will not simply be those of the West. Indeed, as global economic growth becomes driven by new economic actors, it is the views and experiences of those leaders that will hold sway in global institutions, as we have already begun to see in the 2011 debates about leadership at the World Bank. The perceptions and views of other cultures and histories will be at the global economic decision-making table. Those leaders will share the nearly universal view of the benefits of open societies and open markets, but how that common value is expressed in economic policy and priorities will be affected by the diversity of leadership likely come to the fore as new economies grow rapidly in their global role.

The Global Middle Class

By 2030, less than 20 years from now, 2 billion people will join the global middle class.[2] The middle class will then represent 30 percent of the world's population, and 40 percent of the world's incomes, an increase that will dwarf the lost major middle-class explosion in the nineteenth century.

China, of course, provides a striking illustration of the effect, as noted in Exhibit 4.2.

Between 2009 and 2030, the poor will decline from nearly 90 percent to less than 30 percent of China's population. The middle class will rise from being just over 10 percent to being 60 percent of the population. But the middle-class effect will not just be in China. India, Egypt, the Philippines, Mexico, Brazil, and Indonesia will see rapid expansion of their middle classes. Even Africa will experience an expansion of its population entering the global consumption market. This does not, of course, mean that poverty will disappear any more than it has disappeared anywhere else in the world. Rather, the domestic capacity of countries to power their own economies and consequently address their own internal problems in their own ways will rise.

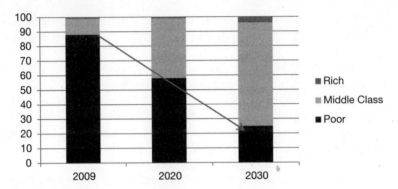

EXHIBIT 4.2 Wealth Distribution of China's Population 2009 through 2030

Source: Homi Karas and Geoffrey Gertz. The New Global Middle Class: A Cross-Over from West to East. In Cheng Li, ed. *China's Emerging Middle Class: Beyond Economic Transformation.* Washington, DC: Brookings Institution Press, 2010

This middle class will power global economic growth and strengthen the industrial and service production sectors in these economies. By 2030, the Asia Pacific region will represent 59 percent of global middle-class consumption, compared to 10 percent for North America and 20 percent in Europe. In turn, then, the eyes of corporations of all types, locales, and sizes will turn to world markets.

The philanthropic implications are twofold. First, this new middle-class expansion, largely occurring within increasingly open societies with emerging nonprofit sectors serving social need, could be the harbinger of a new age of engagement by individuals in structured philanthropic support of local needs. Even now, of course, charity is a part of every culture. But with a rising middle class with discretionary income, the presence of nonprofit structure within society will enable fundraising of all types in support of needs.

Second, the focus of corporate philanthropy and social engagement will be in these new markets attuned to their views and their priorities. The global focus is happening even now, but the sheer numbers and purchasing power of the new middle class outside of North America and Europe will refocus the concerns of firms domiciled in these nations on the social needs, preferences, and causes of these new markets.

Industrial Structural Change

Global industrial structure will also change, beginning more and more to resemble that of the United States. The process will be gradual, but it will be relatively common across global geography. Even now, nations that have

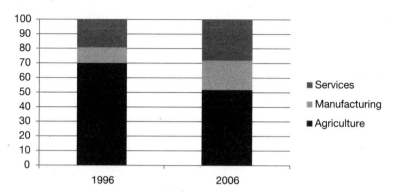

EXHIBIT 4.3 Vietnam's Changing Economic Structure
Source: World Bank Global Indicators

traditionally been thought of as agricultural economies are dominantly industrial. Exhibit 4.3 illustrates this point with Vietnam, but it is true of most
economies. Extractive industries, manufacturing, and even many service industries are a growing, often dominant part of rapidly growing economies.[3]

In some industries, that process has picked up steam since the recession. Steel manufacturing presents an example. Growth in India and China,
which helped to lead the way out of the recession, also created increased
demand for steel. By 2011, steel production was rising, but the global
distribution of its production had changed. In only five years, Asian production (including that of Australia) had risen from half to nearly two thirds
of global production, and U.S. production had fallen from 9 percent to
6 percent. See Exhibit 4.4.

The story will be similar for other primary resource and production
capacities. In the next two decades, nearly 90 percent of the new resource
development in oil and gas will take place in emerging and developing

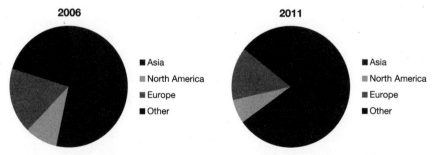

EXHIBIT 4.4 Global Distribution of World Steel Production 2006 and 2011
Source: World Steel Council

economies. Africa will be prime among these foci; indeed, in the post-recession period, three quarters of the globally financed extractive industry deals took place in Africa.

These patterns will increasingly tie global economies together, create new centers of wealth around the world, and change the types of locations of economic leaders who are vested in, and can be mobilized to address, the complex sustainability problems associated with new economic growth and economic expectations in new places.

Capital Integration

As noted in Chapter 2, it was the integration of the financial markets, and their interdependence on mortgage-backed securities, that helped to power the speed of the financial collapse in 2008. While that particular episode is behind us, the integration of capital markets inevitably continues. This provides a huge boost to global economic growth because capital can find opportunity regardless of geographic boundaries.

There are now 237 stock exchanges located in 114 countries around the world. This represents nearly a quadrupling of exchanges in the past decade. They are also increasingly linked. The New York Stock Exchange is now officially the NYSE-Euronext, a European-American entity. Of its 2,433 listed companies, 40 percent are domiciled outside the United States.

Indeed, while the U.S. exchanges account for by far the largest amount of capital and the largest international companies, the total numbers of private companies listed on stock exchanges—and therefore vested in private capital from private investors—are much, much larger in other regions. Indeed, the number of companies listed on the Hong Kong exchange more than doubled in the single decade 2000 to 2010. As noted in Exhibit 4.5, the portion of total listings on the U.S. exchanges has fallen markedly.

It is not just that capital is flowing globally; it is that the numbers of individuals who have a stake in corporate engagement in the global and local economies has grown significantly. There are more people who care about corporate performance around the world, more at stake for these people, and hence more concern over the roles of private capital and private corporations not just in economies but in communities.

The pace of growth of this capital capacity in emerging economic power-houses is striking. The Asia-Pacific region has nearly doubled its share of global market capitalization. The percentage of capital raised through new public offerings of private companies on the world's stock exchanges has heavily shifted toward the Asia region. As noted in Exhibit 4.6, nearly half of the initial public offering (IPO) capital raised globally was raised in the Asia

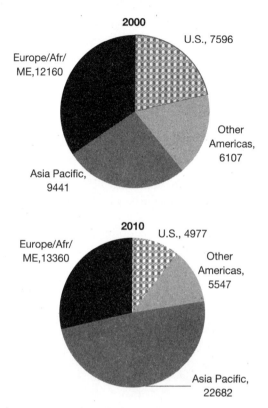

EXHIBIT 4.5 Number of Companies Listed on Stock Exchanges 2000 and 2010
Source: World Exchange Federation, 2011

Pacific region, nearly double the percentage just five years ago. The level of growth and the pace of change have been stunning.

This does not, of course, imply that capital markets and investment capacity in the United States is not important and growing—only that the line of sight of American investors is totally global, and they are joined on

EXHIBIT 4.6 IPO Capital Raised by Region 2005 and 2011 (%)
Source: Ernst & Young

that playing field by investors of all nationalities through all manner of investment exchanges powering private corporations and private business leadership from every corner of the globe. Chapter 8 will return to this theme in examining the consequent changing patterns of wealth around the world.

Trade and Business Patterns

Three decades ago, trade represented 36 percent of the global economy. Today, that has risen to 56 percent. While global trade fell during the Great Recession, and slowed again in the 2011–2012 period in response to the euro crisis and the tepid recovery in the United States, longer-term estimates see the inevitability of rapidly expanding trade as emerging economies diversify and as demand for advanced goods rises with rising middle-class incomes. The strengthening trend toward a multipolar global economy will pull nations together via trade with greater and greater strength. It will be difficult to untangle the corporate and consumer interests of nations from one another, and therefore it will be similarly difficult to make distinctions among local, national, and international issues and problems and hence difficult to isolate resource commitments to those problems simply by geography.

As is true in much of the rest of the global economic structure, emerging market economies will lead tomorrow's trade growth. While developed nations will still represent the largest share of global trade by volume over the next decade, the rate of growth in trade will be highest for emerging economies including not just India, Brazil, and China, but also nations of Eastern Europe.[4] As will be noted in Chapter 6, however, the pattern that is emerging is one of much greater economic interchange between economies outside of North America and Europe rather than between these economies and those of the traditional "developed" world. Trade is the tie that binds economies, but open trade has also been a critical factor—some would say the critical factor in the past 20 years—in powering the growth of the emerging and high-growth economies and hence creating the multipolar global economy.

Foreign direct investment (FDI) is also an integrating tool. And FDI is an increasing power behind economic growth.

Perspective is important. In 1980, only about 30 years ago, the total world stock of foreign direct investment was $500 billion. There was no multinational investment in China and virtually none in India.[5] Today, FDI totals nearly $2 trillion, and developing and transition economies represent half of the inflows and nearly a third of the outflows, the latter being a surprising measure of the strength of private corporate capital seeking investment opportunity that

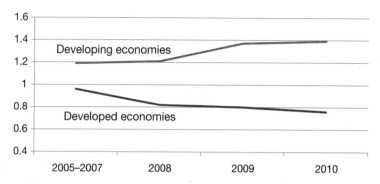

EXHIBIT 4.7 Inward Foreign Direct Investment Performance 2001 through 2010
Source: United Nations Conference on Trade and Development (UNCTAD)

originates in emerging economies. China now enjoys nearly $100 billion of annual FDI inflows and India another $40 billion.[6]

As noted in Exhibit 4.7, since the beginning of the Great Recession, developing economies have accounted for an increasing portion of FDI relative to their economic size. This is consistent with the globalization of the business line of sight relative to economic opportunity.

Again, the pattern is the emergence of a multipolar global economy with corporate and financial strength emanating from a number of nations, and the flow of resources and capacity washing across boundaries. As this takes place, the corporate market, irrespective of where that corporation is domiciled, will be anywhere and everywhere. Since the early 2000s, with a one-year decline in 2008–2009, the sales of foreign affiliates of multinational corporations have soared, nearly doubling in just the last eight years. IBM expects to earn 30 percent of its total revenues from its foreign affiliates in emerging markets alone by 2015. At Unilever, the figure is already at 56 percent.[7] In 1980, over 80 percent of Deutsche Bank's revenues were earned in Germany. In the 1990s, that was still 70 percent. Today, the portion derived from Germany is 38 percent.[8]

With the growth of the global middle class and the expansion of demand and disposable income, such trends are likely to pick up steam in the coming decade.

Again, in a multipolar, integrated global economy, the corporate line of sight, and in many ways the line of sight of public policy, will be along the lines of linkage that tie products and services to multiple markets around the world. This lack of a sense of place, further discussed in Chapter 12, will create leaders who think in terms of social issues that are not tied to a particular setting, and who act on priorities in multiple geographic venues. As Carlos Ghosn, CEO of Renault-Nissan (interestingly, Brazilian born, of Lebanese origin, and a French citizen leading a French-Japanese company) has remarked. "Leaders of the future will also need to have a lot more empathy and sensitivity, not just for people in their own countries but for people from completely different countries and cultures."[9]

Summary and Implications

The global economy, and hence leadership and problem definition, are now multipolar in terms of nodes of economic power, yet highly intertwined. This represents an economic neural system, with clear nodes and synapses, allowing the fast-paced travel of goods, services, finance, and innovation along the nerve system, carrying economic messages and growth among those nodes. It will be increasingly difficult to isolate wealth, capacity, leadership, and societal issues within a single nation or a single economy.

Nonprofits seeking to engage leaders in their work will find that they must relate their work to those multipolar, highly integrated, highly dynamic global institutions. They will not simply be institutions headquartered in the once-called "developed" world of the West. They will be institutions and leaders of many cultures and many societal persuasions. Moreover, they will also be ordinary individuals—the middle class—representing these many cultures and persuasions as well.

On the one hand, this is a challenge for the nonprofit and philanthropic sector. It requires that the aperture of the leadership and strategy lens be opened. Indeed, it requires that the way in which nonprofits even define problems and missions will likely need to accommodate a more global perspective. Change is hard, especially for those institutions that have little knowledge of or experience with globally oriented perspectives. But whether they are universities, secondary schools, health care providers, environmental advocates, human development service agencies, or religious organizations, the fact is that successful nonprofits of the future will need to become global in their understandings and in their funding strategies if they are to attract tomorrow's leaders.

On the other hand, it is also a tremendously positive trend. New corporate institutions, new leaders, and a new global middle class can mean the injection of new energy and new funding into philanthropy. True, this may be funding with different perspectives, different giving methods, and different expectations than in the past. But it has the potential to usher in a new era of philanthropy, a new commitment of private individuals to the common good, and likely even better ways to think about problems and to mobilize resources for solutions.

As challenging as a multipolar, deeply integrated global economy may be for individual institutions in the traditional nonprofit sector, from a philanthropic point of view it could not be more exciting.

Case C: Private Fundraising Strategy in a Newly Open Society

Author: Grizzard Communications Group

Partner: The Salvation Army

Situation

The Salvation Army (TSA) in Russia historically never focused on fundraising due to many challenges including: the government, the Russian Orthodox power, and the population's belief that government takes care of all social problems. Therefore, TSA's International Headquarters has labeled Russia a "grant aided territory" and other countries fund TSA's work there.

Stakes

With a population exceeding 141 million, rare ministry outreach, and a dearth of social service needs met, TSA's work in Russia is both great and integral. Very few nongovernment organizations have the means and infrastructure to provide services for those in dire need.

Strengths

The history of TSA's work in Russia began in September 1917, when seven corps opened in St. Petersburg. TSA and its work flourished in pre-Communist Russia.

(*continued*)

(continued)

The Communist Party came to power through political, social, and economic upheaval. In 1923, the Russian Communist Party closed TSA's operations and demanded it leave the country.

After the fall of Communism in 1991, the Russian Foreign Ministry invited TSA back to fill the void left in the wake of the totalitarian government's demise. Russia became a strong and distinct TSA command. Its work extended to Ukraine, Georgia, Moldova, and Romania.

Despite the TSA's great need and impact, the government continues to restrict its work. A law written for the Russian Orthodox Church categorizes other faiths, including TSA, as nontraditional and restricts them from doing charitable work. In addition, a Russian court ruled that TSA was a paramilitary organization and subject to expulsion. This ruling was later changed.

Though TSA's work and need is extensive, the fundraising program was nonexistent. Because of the lack of government support, and a culture devoid of social service outreach and fundraising, it was critical for TSA to develop its own sources of support. The turning point was when a U.S. officer, Colonel Ken Johnson, was appointed as territorial commander in 2011. He understood fundraising and the strength a focused approach and strategy presented.

Strategy

In 2011, Colonel Johnson reached out to Grizzard Communications Group CEO Chip Grizzard for help in starting the first-ever fundraising program in Russia.

Grizzard has a long history of international fundraising with TSA. The relationship extends for over 68 years and three generations of the Grizzard family, raising more than $3 billion worldwide.

In March 2011, a two-day strategic planning meeting launched the fledgling fundraising effort. Chip traveled to St. Petersburg and Moscow and met with the Territorial Executive Committee, which was made up of three American officers and a Canadian officer. In addition, he invited three experts with fundraising experience in Russia to join the meeting.

The three experts invited were Maria Chertok, Director, Charities Aid Foundation Russia; Tatiana Burmistrova, Fundraising Consultant, Donors Forum Russia; and Dmitry Daushev, Associate Development Director, World Wildlife Fund Russia. The group created a plan for the first-ever Salvation Army Christmas campaign in Russia.

At the end of the meeting, one of the Russian officers commented, "It was a historic two days for the Russian Federation."

Solution

See Appendix 1.

Notes

1. J. O'Neill, "BRIC's rapid growth tips the global balance," *The Telegraph*, November 20, 2011, www.telegraph.co.uk/finance/financialcrisis/8902824 /Jim-ONeill-BRICs-rapid-growth-tips-the-global-balance.html.
2. "The BRICs Nifty 50: The EM & DM Winners," Goldman Sachs, November 4, 2009.
3. "World Economic Indicators," World Bank, 2011, basic reference data.
4. Global Connections Report, HSBC Bank, April 2012, p. 1.
5. G. Jones, "Restoring a Global Economy, 1950–1980," Harvard Business School Working Knowledge Series, August 22, 2005, p. 1.
6. *Global Trends in FDI 2010*, Geneva: United Nations Conference on Trade and Development, 2010, p. 4.
7. M. Dewhurst, J. Harris, and S. Heywood, "The Global Company's Challenge," *McKinsey Quarterly* (June 2012), www.mckinseyquarterly.com /The_global_companys_challenge_2979.
8. D. Barton, A. Grant, and M. Horn, "Leading in the 21st Century," *McKinsey Quarterly* (June 2012), www.mckinseyquarterly.com/Leading__in_the _ 21st_century_2984.
9. Ibid.

CHAPTER **5**

Changing Corporate Context
The United States

The long recovery from the Great Recession, and trends previously under way, will result in marked changes in the industrial and employment structure in the United States over the coming decades. These changes will have larger implications for the corporate perspectives on, and resources to address, larger social issues as well as for the nature and location of the American workforce.

The changes are deep and broad. The purpose of this discussion is not a comprehensive analysis of the economic future of America's corporations. There are volumes of academic literature dedicated to that topic. Rather, the purpose of this chapter is to underscore the degree to which nonprofits and philanthropy should pay attention to and understand such underlying trends in a post-recession world of fundamental change.

To illustrate those changes and their implications, this chapter will focus on four dimensions of change:

- Industrial structure
- Employment and skills
- Corporate and market location
- New firm formation

Industrial Structure

The shift of American industry away from manufacturing and toward services is two decades under way. A larger and larger part of the economy derives from service industries rather than manufacturing. See Exhibit 5.1.

Indeed, manufacturing's share of employment has been falling since the 1950s, and the absolute numbers of manufacturing jobs have been falling

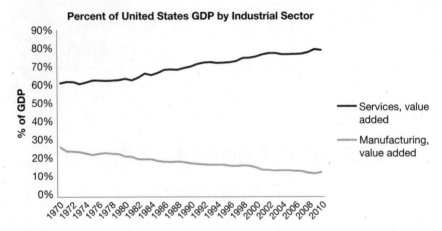

EXHIBIT 5.1 Economic Composition by Industry
Source: World Bank, World Development Indicators

since the late 1970s. The process continues. Between 2000 and 2010 alone, manufacturing output in the United States fell by 11 percent,[1] driven in part by the entrance of China into the World Trade Organization in 2001 and the global opening of markets to Chinese goods.

There is a rising debate about this shift, both in terms of its consequences and in terms of the persistence of the trend itself.

Some argue that this is natural and of little larger economic concern because the economic value of nonmanufacturing jobs in a technology-driven economy is higher in a global context. Indeed, as this argument goes, the type of labor flexibility that allows very quick adaptation to product and market changes is widely present overseas and not in the United States.[2]

Others argue that "manufacturing" no longer means Dickensian jobs on dim, dangerous factory floors. Modern manufacturing is a source of very high-tech jobs with very high value added in electronics, machinery, computer, and similar industries. These industries are globally competitive, and the loss of such capacity is, in fact, dangerous to the economy. These are not jobs one should shrug off, but jobs that should be actively pursued and valued.

There is even evidence that such jobs are returning to the United States and that the decades-long industrial composition shift will reverse. In 2012, The Boston Consulting Group found that the United States now manufactures 75 percent of what it consumes and that, in fact, seven industry groups, including computers and electronics and machinery, will begin to move manufacturing capacity back to the United States in the coming decade, adding $20 to $55 billion in output annually to the economy and as many as two to three million jobs.[3] The combination of higher U.S. productivity relative to foreign locations, rising global logistics costs as the price of fuel and energy rises post-recession, and quality concerns will drive (indeed, are driving) these industries back to American shores.

Such a rebalancing of the economy, however, does not mean a return to old ways. Even if industrial structure diversifies, the jobs that come with that change are not necessarily the kinds of jobs that were lost in the Great Recession, and they will not necessarily restore the geographic parts of the nation that have been most deeply stunned by that unemployment.

Employment and Skills

At this writing, unemployment in the United States still stands at 8.3 percent. It represents perhaps the most important and persistent drag on economic growth. Indeed, long-term unemployment (of more than six months) is at its highest since the Depression. The consequences of such long-term unemployment for recovery are serious; those without jobs are less likely to be considered for newly created jobs, and the longer an individual is jobless, the less likely he or she is to find a job. See Exhibit 5.2.

Indeed, in a 2011 analysis of scenarios for economic recovery, McKinsey & Company found that only a high-job-growth scenario, of the *average* creation of 187,000 jobs per month between now and 2020 would return the United States to 5 percent unemployment by 2020.[4] It would take that sustained effort every month, every year through 2020 to get unemployment back to the levels that the country enjoyed before the Great Recession.

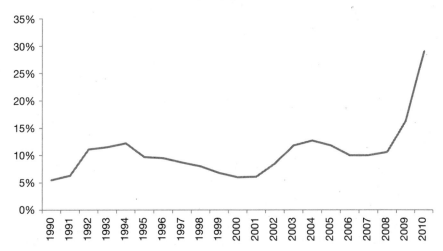

EXHIBIT 5.2 Long-Term Unemployment in the United States, 1990 through 2010
Source: Organisation for Economic Co-operation and Development (OECD), International Labour Organization Key Indicators of the Labour Market (ILO-KILM)

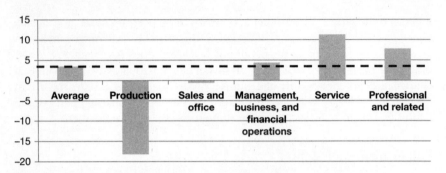

EXHIBIT 5.3 Percent Change Between 2000 and 2005, U.S. Employed
Source: U.S. Bureau of Labor Statistics, Current Population Survey, 2000–2005,
Data Reconstructed by BLS, 2013

The fundamental long-term problem for the United States is not simply jobs—it is the skills to perform the jobs that are being created. The driving issue on the societal commons of the United States post Great Recession is going to be the ability to adjust human capacity to meet changing industrial structure.

The trend has been under way for some time. As noted in Exhibit 5.3, even in the period 2000 through 2005, the creation of management, service, and professional jobs has far outpaced the national average of job creation and job creation in other categories.

In the decade 2000 to 2010, even through the period of the Great Recession, the number of professional, scientific, and technical services jobs in the economy grew by 2.3 million. Some 400,000 of those were actually in the depths of the recession. At the same time, the number of administrative and support services jobs fell by 800,000 in the 2005 through 2010 period.[5] The U.S. Bureau of Labor Statistics predicts that the leading 6 of the top 10 fastest-growing industries for job creation between 2010 and 2020 will be directly technology based, and will alone add over a million jobs.[6]

As a result, the unemployment rate in science-, technology-, engineering-, and mathematics-focused (STEM) jobs never approached that of the overall economy, recovered more quickly, and is now near record lows. See Exhibit 5.4.

Furthermore, over time those jobs pay more, and hence have more economic multiplier power than jobs in other sectors. As noted in Exhibit 5.5, between 2007 and 2010, overall earnings in the United States stagnated, but science and engineering incomes rose, in some cases markedly.

STEM prepared workforce is employed and earns wage levels that can power the economy and, importantly, provides likely end-of-career financial capacity that will enable secure retirement and continued consumption.

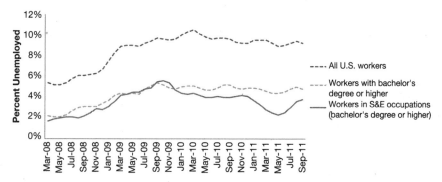

EXHIBIT 5.4 STEM Unemployment Rates in the United States 2008 through 2011
Source: National Science Foundation, Science and Engineering Indicators, 2012

The return of manufacturing, if it happens, will be based on technology skills in even the manufacturing workforce. New job growth will be based on these skills. The numbers of opportunities for those without such skills will decline. This is not just a matter of manufacturing. It is what is behind the decline in administrative jobs, for example, where technology has made administration more productive (e.g., producing more output for fewer units of labor). iPads used for ordering at restaurants will decrease the numbers of waiters and waitresses needed. Curtis Carlson of SRI International, whose laboratory invented Siri, the iPhone digital assistant, has predicted that such digital programs will alter every area of the economy, from services to retail shopping to banking to product design.[7]

EXHIBIT 5.5 Median Annual Earnings in STEM Occupations in the United States 2007 and 2010
Source: National Science Foundation, Science and Engineering Indicators, 2012

If, as McKinsey predicts, we need 187,000 new jobs per month every year until 2020, and if many of those jobs (and certainly the best of those jobs) are STEM-based or STEM-related, then how are we doing?

In short, not well. It is hard to know where to start in describing the implications.

First, where the STEM-based jobs are likely to be created is not where the Great Recession wreaked greatest employment devastation. The highest percentages of jobs that are STEM-based tend to be on the East and West Coasts and in the Central Plains states, not in the core Midwest or the South.[8]

Second, these jobs are likely to require higher levels of education, and that education needs to be technically based. In 1973, 16 percent of employment required a bachelor's degree or better. Seventy-two percent require a high school education or less. In 2018, 33 percent of jobs will require a bachelor's degree or better and only 38 percent a high school diploma or less. In 1973, a third of jobs could be won without a high school diploma. By 2018, that will fall to 10 percent.[9]

In the meantime, only 4.4 percent of U.S. undergraduates earn a degree in engineering, compared with over 30 percent of undergraduates in China and Singapore and over 10 percent in Germany.[10] This problem may become more intense as a larger portion of higher education degrees are awarded to women, but women account for a small portion of engineering and computer sciences degrees. Women now account for half or more than half of undergraduate, graduate, and first professional degrees in the United States. But they remain a small minority of professionals on highly technical computer jobs and in such areas of science as physics. See Exhibit 5.6.

The problem of filling STEM skill requirements in order to expand economic growth extends downward in the education system as well. The United States spends more than other nations to achieve a point gain in the international student mathematics tests, but ranks near the bottom in

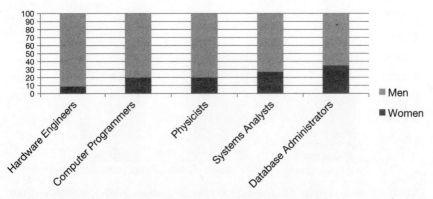

EXHIBIT 5.6 Gender Distribution of Technical Professions, 2006
Source: Bureau of Labor Statistics

achievement.[11] Even as the United States ages and its school-aged population becomes more ethnically diverse, math scores of its minority students remain far below those of its white students.

Third, the role of immigration has been critical in supporting the growth of the technology-based economy. By 2000, 40 percent of science and engineering jobs requiring a PhD were held by immigrants.[12] Indeed, a third of America's software developers, nearly 40 percent of scientists and a quarter of technology company founders and Nobel laureates are foreign born.[13] Yet as other countries increase their focus on attracting highly skilled professionals, immigration remains a divisive issue in the United States. And, simultaneously, growth in the economies of Asia and Latin America, combined with an emphasis on educational expansion, is attracting previous immigrants back to their nations of origin. As we shall see in Chapter 12, this new phenomenon can change the prospects for immigrant-led innovation in industrial economies.

The key issue for the next decade derives directly from economic change that has been propelled forward with more force by the Great Recession. Employment—job creation and workforce preparation—is and will continue to be the driving social issue in the coming decade. It represents a potent illustration of how the combination of post–Great Recession economics and private-sector productive capacity will change the societal landscape and the structure of issues facing nonprofits and philanthropy.

Corporate Markets and Location

Consistent with the globalization trends noted in Chapter 4, U.S. corporate lines of sight are overseas. The sales of foreign affiliates of U.S. corporations have increased rapidly, driven by the differential economic growth in emerging economies and the rapid rise of the global middle class described in Chapter 4. See Exhibit 5.7.

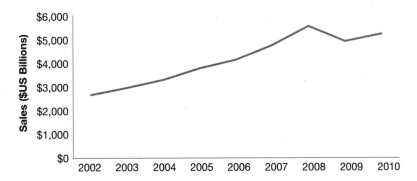

EXHIBIT 5.7 Foreign Affiliate Sales of U.S. Corporations
Source: "Outsourcing and Insourcing Jobs in the U.S. Economy: Evidence Based on Foreign Investment Data," Congressional Research Service, 2012

Similarly, employment in foreign affiliates has grown rapidly, driven not simply by job outsourcing (which has gotten the lion's share of media attention) but by the reality that local production near local markets is often more efficient and less costly than meeting market demands from the other side of the world.

In turn, these global markets now represent the centers of corporate competition for U.S. companies, further fixing the U.S. corporate vision beyond the American shoreline. In 2011, the number of corporate head-quarters of Fortune 500 companies located in the United States declined by 46; the number of headquarters in China rose by 45. Between 2000 and 2011, and driven by growth outside of traditional industrialized economies, the number of Fortune 500 companies headquartered in the combination of China, Russia, India, and Brazil increased by 381 percent, and the number in other emerging economies increased by 200 percent.[14]

This is of much more than passing interest. A 2008 study by Card et al. at Cornell University examined the relationship between headquarters location and corporate giving to local charities. The authors found that location has a significant effect on the directions of giving. For large companies, the change of a corporate headquarters can result in as much as a $25 million change in the philanthropic receipts of local charities.[15]

The geographic line of market sight of American corporations will be even more intensely global in the next decade, and local philanthropy will be affected both by that line of sight and by the growing strength of other markets as headquarters of the world's major corporations.

New Firm Formation

Of course, one could argue that all of this change could be immaterial. If new firms are being formed and are growing rapidly, then the changed focus and shifting nature of larger companies might not be of concern. The problem here is twofold and, again, illustrates the effect of post-recession economic change on the nonprofit operating environment.

First, new firm formation was significantly affected by the Great Recession. Between 2007 and 2010 there was a 23 percent drop in new business creation.[16] This was a steeper decline than in past recessions. Furthermore, the numbers of jobs created by each new firm is also falling, from 8 two decades ago to 6 today.[17] The lack of capital and difficult barriers to capital access, as well as the deep impact of high unemployment on consumption (consumption drives 70 percent of the U.S. economy), have combined to limit business formation. And the lack of formation and growth in turn limit the ability of local business creation to fill in the local line of philanthropic sight traditionally held by local large corporations.

This leaves the local corporate sector and its role in philanthropy weaker than before the recession.

This is not to say that there is still not a tremendous propensity for entrepreneurship in the economy. However, the pace of formal business creation and business growth has been severely impeded by the length and depth of the recession, and their ability to bounce back has been weakened. In turn, the role of new businesses and their founders in community problem solving will also be weakened for at least the coming several years.

Second, there is competition for the entrepreneur. Nations such as the United Kingdom, Singapore, New Zealand, Ireland, and Chile offer visas for start-up entrepreneurs. Indeed, the U.K. visa is for three years, with permanent residency offered if the entrepreneur creates only 2 additional jobs, or three years if he or she creates 10 jobs. In Chile, there is no minimum investment and, indeed, the Chilean government will pay $40,000 into the enterprise.[18] China's National Medium and Long Term Talent Development Plan offers signing bonuses, free housing, and tax breaks to Chinese-born entrepreneurs living in other countries if they bring their talent back home.[19]

Again, it is the globalization of markets and talent, the differential success of high-growth emerging economies, and the deeper understanding in all nations of the value of innovation that are expanding the competition for entrepreneurs and creating a problematic future for new business formation in the United States.

Summary and Implications

The Great Recession gave added power to a series of changes in the U.S. economy that had been under way for a decade, and added additional challenges to economic growth and the private sector that powers that growth. The four challenges in this section can only illustrate the way in which both problems and opportunities addressed by nonprofits and philanthropies are impacted, and the way in which the philanthropic and social engagement perspectives of corporations can be altered.

The effects of economic trends and deep and rapid changes on those corporations is a critical element for nonprofits to understand and anticipate. During the Great Recession, corporate philanthropy held its own more so than did either individual or independent foundation giving. Indeed, the diversification of the definition of *philanthropy* for corporations beyond cash and goods into new mechanisms to link markets and marketing to societal needs and problem-solving opportunities mean that the strategic partnership alternatives for nonprofits are expanding rapidly. But that is true if and only if nonprofits commit to knowing as much about the pressures on corporations as corporations themselves know, if nonprofits anticipate the implications of rapid or deep changes in those pressures, and if nonprofits identify and pursue relationships that reflect a changing reality.

The recession—and the prolonged and painful recovery—has focused corporations ever more on their stability and growth. Social engagement remains a critical element of that focus, but the furrows on the corporate brow will be created by continued economic challenge. Understanding and antici-pating economic pressures, and forging the changing strategies that will adjust to them, is the nonprofit challenge of the coming decade.

Case D: Global Company Seeks Global Engagement

Author: Ketchum

Partner: Room to Read

Situation

Throughout its nearly 90 year history, Ketchum has dedicated significant brainpower and hours to a variety of nonprofit organizations. At the request of Ketchum's global employee base, a decision was made to channel employees' efforts into a common focus area. The goal was to identify a cause for which the entire network—at that time, 69 offices and more than 1,000 employees—could collectively deliver a significant impact. As a result, a strategic pro bono relationship was established in 2008.

Stakes

Identifying one cause for the Ketchum group of companies was no easy task. Its businesses touch numerous industries and sectors and provide a wide range of services for clients around the world. Still, the Ketchum Social Responsibility planning team wanted to "practice what they preach," so they designed the company's corporate social responsibility (CSR) following the same framework used to counsel clients: strategically and creatively. Best practices suggest that CSR efforts have a greater likelihood of success when they are in the "sweet spot" between a company's core offer and an unmet societal need. For Ketchum that sweet spot is communication.

Strength

Ketchum inventoried existing and historical projects within its businesses, conducted an agency-wide survey to gauge employees' interests, and looked at the strategic growth plans for Ketchum overall. It was determined that literacy was the cause that colleagues wanted to get behind, and supporting children was of particular interest. After evaluating more than a dozen potential partners, Room to Read emerged as the clear winner, given its similarity in culture and business approach. This partnership represented a major step forward for Ketchum's corporate responsibility efforts, in terms of the scope, commitment, and opportunity to make a difference in the lives of children across Asia and Africa.

Strategy

Ketchum chose to partner with Room to Read chiefly because part of its mission is fundamentally aligned with literacy, a critical element to its business. In addition, through Room to Read's global headquarters, development hubs, and volunteer chapters, Room to Read and Ketchum have a physical presence in many of the same cities around the world,

(*continued*)

(continued)

which provides optimum opportunities for collaboration and employee engagement. Room to Read was willing to invest in its partnership—the leadership team agreed to spend time in the Ketchum offices and help educate employees about global literacy issues.

Solution

See Appendix 1.

Notes

1. R. D. Atkinson, L. A. Stewart, S. M. Andes, and S. Ezell, *Worse Than the Great Depression: What Experts Are Missing About American Manufacturing Decline* (Washington, DC: Information Technology and Innovation Foundation, March 2012), 4.
2. For a case example of the argument, see C. Duhigg and K. Bradsher, "How the U.S. Lost Out on iPhone Work," *New York Times,* January 22, 2012, p. 1.
3. *Made in America, Again: U.S. Manufacturing Nears the Tipping Point* (Boston: Boston Consulting Group, March 2012), 3.
4. J. Manyika et al., *An Economy that Works: Job Creation and America's Future* (New York: McKinsey Global Institute, June 2011), 23.
5. Ibid., p. 25.
6. R. Henderson, "Industry Employment and Output Projections to 2020," *Monthly Labor Review* (January 2012): 71.
7. T. L. Friedman, "Average Is Over." *New York Times,* January 25, 2012, p. A29.
8. A. P. Carnevale, M. Smith, and J. Strohl, *Help Wanted: Projections of Jobs and Education Requirements Through 2018* (Washington, DC: Center on Education and the Workforce, June 2010), p. 7.
9. Ibid., 14.
10. "Science and Engineering Indicators, 2012." National Science Foundation, 2012.
11. "The Economic Impact of the Achievement Gap in America's Schools," McKinsey and Company, April 2009, p. 9.
12. "Not Coming to America," The Partnership for a New American Economy and the Partnership for New York City, May 2012, p. 6.
13. S. Anderson and M. Platzer, *American Made: The Impact of Immigrant Entrepreneurs and Professionals on U.S. Competitiveness* (Arlington, VA: National Venture Capital Association, November 2006).

14. CTP Changing Headquarter Landscape.
15. D. Card, K. F. Hallock, and E. Moretti, "The Geography of Giving: The Effect of Corporate Headquarters on Local Charities." Working Paper 08-08. Cornell University School of Industrial and Labor Relations, Center for Advanced Human Resource Studies, 2008, p. 5.
16. Manyika et al., p. 3.
17. Ibid.
18. "Not Coming to America," p. 26.
19. Ibid., p. 29.

CHAPTER 6

Changing Corporate Context
The Global "South"

The spread of economic growth around the world is not simply about the rise of China. Throughout Asia, Latin America, and Africa, private corporate strength is building, and in so doing, it promises to bring to the societal commons new resources but, importantly, new perspectives about both problems and solutions.

The power behind this corporate growth and the energy for its continued expansion is a result of a combination of the past three decades of policy shifts toward open markets and open economies that encourage private capital formation (and, in China's case, the role of the state as a private market actor), and the demographic shifts that have created significantly large and increasingly well-trained labor forces in emerging markets. The next two decades will likely see an intensification of these trends, as will be seen in the discussion of corporate growth, labor force expansion, and the increasing role of science and technology innovation within these economies.

Corporate Growth

One cannot separate the growing strength of the corporate sector in emerging and rapidly growing economies of the "South" from the resilience of those economies overall. Emerging and rapid-growth regions of the world went into the recession later than North American and Europe, experienced a less deep turndown, and came out sooner. They were poised to build on the productive capacity established in the previous 20 years and intensify their growth. See Exhibit 6.1.

The rate of growth of incomes in the emerging markets has been higher than ever in their histories. In turn, their private sectors have expanded markedly as capital has been drawn to their prospects. Since 2003, the

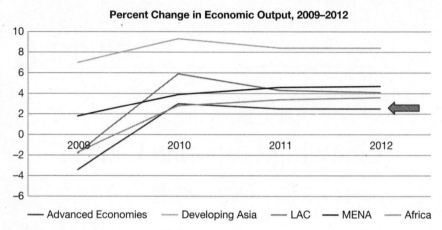

Percent Change in Economic Output, 2009–2012

EXHIBIT 6.1 Regional Recession Climb-Out Differences
Source: International Monetary Fund

Dow Jones BRIC 50 Index (composed of companies in Brazil, Russia, India, and China) has outperformed the Standard & Poor's 500 by 600 percent. Between 2001 and 2010, the return on equity in India and Brazil alone was 400 percent, whereas in Europe, the United States, and Japan it was negative.

In 1960, the United States accounted for about a quarter of the world's gross domestic product (GDP); China represented 4 percent. By 2018, both China and the United States will represent 18 percent of global GDP. Taken together, the combined economies of the BRIC nations are now about a third the size of the G-7 nations.[1] By 2020, the BRIC nations will account for 50 percent of the increase in global GDP. And by 2030, the BRIC nations together are projected to be as large as all of the G-7 economies. See Exhibit 6.2.

In turn, larger firms in the BRIC nations are making a bid for corporate takeovers in the traditional industrial economies as well as in other parts of the "South." Brazil's Embraer, Africa's First Quantum Minerals, China's National Offshore Oil Corporation (CNOOC), and Dubai's Dubai Ports World all have made major global merger and acquisition (M&A) moves in the last decade.[2] As this deal making grows, the financial institutions in these nations will grow in importance as vehicles for facilitating investment flows.

But the strengthening of corporate muscle in the "South" is not simply about the BRIC nations. The Forbes Global 2000 now includes over 730 firms from the Asia Pacific region and 145 from Latin America, compared to 524 for

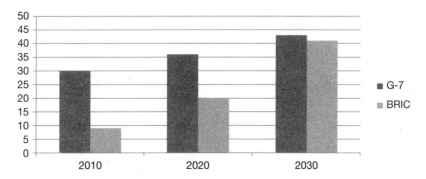

EXHIBIT 6.2 BRIC and G-7 GDP Projections ($ trillions)
Source: Mint, New Delhi

the United States. That represents an increase of 32 firms from Asia in the single year 2011 to 2012, and a decrease of 12 firms from the United States.

Trends in Africa also make the point forcefully that private corporate growth in the "South" will be an engine for global growth in the future.

In 2010, corporate mergers and acquisitions in Africa accounted for 15 percent of all M&A in emerging economies, up from 11 percent just two years earlier.[3] There are 50 global investment funds preparing to invest more than $2.4 billion in African agribusiness.[4] In 2011, South African companies announced or launched 59 new investment projects in other African countries. South African banks moved new project money into 145 foreign direct investment projects across Africa in 2011, compared to 27 in 2007, ranking South Africa fifth across the continent for foreign direct investment, after the United States, United Kingdom, India, and France.[5]

Trade flows also reinforce the rise of corporate power across Southern economies. China has replaced the United States as Africa's largest trading partner. Brazil, home to the largest population of African heritage outside of Africa itself, has more embassies in Africa than does Britain. Brazil's Odebrecht construction company is the largest employer in Angola and Vale, the Brazilian mining giant, is one of the largest employers in Mozambique.[6] In the case of China, Brazil, and Venezuela, the combination of government aid and the pathway it creates for private corporate investment has become both an economic and a political force throughout Africa.

Trade is linked arm-in-arm with investment. "South-south" trade now accounts for over half of all African exports, compared to 25 percent in 1990. In India a decade ago, 13 percent of imports were from southern nations. By 2010, that had increased to 45 percent. Similarly, South African exports to southern nations increased from 12 percent of total exports to 27 percent in 2010.[7]

Labor Force and the New Employee

The capacity of corporations in rapidly growing economies to play this growing role is linked to the changing demographics that have shifted the labor force to Southern nations. In traditional industrial economies, and, in fact, in China the premium will be on productivity. In China in 2011 and 2012, productivity accounted for almost all GDP growth because job growth is at 0.3 percent per year. In the coming decade, with job growth still suppressed by the slow recovery, nearly all GDP increase will need to come from increased labor productivity.[8]

However, over the next 20 years, a significant part of labor force growth will come from developing Africa and Asia.[9] See Exhibit 6.3.

This new workforce will be relatively young and better educated than in the past. Indeed, the traditional stereotypes of labor in developing economies will fall away. Over 80 percent of these young workers will be literate, most will have formal schooling, and many will be well skilled. This is a generation of workers who are likely to be the first in their families to work in larger industrial organizations or to be part of the global competitive economic system. As discussed in Chapter 4, they will be the new middle class of consumers.

The premium will be on the creation of urban jobs, and hence the continued strength of the rising corporate sector to provide that job creation or the opportunity for these new labor force entrants to themselves become

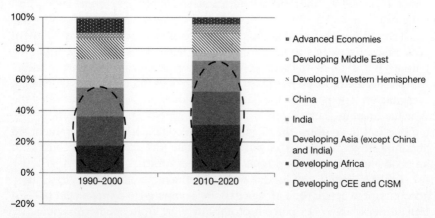

EXHIBIT 6.3 Percent Net New Additions to Global Labor Force
Source: International Labour Organization, 2011

entrepreneurs and business owners. Without this job creation, this very large cohort of young adults runs the risk of becoming frustrated with its inability to progress economically. The larger danger is that, as a consequence, these changes become geopolitically destabilizing at the very moment of promise for economic growth.

Whether or not this group of newly expanding companies in the South will place social engagement on its priority list, and whether or not the equivalent new generation of urban employees will see "employee engagement" as a desired part of employment remains to be seen. Even if this occurs and/or even if corporate and employee engagement advocates can cause it to occur, patterns will not necessarily be familiar. Differing histories and differing cultures almost certainly imply that the way in which corporate and labor force strength interplays with social issues locally and globally will be different than in the past in traditional industrial economies.

Innovation

What truly gives credence to the likely continued growth and economic development of Southern nation economic leadership, however, is the degree to which innovation is beginning to grow within the industrial and academic sectors. Economies are sinking roots into research and development, and creating new products, services, and applications for global markets. This represents a high-value-added dimension to their economic future. China and India alone produce 700,000 engineering graduates per year and another 140,000 higher-degree graduates in engineering and computer sciences.[10]

From an academic perspective, Asia's share of world research article production in science and engineering has risen from 14 percent in 1995 to 24 percent in 2009, led by rapid scientific peer reviewed journal writing from China. See Exhibit 6.4.

Indeed, the Asia-8 (excluding China) increased their scientific article production by 10 percent per year over the 15-year period. China's growing publishing focus on chemicals and South Korea's on biological and medical sciences reflect economic priorities for those nations.[11]

But the fruits of such scientific performance are seen in the applications of innovation in the rapidly growing economies and their private corporations. More than 5,000 Chinese scientists returning form education or employment abroad have set up high-tech firms in China's Silicon Valley, Zhongguancun Science Park.[12] In a McKinsey global survey of multinational corporations with high-performing innovation at the core of their business, 100 percent conduct some of their research and development in emerging economies.[13]

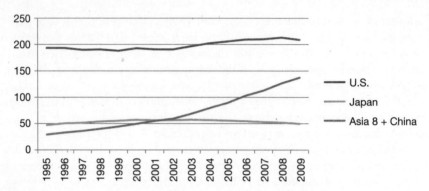

EXHIBIT 6.4 Science and Engineering Journal Articles 1995–2009
Source: National Science Foundation Science and Engineering Indicators, 2012

The result is product development that can strengthen those corporations in global markets while solving local problems in significant ways. Take mobile communications as an example. An analysis of product and service development in the mobile phone banking services industry indicated that 85 percent of the innovations in mobile banking originated in emerging economies.[14] One of the first, M-PESA (*pesa* is the Swahili word for "money") in Kenya was created by Safricom, Kenya's largest mobile phone company, as a cell phone–based electronic payments system. M-PESA now handles 2 million transactions per day for 10 million customers,[15] which represents a quarter of Kenya's population.

Other examples are the Tata Nano, which was developed and engineered in India as a $2,500 automobile alternative and is the world's cheapest car. The market realities of the growing middle class, described in Chapter 4, combined with the deep engineering and production capacity in India have created what is known as the "people's car" to provide transportation to 65 million Indians entering the middle class. The Nano was reverse engineered, with the price determined first and the technology developed in response.

In an increasingly technology-based global economy, this ability of emerging economies to research, develop, and produce innovations means that they are not simply growing from the displacement of traditional manufacturing industries onto their shores, or the production of goods or services developed elsewhere as a means of reducing labor and transportation costs. They are becoming, and will continue to become, the innovators for tomorrow's goods and services, and hence take a stronger and stronger leadership position in the global economy.

The strength of corporate capacity in the global "South" is here to stay.

Summary and Implications

The leadership of the "South" in the global economy is well under way. The Great Recession, and the tepid recovery in Europe and North America, has provided impetus for this role. The transition of these economies into high-value innovation, and the degree to which they are increasingly trading and investing in one another, will create deeper relationships with North America and Europe, but also a more intense web among Southern nations themselves.

The implications for philanthropy and nonprofits are profound.

New leaders will emerge, a topic that is further explored in Chapter 8 regarding wealth. New corporate leaders will become global leaders as well. Aigboje Aig-Imoukhuede, group managing director and chief executive officer of Access Bank Plc in Nigeria, is now co-chair, with Coca-Cola CEO Muhtar Kent, of the Global Business Coalition on Health, a coalition of more than 200 businesses focused on addressing global health crises. These new leaders will bring new perspectives and new personal networks not traditionally known to or tracked by nonprofits and philanthropy in North America or Europe. This will be a huge advantage in an era of declining public funds focused on social problem solving and an increasing reliance on private solutions. It will also be an enormous challenge because many nonprofits, especially in the United States, do not have deep knowledge of nor experience in identifying, cultivating, or relating to corporate leadership from outside the borders of the country.

Second, these leaders will influence their companies. One can only speculate how many will place social engagement as a personal and corporate priority. Increasing that number and that propensity to engage will be an important task for global philanthropic leaders because these new corporate powerhouses, and those to follow, are the pathway to continued engagement and problem solving in the future. Who will take on that challenge is the question.

Third, the growth in the global labor force will take place in emerging and rapidly growing economies. There is little known about how these new workers, at all levels from the shop floor to the sales floor to the C-suite, will view engagement by and through their place of work. Yet, employee engagement is becoming a core and fundamental part of corporate social engagement strategies. There will need to be careful thought about how to translate these strategies into the expectations and preferences of a new cohort of workers from a huge diversity of perspectives around the world.

Finally, the process and meaning of corporate engagement itself is undergoing change of its own, even as the nature of the corporate constellation globally changes. Corporate check writing for charity has given way to strategic engagement of all elements and assets of a corporation deeply tied to market priorities. And that is giving way to "shared value"[16] in which corporations, their products and their services contribute to and profits from their engagement in solving social problems. As the numbers of new corporate entrants into the global ranks from Southern economies increase, the question is whether their strategies will leapfrog old ways and begin with such all-of-resource approaches to engagement, or begin where others have begun in the past, with pure cash and product transfers to charity. If the latter, then the totality of the picture of global corporate engagement may, in fact, begin to look more like the past than the present.

Notes

1. Composed of the United States, United Kingdom, France, Germany, Canada, Italy, and Japan.
2. P. T. Larsen, "Emerging Markets Bite Back," *Financial Times* (November 29, 2006): 5.
3. "More of the Pie," *African Investor* (January–February 2011): 54.
4. "Harvesting Promise," *African Investor* (January–February 2011): 66.
5. "Building Bridges: Africa," Ernst & Young, 2012, p. 6.
6. S. Romero, "Brazil Gains Business and Influence as It Offers Aid and Loans in Africa," *New York Times*, August 8, 2012, pp. A4–A7.
7. Data from the International Trade Center, which covers 220 countries and territories and 5,300 products of the Harmonized Trade System.
8. 2012 Productivity Brief, The Conference Board, 2012, p. 5.
9. Countries designated according to International Monetary Fund groupings.
10. G. Segran, "As Innovation Drives Growth in Emerging Markets, Western Economies Need to Adapt," INSEAD, 2011, p. 2.
11. Detailed examination of the science and engineering innovation status of emerging economies can be found in the data in the National Science Foundation's Science and Engineering Indicators, 2012.
12. X. Liu et al., "Returnee Entrepreneurs, Knowledge Spillover and Innovation in High-Tech Firms in Emerging Economies," *Journal of International Business Studies* 41(7), (September 2010): 1183–1197.
13. C. Barrett, P. van Biljon, and C. Musso, "R&D Strategies in Emerging Economies: Results from the McKinsey Global Survey," *Research Technology Management* 54(4) (July/August 2011): 17–22.
14. P. van der Bor, F. M. Veloso, and P. Oliveira, SSRN Working Paper Series, February 2012, p. 10.

15. "Intuit 2020 Annual Report: Future of Financial Services," April 2011, p. 10.
16. The concept of "shared value" was introduced by Michael E. Porter and Mark R. Kramer. In their article "Creating Shared Value," *Harvard Business Review*, 89(12) (January/February 2011): 62–77.

CHAPTER 7

It Depends on What You Mean by "Give"

Investing in Problem Solving

The distinctions between nonprofit organizations and other institutional forms are blurring as new types of organizations are born to address societal problems, and as philanthropy itself begins to flow in new ways or with new contingencies and expectations. These innovations are partly driven by the views and experiences of new philanthropists who, as will be noted further in Chapters 8, 10, and 15, see their own commercial success as a model for applying similar techniques and approaches to social problems. In some ways, then, innovation is being driven by the "supply" side of philanthropic dollars and expectations. It is also driven, however, by "demand"—by an increase in education, communication, and global awareness. Consumers and investors have changed their views, and they are looking for opportunities to develop and use new tools that are both commercial in their structure and sustainability, yet societal in their impacts.

There is a significant literature building on the nature and implications of these strategies, although, in the sweep of nonprofit and philanthropic history, they are relatively new phenomena. For example, as noted in Exhibit 7.1, although the first microfinance system dates from the 1700s in Ireland, it is just in the past three decades that commercial-modeled innovations have begun to proliferate.

While a full treatment of all of these hybrid structures is beyond the scope of this work, in considering the pace of change and its implications for both nonprofits and philanthropic roles, it is important to appreciate the dimensions of change and the continued relationships between change toward an investment and enterprise optic and the continuity of the role of gift-based

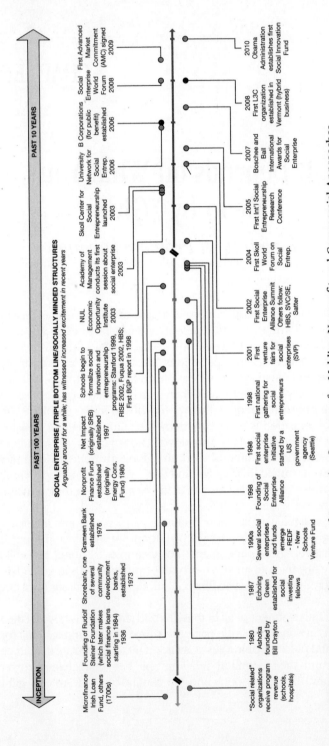

EXHIBIT 7.1 Timeline of Evolution of Innovative Structures for Melding Nonprofit and Commercial Approaches

Source: Changing Our World, Sally Park, Managing Director

philanthropy. This chapter will examine three concrete examples to illustrate the issues that innovation raises.

Social Enterprise

There has been a rapid adoption of the concepts of "social enterprise" across the nonprofit, for-profit, and government sectors over the past two decades. In the context of the Great Recession, the search by nonprofits for new sources of revenue has provided momentum to this trend. Still, nearly every article on the topic begins by defining the term, an indication of how elusive a core, accepted definition is. Indeed, in the United Kingdom, the government estimated in 2007 that there were 61,800 social enterprises. Using a different measure that examined why individuals established their businesses and attributing the desire to make a social difference as the distinguishing feature, a 2011 study by Delta Economics and IFF Research estimated that number to be 232,000, or over three times as many.[1] Taking a different lens to the term results in significant differences in results.

Moreover, where one looks on the organization landscape also matters. A survey of social enterprises in the United States also illustrates that such organizations are to be found under a variety of umbrellas. As illustrated in Exhibit 7.2, most of the organizations surveyed are part of other organizations, for-profit or not-for-profit.

So, although there is consensus that there is a material increase in the number of enterprises established to achieve a social mission through a commercial format, hard data are elusive.

For purposes of this volume, however, the more important point is that such enterprises rarely exist or grow in a philanthropic vacuum. Indeed, what

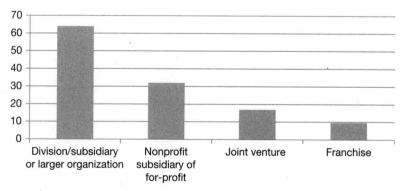

EXHIBIT 7.2 Organizational Form of Social Enterprises
Source: Community Wealth Ventures survey

characterizes the emergence of these organizations, in fact, is their deep financial roots in philanthropy. They do not appear wholly formed in the marketplace. Rather, they are often a function of an initial philanthropic investment and indeed remain dependent on philanthropy for longer than most observers recognize.

In 2010, Changing Our World conducted a financial analysis of 10 years of financial data for 20 social enterprises. The expectation was that, at least for a period of time, social enterprises would be dependent on some type of donated resources before they were able to evolve their financial and organizational structure to more closely resemble a market-driven, sales-compensated operation. As noted in Exhibit 7.3, however, the result showed much more concavity that had been expected.[2]

In 50 percent of the cases, social enterprises relied on philanthropy for the majority of their revenue for a longer period of time than the study had anticipated. Indeed, in one case, the dependence on philanthropy approached 90 percent. A survey of social enterprises in Ireland in 2011 produced similar results. Over half of the enterprises received at least half of their resources from some combination of government statutory grants and philanthropy. Over three quarters got only 10 percent of their funding from their corporate enterprises.[3]

A 2012 study by the Monitor Group and Acumen Fund came to similar conclusions.[4]

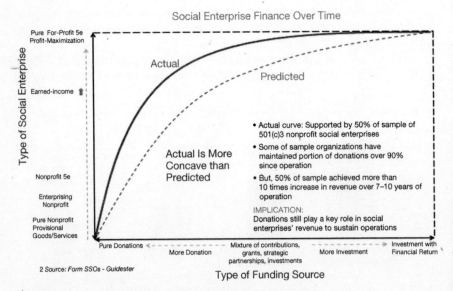

EXHIBIT 7.3 Social Enterprise Revenue Structure Transition
Source: Raymond, Changing Our World

Hence, the innovation in social finance that has gained momentum in the last decade, and especially since the Great Recession, is deeply rooted in the willingness of philanthropy to act as the initial source of funds. Philanthropy has played a critical role as the start-up capital for the organizations that, in fact, are created for the very purpose of not being dependent on philanthropy to accomplish their mission. The final result is a cohort of organizations whose market role blurs the lines between the commercial and the charitable, but it is philanthropy that allows the innovation to take root. We will return to this theme in detail in Chapter 15.

Program- and Mission-Related Investing

While program- and mission-related investing (PRI and MRI) predate the Great Recession by decades, the effects of the recession on foundation grant making capacity has raised interest in how foundations can take an "all of resource" approach to their missions, in ways that are analogous to the ways in which companies are aligning both giving and markets for purposes of social engagement. The enabler for that "all of resource" approach is also the degree to which nonprofits themselves are thinking about their programs in terms of investments rather than grants. Both the demand for investment-type support and the supply of such support through foundation portfolios and assets now represent further opportunity to treat charitable resources in ways that resemble investment capital.

In the United States, funds allocated to PRI (supporting nonprofits through lending) by foundations have tripled in the past 15 years (Exhibit 7.4).

The devastation of the recession on home ownership created an inflow of PRI activity on the part of philanthropic foundations to support housing solutions to mortgage foreclosure, particularly in urban neighborhoods, and especially by very large foundations such as the MacArthur Foundation.

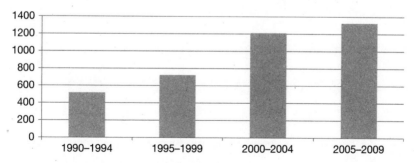

EXHIBIT 7.4 Value of PRI Activity ($million)
Source: Foundation Center PRI Directory. Data for 2008–2009 are incomplete.

In terms of the vehicles used for PRI, over 86 percent of the funds and 78 percent of the PRIs take the form of loans, 5 percent are in equity investments, and the remaining areas (e.g., business start-ups, lines of credit, and charitable use assets.[5]

The levels are likely to increase for three reasons. First, the forms that PRI can take are multiple yet the funds are concentrated on loans. Hence, there is opportunity for diversification of the use of the tool. Second, new nonprofit structures, such as social enterprises, represent more robust vehicles for PRI vehicles than many traditional charities. For example, new partnerships for product development between nonprofit scientific organizations and the government for advancing prevention or therapeutic technologies for tropical or orphan diseases, with ultimate licensing to the private sector for product development, represent robust points for PRI strategy. Third, in May 2012, the U.S. Internal Revenue Service revised its guidance on PRIs to expand applicability of the guidance to enable greater support of social enterprises.

Mission-related investing (MRI) is also growing as foundations attempt to put both their grant making and their asset bases at the service of their missions and core interest areas. In a survey of 1,195 foundations, the U.S. Foundation Center found that 14 percent engaged in MRI. These 168 foundations encompassed $119.2 billion in total assets.[6]

As noted in Exhibit 7.5, half of these foundations allocate 5 percent or less of their assets to mission driven, market-rate investments.

There is an important distinction to be understood here. The blurring of lines between nonprofits and for-profit commerce is not simply occurring in the revenue line of nonprofit financial structure. It is occurring in the way in which capital reaches cause. Social enterprises generate revenue for nonprofit operations. PRI and MRI mechanisms generate capital, and it is capital that many nonprofits lack.

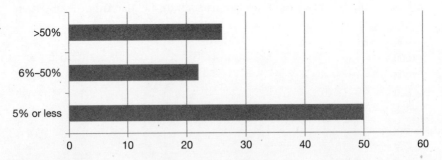

EXHIBIT 7.5 Percentage of Assets of Foundations Held as Market-Rate Mission-Related Investment

Source: Doing Good with Foundation Assets: An Updated Look at Program-related Investments, © 2010 The Foundation Center. Used by permission.

PRI and MRI mechanisms begin to bring the concepts of private capital into the nonprofit sector.

Social Franchising

One of the key problems with social enterprise is scale. Most social enterprises remain for many years—and often permanently—at very small, very local levels. Recently, in the nonprofit sector, there has been great interest in applying the concepts of franchising to nonprofits and to social enterprises. In the United States, there are nearly half a million franchise establishments that employ nearly eight million people. Taking this commercial concept into the nonprofit sector or social space, franchising allows central repositories of a product or service, surrounded by common branding capacity, to be decentralized into local service or product provision through individual entrepreneurs who focus not on product development but on the dimensions and needs of specific markets.

In the United States, nonprofits seeking scale have[7]:

- Purchased a franchise agreement from a for-profit system (Marshall Heights Community Development Organization and the Chesapeake Bagel Bakery; Manna, Inc. and Maggie Moo's).
- Developed a franchise model (Platte River Industries).
- Created training partnerships with a franchise system (PartnerShops and Ben & Jerry's).
- Received in-kind management assistance as part of a larger social engagement strategy of a franchise system seeking a nonprofit system partner (ServiceMaster and On the Job, Inc.).

In Europe, there are about 60 social franchises that employ some 13,000 people. They represent either partnerships between commercial franchises and nonprofits or purely nonprofit franchises operated by a central provider who has developed the systems and quality assurance in areas such as care of the disabled (Aetes in France, which links Augias, a company offering cleaning services, with the Association de Sauvegarde et Promotion de la Personne) or the development of employment opportunities (e.g., CAP-Märkte in Germany). While these franchises are akin to commercial franchises in their revenue flows, they are mission driven and usually not profit maximizing.

There is growing interest in developing economies for the franchise model as well. The Children and Family Wellness Shops (CFW Shops) in Kenya is a franchise model for health services and drugs to far-flung rural villages. Indeed, the first global social franchising conference was held in November 2011, with a keynote speech from the Kenyan Minister of Health arguing that such partnerships are key to expanding health and social services throughout the developing world. By May 2012, the social franchising compendium was 124 pages and included profiles in 35 developing countries in Africa, Asia, and Latin America.[8] The number of countries with social franchises had more than doubled in eight years.

Again, the point here is that the application of commercial concepts and structures to nonprofit service provision allows the strength of the former to be applied to the social causes of the latter. The blurring of the definition of what constitutes commercial and nonprofit; what constitutes a gift and an investment; and what constitutes a donor, a customer, and an investor introduces a future in which the nonprofit "business model" begins to lose its meaning, particularity relative to other ways of organizing effort.

Impact Investing

That flow of capital is taken further along the blurred lines of change by impact investing. Impact investing is the flow of private, market-quality funds (in contrast to the capital out of assets of philanthropic foundations) into commercial-quality investments that have the additional benefit of societal impact through improvement in lives as the base of the economic pyramid. The targets of impact investing are opportunities that are focused on solving common social problems, but the mechanism is private capital rather than charitable grant making or government funds. Often, the return to the investor is limited (e.g., 2 percent per annum), but this is not necessarily the case.

The current spread of impact investing, and the attention paid to it in philanthropy, may be new, but the concept is not. The Acumen Fund, the first multisector resource focused on social impact, for example, was founded in 2001, over a decade ago. However, there is now a wide variety of approaches to impact investing and a wide variety of targets. They are commonly to be found in agriculture, water, housing, and energy, where the sector is commonly and easily characterized by a revenue-producing asset that, with expansion, can create a revenue stream that represents a return on the investment. Indeed, in the United States, nonprofit creation of low-income housing has long been accomplished with impact investing, albeit not always with private, commercial-grade capital.

The international spread of impact investing has extended to a variety of economic development sectors, as noted in Exhibit 7.6.

This international effort is not new either. The International Finance Corporation (IFC) of the World Bank was actually created in 1956 to carry out a form of impact investing by seeking to support private ventures in critical industries in the developing world as a balance to the government-oriented lending of the remainder of the World Bank. Impact investing is not charity.

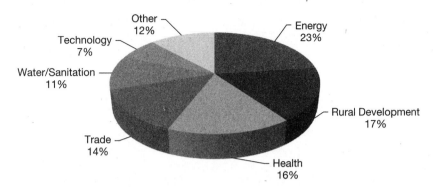

EXHIBIT 7.6 Distribution of Social Impact Investments in the Developing World
Source: J. Simon and J. Barmeier, *More than Money: Impact Investing for Development* (Washington, DC: Center for Global Development, 2010), 17

Indeed, the emerging market equity portfolio of the IFC outperformed traditional emerging market venture capital portfolios in the period 1998 to 2006.[9]

Many of the efforts in international development, however, have historically focused on traditional industries (e.g., timber) with the social benefit being measured in terms of sustained job creation and wealth building. It took nearly 30 years, for example, for the IFC to make its first investment in health care. More recently, "bottom of the pyramid" impact investing has flowed to more mainstream social sectors. For example, in 2012, J. P. Morgan created the Global Health Investment Fund to provide capital for the development of vaccines, drugs, diagnostics and preventatives that address global health challenges disproportionally affecting the developing world. The object is both to improve global health and to generate financial returns. The partners in the Fund include J. P. Morgan, Lion's Head Global Partners in London (whose principals were formerly with Goldman Sachs), and the Bill & Melinda Gates Foundation.

The philosophy behind the Fund, and others like it, is that philanthropic grant making alone will never generate sufficient resources to solve global health or other complex and long-standing societal problems. What are needed are mechanisms to tap the huge reservoirs of private global capital in ways that can pool those resources, target them at critical opportunities, and produce both measurable results in social well-being and attractive (if not maximized) return on capital to the investors.

These are not, of course, simple matters. Impact, or bottom of the pyramid, investing implies that many other prerequisites exist. There must be sufficient organization of a problem for there to be an investing opportunity. There often must be access to other types of resources (roads, utilities) or an investment to be possible. There must be a regulatory environment that welcomes and indeed facilitates the flow of private investment to a problem and allows a financial return on that capital, an issue that often stymies both the health and education sectors. There must be managers and other personnel with the knowledge and experience to manage the investment. The list is long, and it is not, as we have seen in social enterprise, independent of philanthropy. Indeed, the Global Health Investment Fund's investors are often philanthropists using the funds of their own foundations.

Still, the application of traditionally market-oriented concepts and standards to problems that have historically been seen as matters of charity, and the rapid growth and spread of such applications, is testimony to the blurring of lines between the commercial and the social, between private return and social problem solving. Impact investing is not philanthropy. Investments are not grants. The standards, perspectives, skills, and expectations of investors are those of the market, not those of the charitable donor. The hope, however, is that the result will be the creation of sufficient capital, structured and incentivized to be sustainable, that will markedly move the dial on problem solving in ways that are more effective than constant charitable giving. "Giving" and "investing" will blur, and the bottom line will be both private wealth creation and private contribution to social problem solving. In turn, this will open up the opportunity for exponential increases in resources far, far beyond what could ever be expected of philanthropy. Indeed, Nick O'Donohoe and his colleagues at J. P. Morgan believe that impact investment funds have the potential to become an asset-class equivalent to equity or bonds, a huge force to drive private capital to social betterment. Their estimate is that there is the potential for $1 trillion in investment in the next 10 years if they count only five sectors (housing, rural water, maternal health, primary education, and financial services) and only the portion of the global population earning less than $3,000 per year.[10] This is 50 times larger than all of the global health and development grant making of the Bill & Melinda Gates Foundation since its inception in 1994.

Variations and Applications

The preceding areas of the intersection between the way commerce operates and the way new philanthropists and social investors are thinking about problem solving offer but a glimpse of the future.

"Social impact bonds" combine philanthropy and government resources to get social problem solving to scale. Governments commit to pay for performance in problem solving; philanthropists provide the program implementation resources. When results benchmarks are met, governments pay for that performance, and the "bond holders" are repaid (or not, depending on the philanthropic agreements). The intermediating nonprofit covers its costs through the initial philanthropy and gains additional net resources through the performance payment.

Indeed, when the system is robust, the process can segue beyond philanthropy to become government policy backed by public budgets. The state of Minnesota has created human capital performance bonds, which are sold to private investors and backed by state budget appropriations. The proceeds pay for direct service provision by nonprofits once the providers achieve predetermined performance benchmarks.[11]

The Debt2Health program of the Global Fund to Fight HIV/AIDS, Tuberculosis and Malaria is a funding mechanism, seed-financed with a grant from the Bill & Melinda Gates Foundation, that used equities and alternative investments to create multiparty agreements. Creditors of developing countries agreed to forgo a portion of their claims on those countries on condition that the beneficiary country invests an agreed amount in its national health program. Ultimately, Debt2Health generated $170 million in funding for disease control.

Quasi-equity debt security mechanisms have been developed for application to organizations that are structured as nonprofits and so cannot access equity capital. They are structured so that returns are indexed to performance and hence provide incentives to impact and efficiency.

Pooled impact investment funds are being developed that deliver different mixes of risk and return in different levels of investment so that individual investors with different desires can be individually satisfied. IFMR Trust in Chennai, India, and Blue Orchard in Switzerland are examples of these pooled funds.[12]

Corporations are also beginning to think about investment alternatives to simple grant making. Chevron has created its own micro-credit bank in Angola. The Shell Foundation has invested in GroFin. The pension fund Teachers Insurance and Annuity Association–College Retirement Equities Fund (TIAA-CREF) formed a Global Social and Community Investment Department.[13] Abbott Laboratories is investing both executive time and resources in creating self-sustaining enterprises in Haiti that will provide both employment and a product, Nourimanba, which is a vitamin-enriched peanut butter to fight malnutrition.[14] All of this activity is focused on capitalizing on, and providing momentum for, the progress in economic and social condition throughout the world, a theme that is explored in Chapter 9 of this book.

In all of these examples, techniques and approaches common in the commercial financial marketplace are being adapted and applied to flowing capital to social problem solving. The source of the funds may be philanthropy, the assets of foundations, or mainstream commercial investors. As Antony Bugg-Levine has written, "with the right market infrastructure and the legal framework in place, enormous amounts of private capital could be mobilized" for social impact.[15]

Summary and Implications

The blurring of the distinction between the commercial and the social, between the for-profit and the nonprofit, holds promise for tremendous resource growth for nonprofits and social enterprises alike. There will be limitations, of course, tied the actual skill levels in the sectors, the ability to actually measure social returns, and the sophistication of financial capacities within the nonprofit sector itself. Investment of resources assumes investable ideas and capacities. If the returns cannot match the investor expectations, the potential for resource mobilization will not be met, no matter the scope of the promise.[16]

Without concomitant growth in capacity for noncharitable resource management, and without the creativity needed to establish programs and services in ways that are investable, nonprofits will miss the opportunity.

The potential for making a quantum leap in the availability of funds is clearly building. But the capacity of organizations that actually do the work of programming and service execution on the societal commons may not keep up. Moreover, it is not simply a matter of skills and systems. Culture must also change. Nonprofits will have to establish dual cultures internally, driven both by passion for mission and by steely-eyed attention to efficiency and return. This is the overwhelming management challenge that a world of blurred definitions presents. Managers must develop ways to marry passion with performance, to hold their staffs accountable for commitment to cause and for return on investment. Far more than money or systems, it is this lack of management skill that may prove the highest barrier to entry and success for most nonprofit organizations.

Moreover, the more the understanding of the opportunity for scale and sustainability through innovation permeates philanthropy, the more it is likely to attract philanthropic organizations seeking impact. This applies to both corporate and private resource pools. In turn, the harder it will be for nonprofits to find sources of general operating support that is not tied to direct program implementation with measurable results. Resources to pay the utility bill will grow scarce. And resources to simply assuage those in need, not fundamentally alter their prospects, may as well.

Case E: Public Resources and Private Outreach

Author: Kaleidoscope Youth and Family Marketing

Partner: U.S. Consumer Product Safety Commission

Situation

The U.S. Consumer Product Safety Commission (CPSC) is an independent agency of the U.S. government created in 1972 by the Consumer Product Safety Act. The CPSC has a critically important mission: to keep all consumers safe from harm from dangerous products.

Stakes

Unfortunately, certain groups of Americans, such as the elderly, urban and rural low-income families, and some minority groups, often did not hear their safety messages. To address this situation, in 2004 the CPSC created the Neighborhood Safety Network (NSN), with the goal of putting lifesaving information in the hands of these populations. Those individuals who joined the NSN became partners with the CPSC and received safety information online to share with other members of their community offline. The CPSC recognized that it was critically important to grow the NSN to reach these at-risk population groups.

As of January 1, 2012, the NSN only had 2,748 members. CPSC set an aggressive goal to build the NSN network to 5,000 by March 31, 2012.

Strengths

Recognizing that the NSN itself was a grassroots initiative, Kaleidoscope and Stratacomm teamed up to create a recruitment effort rooted in that very grassroots philosophy. Though these hard-to-reach populations were disaggregated from traditional media reach, they were already aggregated within their own communities.

Strategy

While mass-market outreach was considered, the team realized that garnering interest in the NSN through people's current community affiliations would be more personal and ultimately more successful. Recognizing that communities have close connections within themselves,

(*continued*)

(*continued*)

community advocates for the NSN needed to be identified and mobilized. The strategy: focus on recruiting community leaders to which members already had strong loyalty and emotional connections and recruit them as partners to share lifesaving safety information with family, friends, neighbors, and the community. Outreach consisted of phone calls, e-mail, direct mail, public relations, and building relationships with community foundations and networks.

Solution

See Appendix 1
Note: CPSC cannot endorse a contractor or its writings or claims.

Notes

1. *Hidden Social Enterprises: Why We Need to Look Again at the Numbers* (London: Delta Economics and IFF Research, 2011).
2. Changing Our World acknowledges with thanks the work of its first Fellow, Annie Lam, in the development and analysis of these data.
3. G. Prizeman and D. Crossan, *Mapping Social Entrepreneurial Enterprises in Ireland* (Dublin: Centre for Nonprofit Management, School of Business, Trinity College, University of Dublin, March 2011), 3.
4. H. Koh, A. Karamchandani, and R. Katz, *From Blueprint to Scale: The Case for Philanthropy in Impact Investing* (Boston: Monitor Group, April 2012).
5. S. Lawrence, "Doing Good with Foundation Assets: An Updated Look at Program-Related Investments," Foundation Center, 2010, p. xvi.
6. S. Lawrence and R. Mukai, "Key Facts on Mission Investing," Foundation Center, October 2011.
7. Examples are taken from "Nonprofit-Owned Franchises: A Strategic Business Approach," Community Wealth Ventures, Inc. and IFA Educational Foundation, March 2004 (Updated August 204), pp. 15–39.
8. *Clinical Social Franchising Compendium: An Annual Survey of Programs* (San Francisco: Global Health Group, UCSF Global Health Sciences, 2012).
9. N. O'Donohoe, C. Leijonhufvud, and Y. Saltuuk. *Impact Investments: An Emerging Asset Class* (New York: J. P. Morgan, Rockefeller Foundation, Global Impact Investing Network, November 29, 2010), 9.
10. Ibid, p. 6.

11. *From Potential to Action: Bringing Social Impact Bonds to the U.S.* (New York: McKinsey & Company, May 2012), 13.

12. A. Bugg-Levine, B. Kogut, and N. Kulatilaka, "A New Approach to Funding Social Enterprises," *Harvard Business Review* (January–February 2012): 121–122.

13. J. Simon and J. Barmeier, *More than Money: Impact Investing for Development* (Washington, DC: Center for Global Development, 2010), 11–12.

14. D. Wilson, "Making Nutrition a Sustainable Business in Haiti," *New York Times,* November 2, 2011.

15. Bugg-Levine, Kogut and Kulatilaka, p. 123.

16. Simon and Barmeier, p. 10.

CHAPTER 8

Wealth

New Faces and New Places

As global economic structure and demographic structure change, the characteristics of global wealth will change as well. These changes will bring new challenge and new opportunity to both nonprofits and philanthropy itself.

A Glance Backwards for Perspective

In 1982, the first year in which it was compiled, the Forbes 400 list of wealthiest people required just $75 million to get through the door. Today, the entry level is $1.05 billion, an entry fee over 10 times that needed in 1982. This is a rate of increase many times in excess of the rate of inflation. In 1982, in 2010-dollar terms, the total wealth on the Forbes 400 was $720 billion. Only 13 of the Forbes wealthiest were billionaires. Today, the total wealth value on the list is in excess of $1.53 trillion, or more than twice as much, and the 400 billionaires on the list are only a third of the total 1,226 billionaires globally.

But it is not just amount of wealth or the numbers of wealthy that has changed. The characteristics of the wealthy are also undergoing change, reflecting and flowing from the fundamental economic changes described in Chapters 4 and 5. As the global economy becomes more entrepreneurial and interdependent, new economic centers are emerging and providing the engines of global growth, and technological innovation is creating faster and tighter cycles of change in the economic productive capacity. All of these changes in characteristics are likely to continue, and indeed heighten, in the coming decade.

Changes can be seen in the origins of wealth as well. In 1985, 59 percent of those billionaires on the Forbes 400 had inherited their wealth. By 2011, 69 percent of billionaires were self-made. In a 2005 Worth-Harrison Survey of

Wealth in America, only 8 percent of those under the age of 50 had inherited their wealth.[1] Indeed, in the United States, an estimated 81 percent of high-net-worth individuals (HNWIs) have been multimillionaires for less than 20 years.[2] The new wealth in the world is now controlled by the children of middle-class parents.

It is not surprising, therefore, that its emphasis is on entrepreneurship and innovation, or that it looks for new ways to solve problems.

This tendency for wealth to be associated with innovation is supplemented by lenses of geography, gender, and age.

Globalization

Global Wealth and High-Net-Worth Philanthropy

The 2011 billionaires list represents wealth from 58 countries including, for the first time, from Peru, Morocco, and Georgia. Setting one's wealth sights a bit lower, and counting those with a bit less than a billion dollars in assets, global diversity is even more striking. In 2010, there were 10.9 million HNWIs[3] worldwide, an increase of 10 percent over 2009. These individuals controlled $47.2 trillion in assets, topping the HNWI asset levels of 2007 before the Great Recession. See Exhibit 8.1.

The United States, Germany, and Japan account for 53 percent of these individuals, down from nearly 55 percent in 2006. Asia now has the second-largest number of HNWIs, surpassing the number in Europe as well as the total value of European wealth. India now ranks 12th in the world in terms of numbers of HNWIs. And the highest growth rates belong to Asia. China, India, and Australia all outperformed the United States and Europe in the growth of

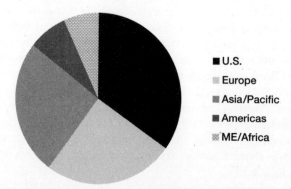

EXHIBIT 8.1 Geographic Distribution of World's Billionaires 2011
Source: Forbes 400, 2011

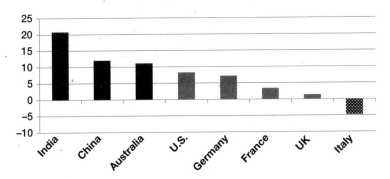

EXHIBIT 8.2 Percent Change in the Number of High-Net-Worth Individuals by Nation
2009–2010
Source: 2011 World Wealth Report from Capgemini and Merrill Lynch

the numbers of the wealthy. Indeed, in 2010 there were nearly 400,000 HNWIs in China alone. See Exhibit 8.2.

This globalization of wealth is not just a matter of the economic tigers of China and Brazil. In Africa, there are over 100 companies, domiciled on the continent and owned by Africans that each have annual sales of $1 billion or more. In the context of the 2010–2011 Third Replenishment of the Global Fund to Fight HIV/AIDS, Tuberculosis and Malaria, African wealth created the first ever regional philanthropic fund. This pooled philanthropy, the Fund from Africa, raised $8 million from African business leaders in just one year, the proceeds to be used within Africa for African disease control needs. Moreover, African wealth is increasingly tied not to natural resources and commodities, but to technology and services. When commodity prices took a nosedive in 2008, African economic growth barely showed an effect.[4] As a result of this increasingly diversified economy, African wealth at all levels will continue to grow.

How will these differing sources of wealth, representing as they do differences in culture and upbringing, affect the practice of philanthropy?

Surveys find that some things will remain familiar and some things may change. According to a 2010 survey by Barclays Wealth, almost a quarter of HNWIs globally say charity is a top spending priority.[5] After two years of decline, the philanthropic commitments of these individuals recovered in 2009. Except in North America, the portions of HNWI assets dedicated to philanthropy returned to their pre-2008 levels, or about 3 to 5 percent of assets.

As a consequence the number of individual, family and corporate foundations has expanded globally. There are over 75,000 foundations in the United States, perhaps as many as 85,000 in Western Europe and another 35,000 in Eastern Europe, 10,000 in Mexico, nearly 2,000 in China, and at least 1,000 in Brazil. The propensity of global wealth to engage in philanthropy is alive and well throughout the world.

Moreover, those philanthropic instincts are overwhelmingly focused on the places where the wealthy primarily live and work. Despite lives that are lived globally, despite businesses that span geographic boundaries, HNWIs of all nationalities find their philanthropic priorities in their own back yards. In a 2008 global survey of HNWIs, Changing Our World and Campden Research found that nearly three quarters of respondents (72.1 percent) ranked local causes as most important in their philanthropy.[6]

While much is held in common, differences are also seen in the data. Young philanthropists are much more likely to focus on poverty than are philanthropists of other ages. Those HNWI philanthropists over the age of 65 are much more likely to focus on health care, and those in middle ages are more likely to focus on education. The Changing Our World/Campden data revealed two very marked differences. First, women's issues are just that— women's issues. Nearly a third of women philanthropists ranked women's issues as "very important" in their philanthropy compared to just 9 percent of men. And in contrast to the philanthropic tendencies in the United States, where 40 percent of philanthropy flows to religion, for HNWIs, religion is a minor philanthropic concern. No other issue ranked as less important for every age group surveyed; religion held least importance as a philanthropic issue. (See Exhibit 8.3.)

Global Giving at All Levels

Philanthropic growth is not simply about the very wealthy, however. Giving within civil society is also an increasingly important phenomenon globally. The mega-gifts of the ultra-wealthy often raise eyebrows, but the consistent giving at all levels of society is usually the more fundamental story.

In December 2010, Azim Premji, India's wealthiest entrepreneur, pledged a $2 billion donation to Indian education, the largest gift of its kind by an Indian billionaire. The gift grabbed understandable headlines. Yet, in that same year,

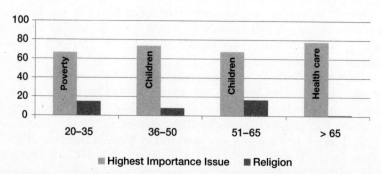

EXHIBIT 8.3 Role of Religion as "Very Important" in Personal Philanthropy (% by Age)

40 percent of India's urban residents and 96 percent of its middle- and upper-income households contributed to charity.[7] The commitment of the average Indian to community needs as the economy grows is the more important story of the globalization of giving that accompanies economic change.

The 2010 Charities Aid survey of global giving noted that 60 to 80 percent of residents of the Middle East give to charity and that Central America ranks seventh out of 13 regions in the world for personal giving. Giving in Chile is more widespread than in Norway. In Thailand, 73 percent of people give to charity, a rate that is higher than virtually anywhere in Europe and nearly triple that of Spain.[8]

Women and Wealth

One of the most striking trends in wealth is the rise of women as the holders of significant wealth in nearly every region of the world.

The United States

In the United States, women account for 43 percent of those with gross assets of $1.5 million or more. This translates into 1.2 million women, $4.6 trillion in wealth, and 41 percent of wealth value.[9] There are at least two factors at work in powering such capacity.

First, education trumps all. Today, American women aged 60-something earned their BA when only 45 percent of girls graduating from high school went on to college. Today, nearly three quarters do. In 1970, 34 percent of women entering the workforce had not finished high school. Today, the portion is less than 8 percent.

As noted in Exhibits 8.4, 8.5, and 8.6, women are beginning to pull even with, and even surpass, men in terms of educational achievement. The

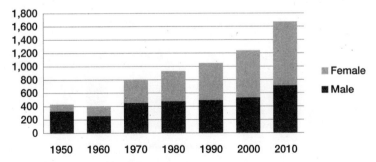

EXHIBIT 8.4 BA Degrees Awarded by Gender (in thousands)
Source: National Center for Education Statistics

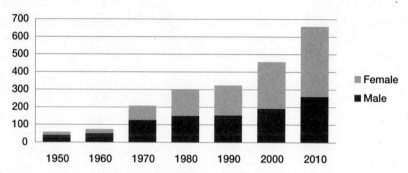

EXHIBIT 8.5 MA Degrees Awarded by Gender (in thousands)
Source: National Center for Education Statistics

majority of undergraduate BAs are awarded to women, compared to a quarter in 1960. Women also earn the majority of MAs, and nearly as many first professional degrees as men. Half of all medical students are women, as are 47 percent of law students. Although, in general, women earn less than men, women with a BA or higher on average earn nearly 95 percent as much as men. See Exhibit 8.4, Exhibit 8.5, and Exhibit 8.6.

Moreover, women's wealth-holding trends are likely to pick up greater momentum in the future. Young women aged 25 to 34 with at least a BA have nearly reached parity with their male counterparts (93 percent of salary), while women aged 45 to 54 with at least a BA are at 77 percent parity.[10] Equally in medicine, time will only accentuate women's wealth roles. Only 15 percent of women physicians are over the age of 55, compared to over a third of male physicians. Conversely, nearly 30 percent of women physicians are under the age of 35, compared to only 12 percent of men.[11] Over time, physicians in their prime earning years will increasingly be women.

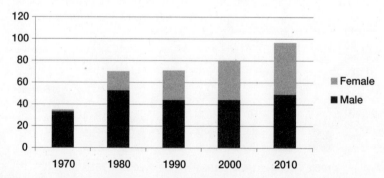

EXHIBIT 8.6 First Professional Degrees Awarded by Gender (in thousands)
Source: National Center for Education Statistics

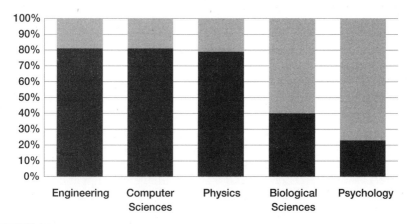

EXHIBIT 8.7 Science and Engineering Employment by Gender 2007
Source: Science and Engineering Indicators, 2010 (Washington, DC: National
Science Foundation, 2010)

Of course, there is a weakness. In a high-technology economy, which, as previous chapters have shown, is likely to characterize the economy of the United States in the future, women are woefully lacking in the ranks of professional scientists and engineers, except in the medical sciences. Only 20 percent of computer programmers and software engineers, 27 percent of systems analysts, and 9 percent of computer hardware engineers are women. All of these portions have declined in the last decade.[12] While 80 percent of psychologists are women, only 20 percent of engineers and physicists are women.[13] See Exhibit 8.7.

Strength in science and engineering may be critical to the continued growth of wealth by women in a technology economy. That impact is best seen in West Coast high-tech companies where salaries are higher than in many other industries. On average, 50 percent of workers in an American company are female. Facebook comes in first among its peers, but at 33 percent. At Microsoft and Intel, only 20 percent of the workforce is female. At Apple, Dell, and Google, women account for only 26 percent, 24 percent, and 29 percent, respectively, of the technical workforce.[14]

If education is a critical wealth engine powering women forward, business is often the vehicle. Women own 41 percent of all private firms in the United States. They employ 12.8 million workers (one out of every seven), and the number of women-owned firms has grown at twice the rate of all privately held companies. If the economic capacity of these firms was a country, it would rank just behind Germany in economic size.

Furthermore, the distribution of those firms is well balanced. Professional, scientific, and technical firms account for 21 percent, financial for 6 percent, communications for 8 percent, and health and welfare for 9 percent. This ability of the women-owned business sector to withstand economic change is aided by its diversity.

Women's Wealth Globally

As women are rising to wealth parity in the United States, they are also doing so abroad.[15] Globally, over $20 trillion in investments are controlled by women, nearly a third of which are outside of North America and Western Europe. As noted in Exhibit 8.8, North America is in the lead, but even in the Middle East, women control more than one in five investment dollars.

Women control more than half of all wealth in Finland, the Netherlands, Denmark, France, Germany, and Britain. In the United Kingdom, women millionaires will outnumber their male counterparts by 2020. Australia and New Zealand rank second behind the United States in terms of the percent of wealth controlled by women.

But women's wealth is not just a Western phenomenon. The annual growth rate of women's wealth in Asia (excluding Japan) equaled or exceeded that in the United States between 2008 and 2009. In the Middle East, women hold $40 billion in personal wealth and make decisions affecting $500 billion in investments. A third of Middle Eastern women-owned businesses earn in excess of $100,000 per year, compared to 12 percent of their U.S. counterparts.

As evidence of the significance of the trend, private bankers have begun to create institutional mechanisms to serve that wealth. This has been a clear trend in the West, but the Middle East provides perhaps the most striking example of the degree to which the wealth of women has emerged from the shadows.

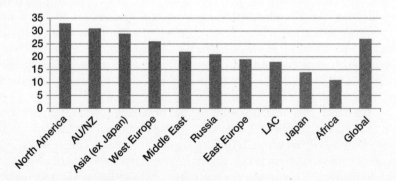

EXHIBIT 8.8 Global Distribution of Women's Wealth 2009
Source: Leveling the Playing Field: Upgrading the Wealth Experience for Women
© 2010, The Boston Consulting Group

Financial institutions in the region are now racing to catch up with and accommodate these trends. Founded in Dubai in 2007 by Dubai World (whose chief financial officer is a woman), FORSA is a specialized investment fund for women only. Its initial capitalization reached AED 300 million. It is managed by women investors and solicits investments from women. Moreover, FORSA has joined with the Mohammed Bin Rashid Establishment to support women entrepreneurs and with INSEAD to expand business management skills for women. Abu Dhabi–based Al Bashayer Investments is a similar fund, offering investments consistent with Islamic law.

But financial clout is not simply limited to women-owned investment companies. The Abu Dhabi Chamber of Commerce now has three women on its 21-member board. The Kuwait Stock Exchange now has a women's trading floor. The Commercial International Bank of Egypt, the third-largest bank in the country, has a female managing director at the helm, a Women's Banking Service with separate women's lounges and specialized staff, and a "Ladies Business Club" for regular discussion of investment options and tailored financial products. Saudi Arabia's National Commercial Bank has opened up 46 women-only branches, up from only 2 in 1980. Saudi Hollandi Bank, Al Rajhi Capital, Al Otaiba Holdings—the list of financial institutions in the region newly committed to providing services to women is increasing rapidly.

Women's Engagement

Women with professional and financial power are now more engaged in the public forums that affect global economic directions. In 2002, the Davos World Economic Forum counted only 9 percent women among its participants and no female panelists. Ten years later, 17 percent of participants and 20 percent of panelists were women, still an underrepresentation at this long male-dominated talkfest, but a significant increase from the past.

Moreover, high-net-worth women are not passive about their wealth. Prudential's Financial Experience & Behaviors Among Women survey found that 84 percent of high-net-worth women are involved in their financial planning.[16] Similarly, a Wilmington Trust survey in 2010 found that two thirds were highly engaged in their own and their family's wealth management and 80 percent had a high understanding of their financial assets.[17]

While emerging high-net-worth women clearly understand and are involved in the management of their wealth, 63 percent would prefer that people *not* know they are wealthy. They are less likely to be overt about their wealth and less likely to seek recognition for their philanthropy. But should there have been any question up to this point, they are no fools. As noted in Exhibit 8.9, they are more likely than men to want to see direct impact from their giving.

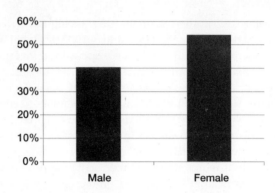

EXHIBIT 8.9 Percent of HNWI Survey Respondents Who Ranked Measurable Impact as "Very Important"

Source: Giving Through the Generations

The Rise of the Young

When Andrew Carnegie pledged to give away his fortune, he was 54 years old. Average life expectancy was 52. He was, for all intents and purposes, giving his money away at the end of his life. When Bill Gates and Jeff Skoll created their foundations, they were 39 and 34 years old, respectively. Average life expectancy was 76. They have at least 40 years of philanthropic strategy ahead of them. The Bill & Melinda Gates Foundation is now almost three times the size of its next-largest peer, and must give away more than $3 billion per year.[18]

Skoll and Gates are not alone. When Google went public, 900 employees became instant millionaires. The entire core executive suite of Facebook is under the age of 45. The average age of Facebook's board is 44, and the median age of its employees is 26. Facebook's 2012 initial stock offering represented a liquidity event for its employees and managers that created more than 1,000 new millionaires in their early 30s. Subsequent weaknesses in the market for Facebook stock dampened the euphoria somewhat, but the betting is still that Facebook founders will be among the wealthiest people of their generation. While such wealth at such young ages does not create instant mega-philanthropists (there is allure to that Ferrari, after all), wealth held from a young age for a long time does build philanthropic resources at levels not previously seen.

The entrepreneurship that increasingly drives the innovation that, in turn, increasingly drives economic growth and change is populated by the young. Global Entrepreneurship Monitor estimates that 42 percent of early-stage entrepreneurs are between 18 and 35 years of age, with a steep increase between the ages of 25 and 34, and that about 1 in 5 is offering an innovative product or service that is completely new and has few other competitors.[19] Survey research in India has shown the same granular pattern as the global data. Over half of entrepreneurs are below the age of 30 when they create their businesses.[20] In India, 77 percent of the philanthropists surveyed by Bain & Company in 2012 had been engaged in philanthropy for less than three years, and 69 percent of these young donors expected to increase their philanthropy in the next five years.[21]

With four or five decades of life ahead of them, the younger generation of philanthropists expects to be actively and personally involved in their philanthropic investments for much longer than past generations of philanthropists. Moreover, many come from industries in which change and innovations are the constant, not the exception. For these philanthropists, new ways of thinking and new approaches are the norm.

Hence, they start with the opportunity for problem solving and tailor resource strategies accordingly rather than starting with resources and seeking problems or causes with which they resonate. Moreover, how resources are organized to solve problems or power opportunities is immaterial. This new generation of funders and philanthropy managers is particularly comfortable operating in the interstices between donations and investments, and they have created an entirely new class of resources which are neither pure gifts nor pure commercial capital, but rather, as discussed in Chapters 6 and 7, a blended mix of resources that now flow to social problem solving.

They are what Paul Schervish calls "agent-animated philanthropists."[22] Young wealth emerging from entrepreneurship and technology is more steeped in business than in charity, and hence tends to think in term of sustainable market-type solutions that can meet needs at scale, rather than in terms of culture or community.

Summary and Nonprofit Implications

Wealth is not simply growing rapidly; its distribution is taking on characteristics quite different from those of the past. The accumulation of high levels of wealth and the engagement in philanthropy is a global phenomenon, and is likely to be ever more so as non-Western economies become engines of economic growth. Education and the opening of professions has propelled women to the front of wealth holding, and the effects of this rise in women's leadership roles is likely to only gain momentum in the future. And, of course, there is ever the energy of youth. The pace of technological change and the mastery of ever newer technologies will continue to create wealth among young entrepreneurs and technologists because the pace of global economic integration will demand ever newer means to boost productivity and lever economic growth.

All three trends will change the face of wealth holding in the future.

In turn, the philanthropy of the wealthy will change. Nonprofits are likely to find that cause is less compelling than results, and gifts are less numerous than investments. But results and investments assume, and will demand, fundamental change in nonprofit structures, management, and skills.

Case F: New Leaders, New Passion, Persistent Problems

Author: Wolff Olins

Wolff Olins

Partner: i2 Institute for Imagination and Ingenuity

Situation

Young people are the world's most important resource. Strong societies depend on them, and the future depends on them. While Saudi Arabian youth have abundant access to education, they do not have enough access to the opportunities to apply it. In 2011, the Saudi Arabian government invested $40 billion in education and training, yet 43 percent of 20- to 24-year-olds in Saudi Arabia are unemployed. With nearly 40 percent of the Arab population being 18 years old or younger, the region needed a solution that's both sustainable and scalable.

Renowned Saudi Arabian scientist Dr. Hayat Sindi came to Wolff Olins with the ambition to translate her passion for science and social innovation into a sustainable solution to bring employment and opportunity to the Middle East, starting in her home country, Saudi Arabia. Dr. Sindi is the first female from the Gulf to earn a PhD in biotechnology.

Stakes

i2 Institute for Imagination and Ingenuity aims to create an ecosystem of entrepreneurship and social innovation for scientists, technologists, and engineers in the Middle East and beyond. Because i2 was taking shape in the midst of the Arab Spring and a post-recession world, there were many variables to consider to ensure that the organization would be as impactful and as adaptable as possible. The stakes for getting this model right were incredibly high. Most important, to enable i2 to build financial strength, we needed to create a brand that would appeal to Western and Middle Eastern donors by championing possibility, not politics.

Strengths

Dr. Sindi believed that by addressing a fundamental social and economic problem, she could achieve lasting positive impact and give young people a sense of hope and possibility. i2 launched in the fall of 2012 in Jeddah, Saudi Arabia, and open applications for its first round of fellows. As it builds a network of innovators, investors, and scholars dedicated to its core purpose, the institute will provide fellows with the inspiration, training, and tools to contribute to society and to the market. i2 is trying to connect the dots by putting the right resources with the right issues so that every young innovator has the opportunity to reach their potential and contribute to their society.

Strategy

i2's strategic imperatives were to create sustainable, scalable impact, which meant any strategy would need to connect people, resources, and opportunities on an ongoing, synergistic basis. Any other solution would be creating one-off opportunities instead of addressing the fundamental problem of overeducated, underemployed young people. The name i2 boldly expresses a formula for innovation and self-realization—imagination activated by ingenuity. The Middle Eastern origin and universal relevance of i2's mission is expressed by an Arabic-inspired logo created with Roman characters, and a verbal system employing Arabic and English integrated with the i2 name. The strong, vibrant color palette expresses optimism, the diversity of minds i2 hopes to attract, and a spectrum of opportunity for the youth, both for the country and region.

Solution

See Appendix 1.

Notes

1. "The Status of Wealth in America," *Worth* (November 2005): 31.
2. A. Trachtenberg and D. Ehrlich, "America's New Ultra-Wealthy: Not the Same Old Rich," Ivory River Group Wealth Management Report, 2006, p. 1.
3. Defined by private banking as those with financial assets in excess of $1 million, not including the value of a primary residence and consumables. Data are from the 2011 World Wealth Report of Capgemini and Merrill Lynch Wealth Management, which provide an annual analysis of global wealth trends.
4. "Africa's Hopeful Economies: The Sun Shines Bright," *The Economist* (December 3, 2011): 83.
5. *Global Giving: The Culture of Philanthropy* (London: Barclay's Wealth and Ledbury Research, November 2010), 2.
6. S. Raymond, B. Love, and J. Moore, *Giving through the Generations* (London: Campden Research, 2009), 36.
7. A. Sheth, "An Overview of Philanthropy in India." Presentation at the Indian Philanthropy Forum, March 19, 2010.
8. World Giving Index 2011, Charities Aid Foundation, 2012.
9. U.S. Department of Commerce and Bureau of the Census, 2009.
10. U.S. Bureau of Labor Statistics, 2009.
11. American Medical Association data, 2008.
12. Bureau of Labor Statistics, 2010.
13. *Science and Engineering Indicators, 2010* (Washington, DC: National Science Foundation, 2010).
14. Technology Company Salary and Job Satisfaction Report. PayScale, 2011. Various.
15. Unless otherwise cited, data on global distribution of women's wealth are taken from "Leveling the Playing Field," Boston Consulting Group, July 2010; and "Women and Wealth," GenSpring Family Offices, 2010.
16. "Financial Experience & Behaviors Among Women: 2010–2011 Prudential Research Survey." Prudential Insurance, 2011, p. 5.
17. "The New Wealth Paradigm," Wilmington Trust and Campden Research, 2010, p. 3.
18. E. Skloot, "The Gated Community," *Alliance* 16(3) (September 2011): 32.
19. D. J. Kelley, S. Singer, and M. Herrington, "Global Entrepreneurship Monitor 2011 Global Report," Global Entrepreneurship Research Association, 2011, pp. 4, 17. Note that a study by the Kauffman Foundation specifically in the United States found that the Great Recession may have resulted in a surge of entrepreneurship among those in middle ages rather than in the young. See D. Stangler, "The Coming Entrepreneurship Boom," Ewing Marion Kauffman Foundation, June 2009.

20. S. K. Rai, "Indian Entrepreneurs: An Empirical Investigation of Entrepreneur's Age and Firm Entry, Type of Ownership and Risk Behavior," *Journal of Services Research* 8(1) (April–September 2008): 213–228.
21. *India Philanthropy Report 2012* (Boston: Bain & Co., 2012), 37.
22. P. G. Schervish, M. A. O'Herlihy, and J. J. Havens. "Agent-Animated Wealth and Philanthropy: The Dynamics of Accumulation and Allocation among High-Tech Donors," 2001, www.bc.edu/swri.

CHAPTER **9**

The Global Benefits of
Rising Well-Being

Because nonprofits often are focused on problems, and hence because philanthropy often flows to problem solving, the sector often loses sight of the fact that, in many ways, people around the world are better off than they were decades ago, and are likely to be even better off in the future. Indeed, the World Bank estimates than in 2008 the percentage of the global population living in extreme poverty had declined to 22 percent from 43 percent in 1981. In East Asia and the Pacific, extreme poverty has declined to 14 percent from 77 percent in 1981—an extraordinary accomplishment. With that progress, achieving the Millennium Development Goal of halving extreme poverty by 2015 is well in sight.[1]

While Chapters 3 and 8 noted the spread of global economic progress, related progress can be seen on a variety of other indicators, all of which will change the patterns of both needs and opportunities in the nonprofit sector, and the ways in which philanthropists—corporate, foundation, and individual—will think about the nature and use of their resources.

This does not mean that there are not serious deficiencies in almost any indicator of progress. Poverty and needless suffering, lack of access to basic human needs, continued challenges meeting global, national, and local challenges of all sorts continue everywhere in the world. Much remains to be done, whatever your line of sight. But the pace of advancement has been marked, and is often lost for the focus on problems. Furthermore, that pace of advancement opens up new opportunities to spur philanthropy itself. Three examples of the elements of rising well-being will illustrate the implications of change: education, health, and civic participation.

Education

In 1970, 47.1 percent of Americans over the age of 25 had not completed a high school education. By 2010, that had dropped to 14.4 percent. The equivalent percentages for those holding a bachelor's degree or higher was 10.7 percent in 1970 and 28.2 percent in 2010. Indeed, the portion of the population with holding a bachelor's degree or higher rose by 8 percentage points in just two decades, 1990 to 2010.

Viewing such progress in gross, point-in-time terms, however, does not provide the full picture of actual implications. One must first look toward future trends and second toward the broadening effects of education across the population.

In 2010, less than a quarter of those aged 65 and older had a college degree or higher, compared to 31.1 percent of those aged 25 to 34. And of the next cohort, aged 18 to 24, over half (53.8 percent) were either in college (bachelors and associate levels) or had completed a college degree.[2] This wave of educational achievement has built over the generations and will continue to build. The educational levels of future generations in aggregate will be higher than in the past, driven by the expectations of higher levels of education in younger generations. See Exhibit 9.1.

These levels will also be driven by the role of technology in making higher education available to larger numbers of people at lower cost, and in ways that will even begin to adjust the numbers of college graduates in older age groups. Indeed, more than half the students enrolled in for-profit higher education institutions (most of which have predominant online access) are over the age of 25.[3] Indeed, there are now nearly four million students pursuing bachelor's degrees exclusively online, and 25 percent of all college students are taking at least one online course.

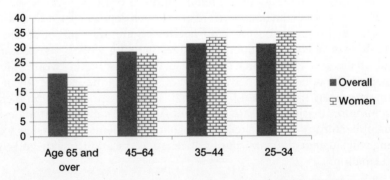

EXHIBIT 9.1 Percent Age Group with College Degree or Higher, 2010
Source: Bureau of the Census, 2010

Two thirds of two-year and four-year postsecondary institutions offer online courses or other distance education programs.[4] In an Instructional Technology Council survey of 2012, moreover, 62 percent of institutions reported that demand for distance learning class offerings exceeds program supply.[5] Between 2002 and 2011, the percentage of a survey of higher education institutions who believed that online education would be critical to long-term strategy for their institutions increased from 48.8 percent to 65.5 percent.[6] The demographic structure of those with higher education, therefore, is likely to change markedly in the future. Technology will enable people globally to obtain knowledge and skills (and therefore move up the job and financial ladder) at ages and in places different from the past. A college degree will not pass only through the hands of 20-somethings. It will be earned at all ages and by people from all types of job backgrounds, at prices that are a fraction of those on the ivy-covered campuses of the past.

Second, education has broadened within the U.S. population. Indeed, the broadening is striking in scope and time frame.

In terms of gender, only 16.8 percent of women aged 65 or older hold college degrees. Double that percent are degree holders in the 35-to-44 age group, and more than double that percentage (35 percent) have college or advanced degrees in the 25-to-34 age group.

In terms of ethnicity, the story is equally compelling. In 2003, the Pew Hispanic Center issued an education report with the title "Hispanic Youth Dropping Out of U.S. Schools: Measuring the Challenge."[7] The report noted that, while dropout rates for Hispanic youth had declined in the 1990s apace with the declines for other ethnic groups, Hispanic youth were more likely to have dropped out of high school than other groups. Just eight years later, in 2011, The Center issued a report entitled "Hispanic College Enrollment Spikes, Narrowing Gaps with Other Groups."[8] This report noted that, for the first time, young Hispanics outnumbered young blacks on college campuses. The percentage of Hispanic youth who had completed high school and were in college now approaches the percentages of whites and blacks. See Exhibit 9.2.

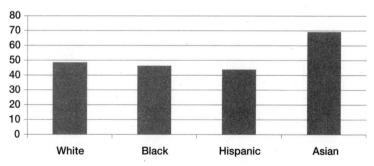

EXHIBIT 9.2 Percent High School Completers in College 2010
Source: Pew Research Center

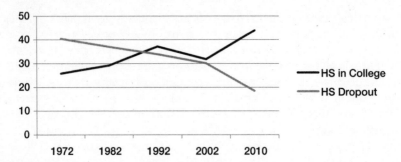

EXHIBIT 9.3 Percentage of Hispanic 18- to 24-Year-Olds: Graduated High School and in College versus High School Dropout

Source: Pew Research Center

Moreover, the percentage of Hispanic high school graduates now far exceeds the percentage of Hispanic youth dropping out of high school. In only eight years, the picture changed markedly. See Exhibit 9.3.

The contexts created by past and current educational achievement are an important harbinger of the future. In 1979, only 4.9 percent of black children had parents who had completed a college education. By 2006, just a decade and a half later, that portion had nearly quintupled, to 21.2 percent.[9]

While there remain serious educational problems in America, not the least of which is the continued need to address problems of inequality of access and quality, the educational picture for American youth has changed for the better. In the past three decades the percentage of 18- to 24-year-olds enrolled in college has risen from under a quarter to nearly half. And the higher education numbers of all ethnicities are rising. These rising numbers hold the potential for rising incomes across ethnicities, and hence perhaps patterns of philanthropy that will, in the future, be much more highly diverse at levels of major giving and high-net-worth philanthropy.

Internationally, progress is also to be seen. International development has long been focused on literacy as a critical prerequisite for economic and social progress. While much remains to be done, and very, very much in some places, as seen in Exhibit 9.4, many nations have markedly increased their literacy rates in the past three decades. These data for youth 15 to 24 years of age are higher than for entire populations because previous generations were unschooled. Again, from a trajectory point of view, this progress foreshadows a very different future in terms of population capacity and expectations.

While in many countries overall women's literacy has not kept pace with national averages, in many nations the current generation of young people does show increasing gender balance in terms of literacy. In the countries noted in Exhibit 9.4, girls' literacy rates were within two or three percentage points of the overall average and, in some cases, exceeded them.

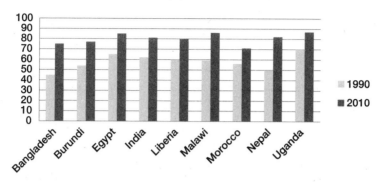

EXHIBIT 9.4 Percent Literate Ages 18 to 24, Selected Countries
Source: World Bank, World Development Indicators

School enrollment rates have also increased. Primary school net enroll-ment rates a decade ago that were in the 70 percent range, now are in the 80 to 90 percent range. Even in sub-Saharan Africa, net primary school enrollment approaches 80 percent. While enrollment rates for girls lag totals, the gap is closing. This tends to be true even where cultural barriers exist. In the Arab states, for example, only 79 percent of girls were enrolled in primary school in 1998. By 2009, that had increased to 93 percent. Secondary school enrollment rates, however, have generally not kept pace, with only 60 to 70 percent of young people enrolled, sinking to 27 percent in Africa. (See Exhibit 9.5.)

In addition, and obviously, questions of quality must be raised. To sit in a seat in a classroom is very different from acquiring knowledge and under-standing. Nonetheless, progress is apparent, and today's generation of young people in developing economies will have a very different educational

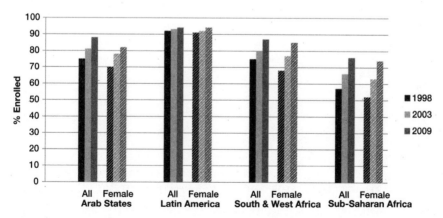

EXHIBIT 9.5 Net Primary School Enrollment Rate, Selected Global Regions
Source: UNESCO Statistics

experience than their parents or grandparents, with associated differences in personal economic capacities and expectations.

Health Status and Its Consequences

Just as with education, progress in health status has been marked in the past decades, and has created both new capabilities and new challenges.

In the United States, life expectancy at age 65 now approaches or exceeds 80 years of age. The nation is aging, which is the fundamental force behind health care costs and the fundamental turning point on which health care policy and finance must turn. (See Exhibit 9.6.)

But that progress is also a product of other changes, in both health behaviors and in medicine. In the past three decades, for example, cardiovascular death rates have fallen from over 500 per 100,000 population to 260 per 100,000.[10] In no small measure, this reflects both new therapeutics to prevent and reverse heart disease, and also behavior change. Smoking rates have fallen from nearly half the population (42.4 percent) in 1965 to less than one in five (19.3 percent) today. Indeed, after World War II, more than half of men in America smoked cigarettes, driving up cardiovascular and other chronic diseases at early ages. In 2010, only 21.5 percent smoke, as do only 17.3 percent of women, down from a third in 1965.[11]

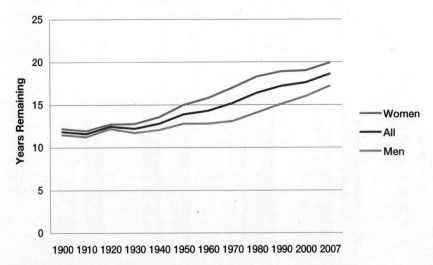

EXHIBIT 9.6 U.S. Life Expectancy at Age 65

Source: CDC National Vital Statistics Reports, 2011/CDC Health, United States, 2010

As a result, the "aging" of the population has not necessarily meant an immediate and equivalent rise in personal dependency, even if it means an increase in Social Security payments. Indeed, a combination of better health status (35 percent of those 65 to 74 exercise regularly, as do 34 percent of those over the age of 75), less demanding working conditions, and the 2000 Social Security reform that rolled back penalties for older workers now means that over a third of men aged 66 to 69 continue in the full-time workforce.[12] This is nearly double the rate in the 1980s, and provides not only income to individuals, but an economic boost because part of those earnings become consumption, which itself represents 70 percent of the economy.

There are new problems that come with progress, regarding both costs and diseases. The aging of the population, together with technological advance, is the engine for health care cost inflation. Those 65 years of age and older are three times more likely to be hospitalized than younger groups, with longer lengths of stay and higher costs.[13] With an increasingly elder population also comes change in epidemiology, with most older persons having at least one chronic condition and a recent significant rise in obesity throughout the population that is associated with a range of other health problems.

Hence, the need to be continuously attuned to changes in the health and well-being of the population is critical to keeping both philanthropy and nonprofits positioned to take advantage of positive trends, and adjust to the consequent changing nature of problems.

Internationally, the patterns are similar. In industrialized countries, the aging of the population is even more marked than in the United States. In Germany, for example, 20 percent of the population is over the age of 65, and the birth rate is 1.4, well below the replacement level of 2.0 per woman of childbearing age. Today in Germany, there are 34 retirees per 100 working-age people; by 2030 that will rise to 50/100. Every two workers will support one retiree. Those needs for budgets for social support will drain resources away from reinvestment in the productive capacity of the economy and hence risk the creation of limits to growth.

The consequent future economic and social challenges are daunting. For Europe, the past social safety guarantees mean that financial supports that begin at 50 years of age must continue on for decades for larger and larger portions of the population. These trends are fundamental building blocks for economic and social policy challenges in the coming decade—challenges that will affect government expectations of the role of philanthropy in society and the nature of the populations and problems addressed by nonprofits.

In developing nations, changes in health have also been marked, tied to both changes in demography and changes in health capacity.[14] As noted in Exhibit 9.7, life expectancy has risen rapidly and will be within nine years of industrialized nations by 2025. This aging has been accompanied by falling birth rates, such that the percentage of the population over the age of 60 and

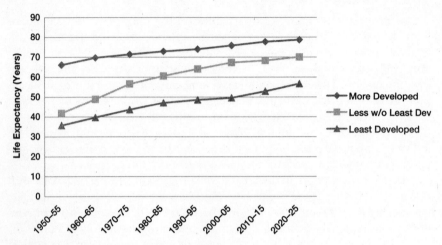

EXHIBIT 9.7 U.S. Life Expectancy at Age 65
Source: World Population Prospects

under the age of five will cross over in approximately 2015. The absolute numbers of children under the age of five in developing economies will begin to fall by that time as well. Indeed, in some regions this crossover between the elderly and the young has already taken place. In South America and the Caribbean, for example, the portions shifted in the 1980s. Also see Exhibit 9.8.

These changes will in turn change the nature of health care problems and opportunities, a subject discussed in more detail in Chapter 14. With economic progress and longer lives has come the need to expand the lens of health into disease areas that are deeply entwined with the behaviors that accompany that progress. This is a fundamental and inexorable change that will affect the health context of progress for decades, even generations, to come.

In between these changes, and due to falling death rates at early ages, in the middle of the demographic sandwich if you will, there is the rise of the young working-aged population, a theme to which the author will return in

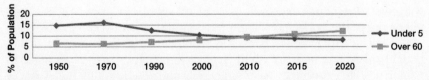

EXHIBIT 9.8 The Aging of the Developing World
Source: World Population Prospects

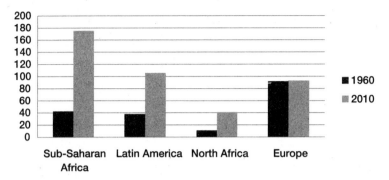

EXHIBIT 9.9 Population Aged 15 to 24 by Global Region
Source: World Population Prospects

the discussion of civil engagement later in this chapter. In short, the population aged 15 to 24 has increased markedly in the developing world. The numbers of young people of working ages have quadrupled in sub-Saharan Africa and more than doubled in Latin America, while stagnating in Europe. This will have immeasurable effects on economies and political systems in the immediate future. See Exhibit 9.9.

Young, healthy, educated workforces could create huge economic opportunities in these nations. They have the potential to attract significant investment in labor-intensive industries by global companies as well as spur greater enterprise creation within nations. Indeed, small and medium-sized enterprises in most economies, including those in developing economies, account for 60 to 70 percent of jobs.[15] In addition, foreign investment, reacting to emerging economy capacity, will continue to create jobs abroad; the U.S. multinational sector has over 10 million employees around the world.[16] The growth of the workforce and private enterprise will create new priorities on job creation for global development, as well as new human resources for philanthropy and volunteerism.

In addition and as a consequence of the growing labor force and the growing presence of private employers, the concepts of corporate engagement will also increasingly be found in developing economies. However, they will adjust to local culture and local expectations. As noted in Chapters 6 and 7, this adaptation continually adjusts the nature of, and opportunities for, the alignment of what is now "corporate social engagement" or "corporate social responsibility" with the changing nature of community assets and needs in developing economies.

This progress has and will continue to fundamentally change the nature of policy priorities, problems, and opportunities in the international development space.

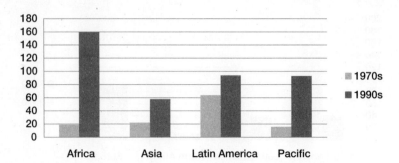

EXHIBIT 9.10 Total Number of Presidential and Parliamentary Elections by Global Region

Source: International Institute for Democracy and Electoral Assistance

Participation and Connectivity

The additional dimension of change that has come with, and in some cases has been fueled by, these changes in education and well-being is civic engagement. Beginning with the end of the Cold War in the 1990s, former authoritarian societies became increasingly open, and civic participation is increasingly expected. In the 1970s there were 237 presidential and parliamentary elections worldwide. By the 1990s, that number had nearly tripled, with nearly all of the growth coming outside of North America and western Europe.[17] See Exhibit 9.10.

The Gallup Organization annually publishes a Civic Engagement Index that combines volunteerism, donations, and general assistance to communities. The 2010 Index found that 9 of the countries ranked in the Top 20 were non-Western.[18] In an assessment of voter turnout, The Institute for Democracy and Electoral Assistance found that only 6 of the top 20 countries in terms of voter turnout were from western Europe. The rest were from central and eastern Europe, Africa, South America, and Asia.[19] Participation in decisions that affect community, and participation in problem solving itself, is increasingly a global phenomenon. Expectations about participation go hand-in-hand with that trend.

The future is likely to see more of the same. Of course, the transition will not be smooth or even. The elevated expectations of the Arab Spring of 2011, for instance, quickly gave way to the messiness of actual government formation and the often unpopular decisions entailed in governing. The openness and freedom of ideas and action that can be generated by the boundless potential of digital strategy and communications ultimately becomes lassoed to earth by the decidedly bounded details of putting bodies in governing chairs and making practical decisions about how to allocate resources to competing needs. All of this is natural. But the pure oxygen of open societies and civic participation, once uncorked, will not be forced back into its former confines.

It appears that this is particularly true for the young. And hence it will be particularly true for the future. Formed in 2011, its recentness perhaps also a measure of the pace of change, the Youth and Participatory Politics research group found that youth are disengaged from traditional forms of participation but drawn into engagement through the Internet and digital media. Digital media are creating, and have the potential to increase, civic engagement.[20] Indeed, an international survey of universities found that over 50 percent of students participate in civil engagement activities, with some of the highest levels coming from places like Indonesia and Ghana.[21]

Nonprofits and philanthropies must pay attention to these trends.

On the one hand, the members of society globally want a say. And hence the views and expectations of communities will need to be the premise upon which philanthropy acts. The days of top-down resource flows are coming to an end. The demands for engagement mean that priorities must reflect the views of the people, wherever they are, not simply the views of philanthropy wherever its offices.

On the other hand, engagement also means that there is greater opportunity to build volunteerism and giving. An age of broad expansion of participation on the societal commons, albeit likely digitally mediated, is ahead. There is no better news for the nonprofit sector.

Summary and Nonprofit Implications

Progress is to be seen on a wide variety of measures of the human condition. In turn, this has created both unprecedented opportunity and a changed set of problems.

In this context of continued change, the real challenge for philanthropy and nonprofits is to embed constant flexibility into priorities and programs. Yesterday's portfolios will not reflect tomorrow's realities. Yesterday's priorities, however compelling at the time, will not reflect either tomorrow's problems or tomorrow's opportunities. This is the real problem for the nonprofit and philanthropic sectors facing change.

Commercial organizations are accustomed to being ever responsive to markets, knowing when the consumer's view changes, anticipating that change, and acting quickly. Nonprofits and philanthropies are not. They are more likely to be tied to core commitments of long-standing importance. This tethers them to the past, rather than positioning them for the future. They have not built deep capacity to think about the need for change simultaneously with carrying out their missions.

That great American Oracle, Yogi Berra, once remarked, "Think? How ya gonna think and hit at the same time?" This is the fundamental problem and opportunity for the nonprofit sector. Progress provides both increasing opportunity and a changing problem set. Both exist within the continued need to address community needs. The key is learning how to think and hit at the same time.

Notes

1. Povcalnet, http://econ.worldbank.org/povcalnet.
2. U.S. Bureau of the Census, 2010 American Community Survey 1-Year Estimates, Table S1501.
3. D. L. Bennett, A. R. Lucchese, and R. K. Vedder, *For-Profit Higher Education: Growth, Innovation and Regulation* (Washington, DC: Center for College Affordability and Productivity, July 2010), 11.
4. "Distance Education at Degree-Granting Postsecondary Institutions: 2006–07," U.S. Department of Education, National Center for Education Statistics, 2008, p. 2.
5. "2011 Distance Education Survey Results," Instructional Technology Council, March 2012, p. 19.
6. I. E. Allen and J. Seaman, *Class Differences: Online Education in the United States, 2010* (Boston: Babson Survey Research and The Sloan Consortium, November 2010), 29.
7. R. Fry, Pew Hispanic Center Report, June 12, 2003.
8. R. Fry, Pew Hispanic Center Report, August 25, 2011.
9. Vital Statistics, *The Journal of Blacks in Higher Education*, 60 (Summer 2008): 2.
10. *Morbidity and Mortality: 2009 Chartbook on Cardiovascular, Lung and Blood Diseases* (Washington, DC: National Institutes of Health, 2009), 25.
11. U.S. Centers for Disease Control and Prevention, 2010.
12. E. L. Glaeser, "Goodbye, Golden Years," *New York Times,* November 19, 2011, Sunday Review Opinions, p. 1.
13. Department of Health and Human Services, Administration on Aging, 2010 profiles on utilization.
14. Demographic projections data are from the United Nations Populations Prospects, 2009 database.
15. International Labor Organization, *Global Employment Trends 2011: The Challenge of a Jobs Recovery* (Geneva: International Labor Office, 2011).
16. J. K. Jackson, "U.S. Direct Investment Abroad: Trends and Current Issues," Congressional Research Service, February 1, 2011, p. 6.
17. International Institute for Democracy and Electoral Assistance, 2009.
18. C. English, "Civic Engagement Highest in Developing Countries." *Gallup World* (January 18, 2011), www.gallup.com/poll/145589/civic-engage-ment-highest-developed-countries.aspx.

19. International Institute for Democracy and Electoral Assistance.
20. Youth & Participatory Politics, www.ypp.dmlcentral.net.
21. Report on the conference Fulfilling the Civil Roles and Social Responsibilities of Higher Education, Tallories, France, September 2005, as contained in the comments of Robert Hollister, Jonathan M. Tisch College, New York.

CHAPTER 10

Next-Gen Leaders
The Emerging Corporate-Nonprofit Gap

With the aging of the population comes opportunity for leadership. Baby Boomers are retiring at a rate of one every eight seconds, and some companies will have up to 60 percent of their workforce eligible for retirement by 2015. What is true on the shop floor is also true in the C-suite. Leadership in nonprofit and commercial institutions will begin to exit the stage, and a new set of leaders will step forward. But these leaders will be of a different stripe, with different skills and different perspectives than their forebears. The nature and pace of that change will deeply affect the future of philanthropy, private and corporate, and the future of nonprofit strategy.

Corporate Leaders

In 2010, the average age of a chief executive officer (CEO) of a major U.S. corporation was 52.9 years, compared to 54.7 years only four years previously.[1] The average age of a CEO in India is now between 47 and 50. The same is true in China, where a majority of CEOs of the largest 500 corporations are under 45 years of age.[2] In Brazil, the CEOs of most of the high-flying, high-tech companies spearheading economic growth are under 40 years of age. The average CEO in Russia is 46, six to seven years younger than his or her counterpart in Europe.[3] See Exhibit 10.1.

While women continue to be scarce in the ranks of corporate CEOs, they are increasingly to be found at the helm of non-U.S. companies. In the United States, only 3 percent of Fortune 500 CEOs are women. In Turkey, 12 percent of CEOs are women (and so are 31 percent of senior managers), as are 11 percent in India. By 2012, 41 percent of the Young Global Leaders designated by the World Economic Forum at its Davos meeting were women. Hence, the corporate leadership ranks are not only getting younger, they are

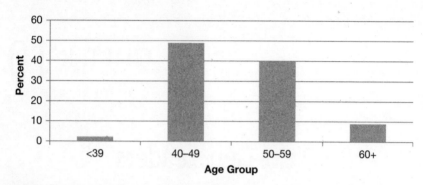

EXHIBIT 10.1 Age Distribution of Top CEOs in China, 2005
Source: Cheng Li, China Leadership Monitor

becoming more diverse. With women now representing half of all MBA students in the United States, these trends are likely to follow suit in America's corporate halls as well.

These young leaders, and the vice president and senior vice presidents below them who are themselves poised to take the leadership reins, have had broadly different experiences than their peers of 20 years ago.

In the United States, young corporate leaders are matriculating from business curricula that underscore triple-bottom-line thinking and global experiences. As Garth Saloner, dean of the Graduate School of Business at Stanford University, has pointed out, "Finance and supply chain management and accounting and so on—those have become . . . kind of a hygiene factor that everybody ought to know."[4] The business school curriculum is adding societal context to the meat-and-potatoes subjects of finance and management for the next generation of business issues. Forty-five percent of business schools have at least one required course on ethics or social responsibility.[5] In part, this may be because of the expectations of students. But it is also because of the demands of corporate employers. A 2008 survey of corporate CEOs by Arthur D. Little found that 90 percent felt that "sustainable development was important to their company's future" only 30 percent felt they had the internal corporate skills and personnel to carry out that priority.[6]

The Aspen Institute's Beyond Grey Pinstripes program evaluates business schools on their curriculum for social and environmental issues. Since the Great Recession, the program's survey shows a marked increase in the number of business school courses focused on social responsibility and social impact. The trend appears to flow across the curriculum, from finance to accounting to operations management. The average business school student today, and therefore the business leader tomorrow, is exposed to the relationship between business and society in ways that did not exist in the past. See Exhibit 10.2.

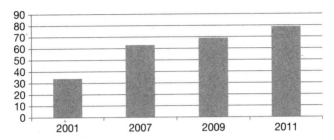

EXHIBIT 10.2 Percentage of MBA Programs Requiring Dedicated Business and Society Course

Source: **Aspen Institute**

In turn, this will mean that the ways in which corporate leaders engage their businesses in social issues in the future will likely be different than in the past or even than in 2013. Environmental sustainability, government and nonprofit expectations, alternative metrics for measuring business accomplishments, measures of shareholder value that embed societal impact—all are likely to become the core of executive expectations in the future. And the students going through those revised curricula are not just American, and so the perspective will be shared across the world not just in American C-suites. In many U.S. business schools, a third or more of students are international. This is not just a matter of the schools on the East and West Coasts. Forty percent of the students at the Kelley School of Business at Indiana University are international. The next generation of business leaders will share a greater exposure to the corporate-societal intersection.

And that perspective will be borderless because global experience is also a business school prerequisite. A 2011 survey of *Financial Times* top-ranked business schools by George Washington University found that 85 percent had some form of international exchange program, although only 14 percent made that international experience mandatory.[7] Stanford does. Stanford's business school now requires that every student study in a country in which he or she has not grown up and/or has not had significant work experience. This demand that every student's MBA study includes a never-before global experience means that every graduate comes out of the program with a worldview.

Abroad, the story is much the same. Fifty percent of the students in the MBA program of the University of Melbourne are international. At the Hong Kong University of Science and Technology, 80 percent of MBA students are from outside Hong Kong, and the faculty and scholars are from 16 countries. The vast majority of CEOs of large Chinese firms have either studied abroad or have had a corporate management position abroad. Indeed, for most Chinese executives, the global stage is more familiar than the domestic one. Very few Chinese CEOs have any rural experience in their own country.[8]

In sum, corporate engagement, and even—as discussed in Chapters 7 and 15—the line between the commercial and the societal will be deeply affected by these new leaders. Hence, the terms under which they engage with the nonprofit sector will be different. The future will not be one denominated in gifts; it will be defined by complementary roles and hence complementary responsibilities as corporations forge partnerships that are not simply at the heart of their philanthropy, but are at the core of their businesses.

Nonprofit Leaders

Today, the majority of nonprofits in the United States are led by executives 50 years of age or older. Yet, even here the realities of aging cannot be avoided. Various surveys estimate that between 50 percent and 80 percent of executive directors of nonprofits will be leaving or retiring from their nonprofit leadership positions within the decade.[9]

What is the younger generation of nonprofit up-and-comers like? There are two cohorts to be considered, those who are in traditional nonprofits and those who have eschewed the traditional and are creating entirely new categories of nonprofits and blended enterprises that are increasingly populating the societal commons.

In 2011, Changing Our World completed a survey of young professionals in the traditional nonprofit sector in an effort to understand how they see their careers and how likely they are to remain in the sector long enough to accede to the leadership positions that will be vacated by Baby Boomer retirees.[10] Three critical issues emerged.

First, it may prove difficult for the nonprofit sector to retain and grow the careers of the young people now beginning their careers in nonprofits. Over time, satisfaction with their professional development declines. And eroding satisfaction can gradually sap commitment to cause.

By the five-year point of employment, over a third of survey respondents were "very" or "somewhat" dissatisfied with their professional development, up from 20 percent at the three-year point. While over time those dissatisfaction rates decline somewhat, levels of satisfaction never return to those of the early years of experience in the nonprofit sector. Moreover, those who are dissatisfied with their professional development find that they become less committed to the cause or field for which they work. (See Exhibit 10.3.)

The second problem layers on this first. Those who enter into the nonprofit sector bring deep concern for the issues on which they work. But it is not just professional development that undercuts this commitment; organizational effectiveness within the sector also begins to separate commitment from cause. By year three of working in nonprofits, a quarter of respondents were dissatisfied with the effectiveness of the organizations for which they work. By

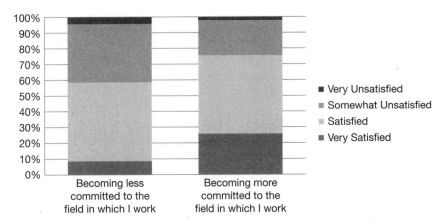

EXHIBIT 10.3 Young Nonprofit Leaders' Satisfaction and Commitment
Source: Changing Our World, Future Leaders in Philanthropy Survey

year 10, that portion rises to 37 percent, nearly two in five. Moreover, organizational dissatisfaction reinforces professional dissatisfaction. Half of those dissatisfied with organizational performance find themselves becoming less committed to the cause for which they work. (See Exhibit 10.4.)

Finally, and perhaps as a consequence, there is tremendous restlessness. Over half of survey respondents under the age of 30 expected to leave their current position within the next five years. One in five of those aged 25 to 38 expected to move to a for-profit setting, either commercially or in the social enterprise space. The younger the respondent the more likely he or she was to

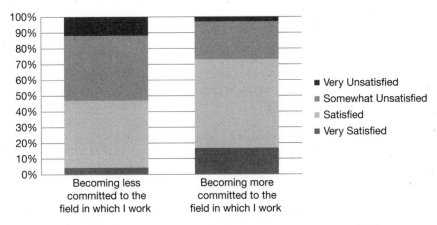

EXHIBIT 10.4 Young Nonprofit Leaders' Satisfaction with Organizational Effectiveness
Source: Changing Our World, Future Leaders in Philanthropy Survey

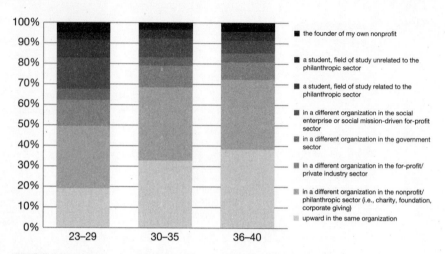

EXHIBIT 10.5 Young Nonprofit Leaders' Plans for the Next Five Years
Source: Changing Our World, Future Leaders in Philanthropy Survey

be looking outside of the current work setting and indeed outside of the nonprofit sector itself. (See Exhibit 10.5.)

This sense of dissatisfaction is not unique to the Changing Our World survey cohort. Professionals for NonProfits surveyed the sector in New York and Boston and found equivalent concern. In that survey, 40 percent of professionals said that their work is not valued, and a whopping 70 percent felt that their jobs were disappointing or only somewhat fulfilling.[11]

The question then becomes, how will the innovation and change that is so clearly becoming part of the training and thinking of the next generation of corporate leaders match up with the dissatisfaction that seems to characterize the next generation of nonprofit leaders? There is tremendous need for the nonprofit and philanthropic sectors to pay close attention to the directions being taken by those now in and graduating from business schools. The latter will open up entirely new ways for corporations to relate to social problem solving. But the skills and enthusiasm for being partners to that innovation will also need to reside in nonprofits. Nonprofit leadership that is energized and innovative, not dissatisfied and restless, will be needed. And paying attention to the views of the young who are those very future leaders is a critical priority for today.

Summary and Nonprofit Implications

The next generation of business leaders is now being prepared in schools and with curricula that emphasize a broader view of corporate engagement than in the past. Indeed, leadership in the corporate sector is itself becoming younger.

Globally, a new generation of leaders is even now entering the executive suite and beginning to make decisions about how markets will intersect with societal problem solving simultaneously with producing the goods and services that fuel the global commons.

The challenge, however, is in the nonprofit sector. The opportunity to forge new and robust partnerships lies at the feet of the sector. The question is whether the nonprofit sector is growing the innovative, enthusiastic young leaders who will take up that opportunity and develop new and effective ways to combine the causes that nonprofits lead with the strengths and resources of commercial leadership.

It is here that there may be cause for concern. What is needed is a nonprofit and philanthropic sector that has an expressed commitment to the next generation of its own leaders, an encouragement of innovation, and a willingness to invest in both professional development and organizational effectiveness to keep those young leaders excited and engaged. Partnership is a two-way street. If there is innovation and outward-facing perspective in the schools that produce tomorrow's corporate leaders, then those leaders will need to find equivalent perspectives in the socially driven organizations to which they will be turning. The failure to find such peers will represent a hugely costly missed opportunity.

Case G: Strength to Strength: Partnership to Boost Engagement

Author: The Marketing Arm

⊕themarketingarm

Partner: United States Olympic Committee

(*continued*)

(continued)

Situation

"What can our brand do for Team USA?"

That's a unique question brands with successful partnerships with the U.S. Olympic Committee (USOC) often attempt to answer. That can differ from other sponsorships, where brands only enter into it with the goal of determining what the property or event can do for their brand.

And because the USOC receives no government funding, unlike other competing countries, consumers are positively influenced by brands that help Olympic and Paralympic athletes pursue their dreams and succeed in competition.

Stakes

As an official sponsor of Team USA, AT&T set out to help U.S. Olympic athletes while utilizing the sponsorship to achieve core brand objectives such as driving usage of its products and services and enhancing brand perception.

Ultimately, the public would judge AT&T not only on the program benefits, but on how well AT&T helped Team USA be competitive in Beijing and beyond.

Strengths

By providing exclusive "behind-the-scenes" content of artists and athletes, the story spread through top print and broadcast media outlets and became a hot DJ chatter item. Consumers helped spread the word by uploading music videos to YouTube and discussing the program in blogs and on Facebook and MySpace.

Strategy

Against the spectacular backdrop of the 2008 Beijing Olympic Games, AT&T launched a campaign that aimed to engage the consumer while enhancing the entertainment of watching the games. To achieve both, AT&T negotiated in-broadcast, 40-second primetime features on each of the 15 core nights of the Olympic Games telecast.

And while this opportunity provided a great vehicle for AT&T to connect with Olympic viewers, it posed many sizeable challenges for the brand:

- AT&T's 18- to 24-year-old core audience is younger than the traditional Olympic viewer (median age: 47.1), creating the need to build a multifaceted program to extend beyond Olympic coverage, draw in younger consumers and inspire them to take action.

- The program needed to seamlessly integrate into the environment and tonality of Olympic programming in order to receive the critical endorsement of both NBC and Team USA.
- The public would judge AT&T not just on program benefits but also on how well AT&T helped Team USA achieve its goals.

Solution

See Appendix 1.

Notes

1. S. E. Ante and J. S. Lublin, "Young CEOs: Are They Up to the Job?" *Wall Street Journal,* February 7, 2012, online edition. http://online.wsj.com/article/SB10001424052970203315804577207131063501196.html.
2. C. Li, "The Rise of China's Yuppie Corps: Top CEOs to Watch," China Leadership Monitor No. 14, http://media.hoover.org/sites/default/files/documents/clm14_lc.pdf.
3. Booz & Company, "10th Annual Global CEO Succession Study," May 18, 2010, p. 20.
4. Interview with Garth Saloner, "Building the Next-Generation Business Leader," *McKinsey Quarterly* (April 2010): 2.
5. A. Weeks, "Business Education for Sustainability: Training a New Generation of Business Leaders," *Green Money Journal* (Spring 2012), www.greenmoneyjournal.com/article.mpl?newsletterid=29&articleid=309.
6. Ibid.
7. R. Dyer and M. M. Tarimcilar, "What's Your Global IQ?" *BizED* (May/June 2011): 47–50.
8. Li, "The Rise of China's Yuppie Corps."
9. R. P. Halpern, "Workforce Issues in the Nonprofit Sector," *American Humanics* (February 2006): 10. See also "Aging Workforce Survey," *Nursing Management* (December 31, 2006).
10. S. Raymond, S. Schiff, and K. Amore, *The Young and the Relentless: An Original Survey of the Next Generation of Philanthropy and Nonprofit Leaders* (New York: Changing Our World, Inc., 2011).
11. P. Bolton, "Nonprofit Employers Don't Meet Workers' Needs for Job Satisfaction, Surveys Find," *Chronicle on Philanthropy* (October 24, 2011): 5.

PART III

Requisite Change in the Nonprofit Sector

The opportunities created by changing philanthropic approaches and new generations of leaders also create huge challenges for nonprofits. New expectations about financial accountability, new needs for organizational flexibility, and new categories of skills to manage financial and program innovation all demand of nonprofits constant and continual innovation. The change in corporate engagement strategy provides a particularly important challenge. Nonprofits must learn to be partners, not recipients, if they are to engage with next-generation corporate leaders and strategies. But they must do so in ways that sustain their own missions and purposes, while accommodating corporate goals and objectives. This will require creativity on the part of both nonprofit executives and their boards. Similarly, the demand of philanthropists for deep engagement in strategy, and for flexibility and innovation in programs and finance, will again require that nonprofits become partners, not simply recipients.

Requisite Change in the Nonprofit Sector

CHAPTER 11

The Globalization of Philanthropy in the United States and Abroad

For the past decade, one of the most consistent trends in U.S. philanthropy has been the rise in giving to international causes. While that still represents less than 3 percent of total resources, the last ten years have seen consistent increases, a total of 73 percent in inflation adjusted terms over the decade. As a result, and perhaps as a cause, the number of U.S. nonprofits dedicated to international causes has tripled in the last decade as well. See Exhibit 11.1.

These data on giving and organizational infrastructure, however, only hint at the trend of globalization. The reality, in the United States and elsewhere in the world, is far, far more complex and far, far more impressive. This chapter can only begin to portray at the scope of the trends, but even within the limitations of this space, the scope is undeniable and the implications profound.

Individual Giving to the World

U.S. private philanthropy flowing to developing countries now exceeds the total of U.S. government–provided development assistance by nearly $9 billion. Official development assistance (ODA) in 2010 was $30.4 billion, compared to $39 billion in U.S. private philanthropy.[1] See Exhibit 11.2.

More than half of that total came from corporations, further discussed later in this chapter, and private voluntary organizations combined. The individual donors to private voluntary organizations themselves supply nearly a third of the total.

This giving total is supplemented by almost $100 billion in remittances from U.S. immigrants from developing nations back to their home communities.[2] Those funds are used in as many ways as there are families that receive

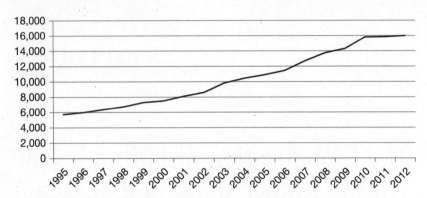

EXHIBIT 11.1 Growth of Nonprofits Focused on International Work
Source: National Center for Charitable Statistics

the funds. So, although not "philanthropy" in the strict sense of the work, these transfers do increase incomes, send children to school, improve diets, better communities, and reduce poverty. Indeed, the value of all remittances from all immigrants around the world is estimated to be $325 billion, a figure that is expected to grow by as much as 8 percent per year over the next decade.[3]

Remittances reflect individual immigrant concern for the well-being of families or communities at home. But they can also have tremendous leverage when they flow through organized effort, and that effort is often focused not simply on individual family well-being, but on larger community effort. Remittances then become development finance in much the same way that

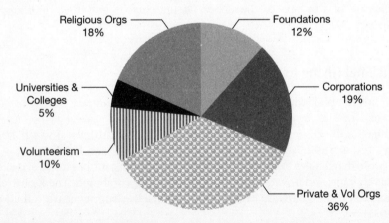

EXHIBIT 11.2 Sources of $39 Billion in Private Philanthropic Flows to Developing Countries
Source: Index of Global Philanthropy and Remittances, 2012

large-scale U.S. institutional philanthropy has funded community development abroad. The Ayala Corporation Foundation in the Philippines, for example, has created the Philippine Development Foundation (PhilDev). Since 2000, PhilDev has raised more than $10 million in philanthropy from thousands of Philippine Americans for development projects in their homeland. For their parts, governments abroad are not unaware of the resource implications. The Mexican government, for example, recognizing that remittances from Mexican immigrants to America represent 40 percent of all U.S. remittances flowing to Latin America, instituted the 3×1 program. It would contribute $1 for every $3 raised by Mexican hometown associations in the United States for aid to their hometowns. Since its inception, the 3×1 program has raised more than $300 million for 1,000 projects in Mexico.[4]

Moreover, immigrants do not just remit their earnings to their home countries. In general, research has shown that immigrants are more likely to give to international charitable activities in general, when all other philanthropic characteristics are held constant.[5]

Globalization also works to the advantage of the charities in the United States. Immigrants do not just flow their giving abroad, they are sources of philanthropy within their own adopted communities. Work at the City University of New York examining New York's ethnic populations found that the median giving level for Latino and Asian American households was $5,000, the majority of which flowed back to the local community.[6] Moreover, immigrant philanthropy is increasingly flowing through organized institutions. The number of Chinese American family foundations in the United States increased from 11 with $23 million in assets in 1990 to 47 with assets of more than $218 million in 2007, a fourfold increase in less than two decades.[7]

Time and age, however, matter. Younger immigrant generations flow funds very differently than their parents, moving their philanthropy outside of their own ethnic communities. As noted in Exhibit 11.3, younger generations are less prone to think of their own ethnic groups and much more prone to focus on education.[8] Over time, then, immigrant giving will lose its "immigrant" characteristics and become part of larger community philanthropic priorities. Ethnicity will remain, but the larger community will be the giving focus.

Corporations: Giving Where the Markets Are

As noted throughout Section II, corporate philanthropy increasingly flows to issues and problems that align with corporate interests, products, and services. It also flows to markets that are important. For the small and medium-sized business, this continues to be within the community it serves. This is a reliable anchor for the local nonprofit. For the large multinational

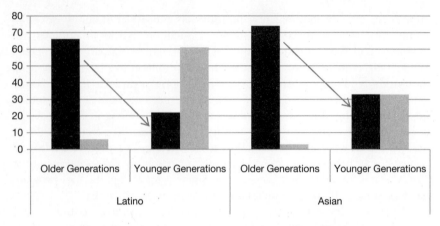

■ Orgs serving own ethnic community   ▪ General educational programs

EXHIBIT 11.3 Younger Immigrant Generations Diversify Philanthropic Interests
Source: F. Mottino and E. D. Miller, *Pathways for Change* (New York: Center on Philanthropy and Civil Society, City University of New York, 2005), v.

corporation, however, it may no longer be dominantly where its headquarters are located. For the local nonprofit, this change in the corporate line of sight is important to appreciate.

Today, about 40 percent of the profits of U.S. corporations come from abroad.[9] For the Standard & Poor's top 500 firms, nearly half (46.3 percent) of sales are abroad.[10] For U.S. firms with majority-owned foreign affiliates, those foreign affiliates represented about a third of the total corporate workforce.[11] These affiliates are relatively prevalent in manufacturing, trade and information. Moreover, these jobs are not just low-skilled, low-pay jobs. Large U.S. technology companies have 30 percent of their research and development staff abroad. More than 85 percent of research and development employment growth of U.S. multinationals has taken place abroad.[12]

Because the corporation is global, so are its executives. Executives at headquarters may not actually be from the city in which the headquarters is located, nor will those executives necessarily spend more than a few years in the headquarters city. They came to Peoria from a posting in Paris and will move on to a posting in Paraguay.

The story within some large firms is even more striking. In 2000, only a bit more than a decade ago, 30 percent of the business of General Electric was abroad. Today, that is 60 percent. In 2000, 46 percent of the workforce was outside the United States. Today, that portion has grown to 54 percent. In the same period, Caterpillar's U.S. workforce has grown by 7.8 percent in the United States and by 39 percent overseas. Oracle's business hardware and software operations are carried out with 63 percent of its workforce abroad.[13]

All of this means that the geographic aperture of the corporate social engagement and philanthropic lens is also increasingly wide. In only four years, from 2006 through 2009, aggregate U.S. corporate international giving from large companies increased from $1.95 billion to $2.72 billion, or by nearly 40 percent.[14] The distribution of that giving tends to concentrate in companies with a significant geographic of employee "footprint" abroad or those for whom foreign markets (and often regulatory issues) are critically important, or whose products are critical inputs to relief. So, for example, pharmaceutical companies have long been leaders in international philanthropy, donating millions of doses of medicine for relief annually. Similarly, manufacturing and extractive industry companies allocate higher portions of their philanthropy resources abroad than do service companies. Exhibits 11.4 and 11.5 illustrate the differences between these two industries.

It is important to remember that global presence is not static; changes in treaties and geopolitics can open new eras. For example, trade barriers have impeded the growth of U.S. service industries abroad by establishing regulatory and financial disincentives that protect local service providers from foreign competition in such areas as insurance. However, considerable effort is under way to strengthen the global General Agreement on Trade in Services (GATS, which is the equivalent of the General Agreement on Trade and Tariffs [GATT]) to create a more dynamic global services economy. As that comes to pass, U.S. service multinationals will greatly increase their global presence and, in turn, also begin to turn their philanthropic lines of sight to non-U.S. markets.

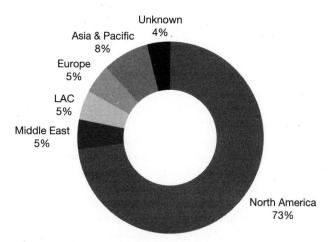

EXHIBIT 11.4 U.S. Manufacturing Industry Giving Abroad 2009
Source: CECP, Giving in Numbers, 2010

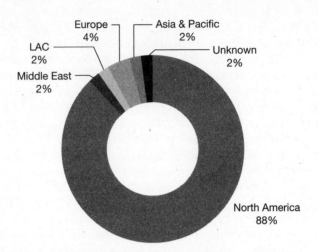

EXHIBIT 11.5 U.S. Service Industry Giving Abroad 2009
Source: CECP, Giving in Numbers, 2010

The Rising Strength of Philanthropy around the World

Globalization clearly is not simply about the broadening of the U.S. perspective. Indeed, that is the least of the story. Charitable giving—the commitment of individuals to their communities and to their neighbors—is fundamental in every culture and every religion. There is nothing new about that behavior.

In the past several decades, however, the combination of broad economic growth, the opening up of legal systems to the formation of formal nonprofits and foundations, and the general global (and instantly communicated) consciousness of complex shared problems has been the impetus for rising philanthropy and the creation of formal institutions to channel that philanthropy into social and economic action. The subsequent funding flows are both within nations and among nations, supporting both community development in, and economic development across, borders.

A surrogate measure of the robustness of philanthropy is the explosion of organizations created to serve it. A great variety of associations and gathering places have arisen to provide voice, research, platforms, and leadership for philanthropic members. Thus, although precise data on the numbers of foundations and the levels of philanthropy globally are elusive, all regions are now populated with a multitude of associations and organizations designed to encourage and organize that giving. Exhibit 11.6 illustrates how dense this network has become, including in Africa, where the growing role of African philanthropists in Africa's development is real and largely unrecognized in the global philanthropic community.

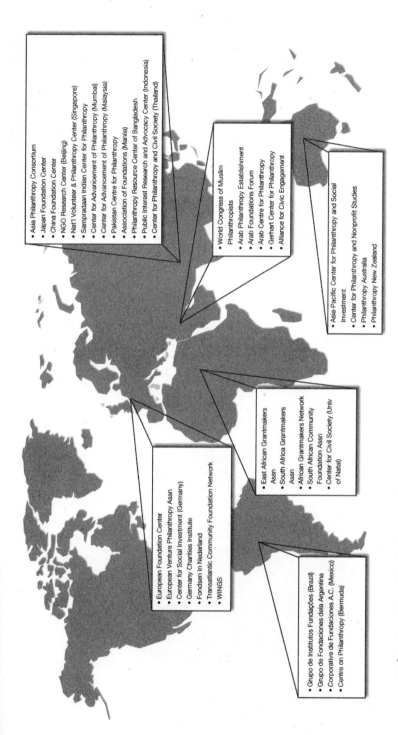

- Asia Philanthropy Consortium
- Japan Foundation Center
- China Foundation Center
- NGO Research Center (Beijing)
- Nat'l Volunteer & Philanthropy Center (Singapore)
- Sampradaan Indian Center for Philanthropy
- Center for Advancement of Philanthropy (Mumbai)
- Center for Advancement of Philanthropy (Malaysia)
- Pakistan Centre for Philanthropy
- Association of Foundations (Manila)
- Philanthropy Resource Center of Bangladesh
- Public Interest Research and Advocacy Center (Indonesia)
- Center for Philanthropy and Civil Society (Thailand)

- World Congress of Muslim Philanthropists
- Arab Philanthropy Establishment
- Arab Foundations Forum
- Arab Centre for Philanthropy
- Gerhart Center for Philanthropy
- Alliance for Civic Engagement

- Asia-Pacific Center for Philanthropy and Social Investment
- Center for Philanthropy and Nonprofit Studies
- Philanthropy Australia
- Philanthropy New Zealand

- European Foundation Center
- European Venture Philanthropy Assn
- Center for Social Investment (Germany)
- Germany Charities Institute
- Fondsen In Nederland
- Transatlantic Community Foundation Network
- WINGS

- East African Grantmakers Assn
- South Africa Grantmakers Assn
- African Grantmakers Network
- South African Community Foundation Assn
- Center for Civil Society (Univ of Natal)

- Grupo de Institutos Fundações (Brazil)
- Grupo de Fondaciones dela Argentina
- Corporative de Fundaciones A.C. (Mexico)
- Centre on Philanthropy (Bermuda)

EXHIBIT 11.6 A Growing Global Network of Philanthropy Associations

Europe

In Europe, the traditions and institutions of philanthropy are well developed, although two thirds of all foundations have been founded just since 1970. The European Foundation Center estimates that there are 85,000 foundations in western Europe and another 35,000 in eastern and central Europe. However, because the term *foundation* applies to many types of nonprofits that raise money for their own programs but retain all of that funding internally, the number of grant-making foundations is almost certainly lower.

From a size perspective, Italy and the United Kingdom account for the vast majority of large foundations and significant assets, as noted in Exhibit 11.7.

In the U.K., private foundations have a long history, of course, but the growth in Italy is more recent and striking and illustrates how economic policy can trigger the creation of formal philanthropy and why, therefore, it is critical for nonprofits to understand the larger economic environments in which they operate. In Italy, the trend toward economic privatization, which has characterized most European and emerging economies over the past two decades, led to the privatization of a large number of banks that had been operating since the nineteenth century. These banks had combined commercial banking with a form of community engagement and investment that was more akin to social investing. Therefore, upon privatization, a series of foundations was established to hold new stock shares and continue this role through philanthropy. That single policy nearly doubled the size of the Italian foundation sector.

As economies and societies have become more open in the past two decades, the trend toward philanthropic formation has gathered speed in

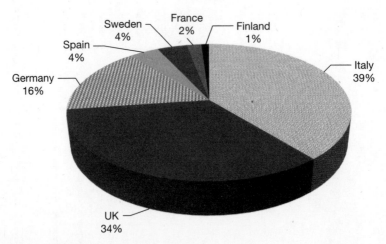

EXHIBIT 11.7 European Foundation Assets by Country
Source: European Foundation Center

nations of the former Soviet Union. In Russia, for example, in the mid-1980s, there was virtually no organized philanthropy. Today, the largest Russian companies donate over $2.5 billion per year and there are over 40 relatively large private foundations. Regulatory and legal limitations are not inconsequential, but, as the Russian economy grows, the upward trend is clear.

European foundations, and philanthropy in general, largely focus resources within Europe. Unlike in the United States, human service organizations garner the largest portion of funding because both health and education (long dominant in U.S. giving) are significantly publicly funded. However, in places like the United Kingdom and Germany, this is likely to change as both governments have put in place aggressive policies to deeply incentivize (even require) higher education institutions to engage in private fundraising.

Again, economics matter and hence nonprofits need to pay attention. Two elements are at work in this regard.

First, the European population is aging rapidly. The demands on social security to meet this reality have created pressures on public budgets that are overwhelming. Moreover, those demands are difficult to scale back because the political repercussions would be quick and vocal. Hence, European governments have a need to offset those budget demands by encouraging private philanthropic support of other services and institutions (e.g., education), which have long been publicly funded.

Second, the echoes of the global Great Recession in Europe continue to reverberate. Austerity programs, the price of financial support from both stronger European nations and from international financial institutions, have cut deeply into public funding. Again, philanthropy has been asked to step up to fill the gap. Doing so at levels sufficient to offset public budget reductions is no more possible in Europe than in the United States. Indeed, in the United States, cutbacks in social funding at the state level would require as much as a 60 percent *per year* increase in private philanthropy.[15] Nevertheless, the polities and needs will likely continue to fuel philanthropic growth.

Only about 2.4 percent of European foundation funding flows to international causes and institutions, a portion that is slightly lower than in the United States. Still, private giving for international development is significant. There is dispute about levels, but the best estimates are that private giving for development from Europe totals about $16.9 billion annually.[16] The distribution of that funding is shown in Exhibit 11.8.

Latin America, Africa, and Asia

Perhaps the most exciting news in philanthropy is the growth and institutionalization of philanthropy in both emerging economies and developing nations. The spread of philanthropy associations and collaborating

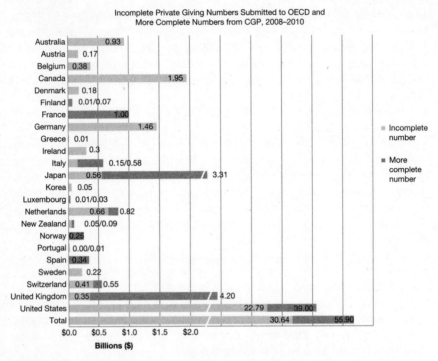

EXHIBIT 11.8 European Private Philanthropy for International Development
Source: Index of Global Philanthropy and Remittances, 2012

organizations previously illustrated in Exhibit 11.6 illustrates how domestic philanthropy is becoming institutionalized in Latin America, Africa, and Asia.

Of course, individual giving has always been a tradition in all of these cultures and continues true to history. Indeed, the Charities Aid Foundation estimates that the rates of giving in many countries in these regions exceed those in industrialized countries. An additional survey by Nature Conservancy in Brazil found that a quarter of the population was making monthly gifts to nonprofit causes.[17] As indicated in Exhibit 11.9, between 30 and 40 percent of the population of these regions contributes to charity, a rate which is far exceeded in nations that are the philanthropic leaders of their regions.

Indeed, in places such as Thailand and the Philippines, per-capita giving ($93 and $28, respectively) now far exceeds Official Development Assistance (ODA, the term used for the official aid flows of government to developing countries), which is $2.80 and $5.83 per capita. Many "developing" countries are growing domestic private philanthropy to many multiples of foreign government aid.

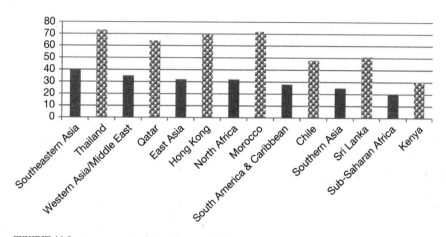

EXHIBIT 11.9 Percentage of Population Giving Cash to Charities—Region and Highest Country 2010
Source: Charities Aid Foundation, 2010

Confirming these trends, MasterCard Worldwide, which conducts a series of consumer surveys and publishes the results at www.masterintelligence.com, found in 2010 that 55 percent of consumers across Asia, the Middle East, and Africa planned to make a charitable contribution in the past six months of 2010, up from 50 percent in mid-2009.[18] Those rates reach 65 to 75 percent in Hong Kong, Malaysia, Bangalore, parts of the Middle East, and Nigeria.

Beyond individual charitable giving, these regions are also growing large cohorts of private philanthropic foundations. In July 2010 the Foundation Center of China was inaugurated in Beijing. It opened with 1,800 foundations registered. There are approximately 10,000 foundations in Mexico and several thousand in Brazil. In the case of Brazil, the number of private philanthropic foundations doubled in just five years, from 1998 to 2003. In Latin America, formal foundations and major philanthropists are focusing their philanthropy not on traditional issues of poverty and social support, the historical purview of religious donations, but on employment and entrepreneurship, seeking to strengthen economic sustainability through philanthropy just as through their commercial investments.[19]

While younger and less well developed than in other regions, the internal philanthropic capacity of Africa is also growing apace with its continent-wide economic growth, which, as noted in Chapter 3, has been and is expected to continue to exceed that of industrialized nations.

Indeed, in 2009, the Gift from Africa was created in the context of the third replenishment of the Global Fund to Fight HIV/AIDS, Tuberculosis and Malaria (Global Fund). The Global Fund's work to address the disease burden in Africa had long been financed exclusively by multilateral and bilateral aid agencies and the philanthropies of wealthy countries. In 2009, the business and philanthropic leaders within Africa made a statement. They would be a financial part of Africa's solutions. This was the first ever continent-wide philanthropic leadership fund for health advancement funded by leaders of the region. Gift from Africa now has raised $8 million to contribute to the work of the Global Fund in Africa.

In just the past decade, community foundations have also become a force in philanthropy in these regions. There are now about 1,680 community foundations around the world,[20] and in emerging economies, Asia has taken the lead. There are now six community foundations in China, two in Japan, one each in Singapore and South Korea, four in Thailand, and at least three in the Philippines. In South Africa in 2008, the community foundation movement was so well developed that the organizations founded the South African Community Foundation Association to begin to learn from one another. Community foundations are not widespread in Latin America, but there are perhaps two dozen in Mexico, all of which have been formed since 1993.[21] In the Middle East, addressed more specifically below, community foundations are rarer because of the tradition of religious giving, although some community giving structures do exist, such as the Wakfayit El Maadi (El Maadi Community Foundation) in Egypt. However, one innovation, Dubai Cares, was created by Sheikh Mohammed bin Rashid Al Maktoum, the constitutional monarch of Dubai and Vice President of the United Arab Emirates, and is funded by his own philanthropy and contributions from throughout the United Arab Emirates and by corporations. Dubai Cares focuses not just on the local community, but on poverty in the larger global community.

The trend toward the creation of community foundations around the world is likely to continue and the momentum to build. In 2006, the World Bank, the Ford Foundation, and the Mott Foundation joined together to create the Global Fund for Community Foundations to broaden the development of these institutions. The fund has made grants for foundation formation in nearly 40 countries since its formation.

Corporations are also a growing part of philanthropy in these regions. In Latin America, most banks and telecommunications companies now have some type of formal philanthropic structure, and nearly all have engaged in cause related marketing. In October 2010, a new Ibero-American Forum for Corporate Foundations was convened in Spain, bringing together both corporate foundations and foundation associations from throughout Latin America and Spain to share experiences and strategies and grow the sector.

In Asia, especially in China and India, corporations domiciled in the region are both increasingly global (and therefore attuned to the growing global expectations for social engagement) and increasingly engaged in philanthropy within the communities they serve. In China, for example, corporations represent an estimated 40 percent of philanthropic contributions

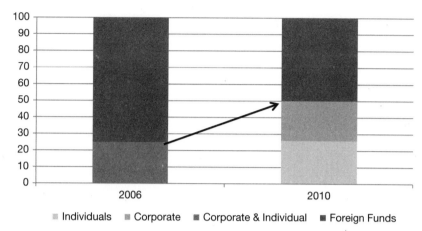

EXHIBIT 11.10 Increased Corporate and Individual Giving in India
Source: Bain & Company, 2011

compared to less than 15 percent in the United States and less than 20 percent in the United Kingdom.[22]

In India, corporations are as critical to philanthropy as are individuals, representing perhaps 30 percent of all giving. See Exhibit 11.10.

Indian corporate philanthropy also tends to focus on innovation and scale, reflecting the venture-capital nature of the new business executive. Indian corporate philanthropy looks for social enterprise opportunities, and sustainable revenue models in the nonprofit sector, and hence has flowed to microfinance, program-related investing, and social entrepreneurship rather than to traditional nonprofit service models.

The Middle East

A special note on the Arab Middle East is in order and applies in many ways to nations with majority Islamic populations. One of the five pillars of Islam, a requirement for adherence to the faith, is *zakat* or charitable contributions.[23] All faithful Muslims must donate zakat to the needy. Because of this religious requirement, individual giving in the Arab Middle East is very significant. The 2010 Charities Aid study estimates that 60 to 80 percent of adults in the region contribute to charity.[24] A similar study by MasterCard found equivalent results.[25]

Within these religious structures, however, philanthropy is also very individual and very informal, often mediated by mosques. The rise of formal private foundations is relatively new in these nations, now most pronounced in Egypt, Jordan, and the United Arab Emirates. Issues of poverty and human well-being are usually the focus of zakat giving, while the newer foundations tend to focus on economic issues such as job-skills education and youth entrepreneurship.

Philanthropy by corporations domiciled in the region is similarly without formal foundation structures, in keeping with the zakat tradition. There is a growing emphasis on formal philanthropic effort, however, led by the Arab Foundations Forum, which for over a decade has sponsored an annual meeting of corporations to encourage community social engagement and the formation of structured independent foundations in the corporate community.

Summary and Implications

The globalization of the economy, the emergence of new foci of wealth, and the opening of political and social processes to wider citizen participation have all combined to produce three results. First, institutions that have long been U.S.-centric are now global in their concerns and their philanthropy. This is most clearly seen in the corporate community but also extends to the experiences and views of high-net-worth individuals whose lives and experiences are increasingly international. Second, immigrant communities are large and far-flung throughout the United States, and they are actively involved in supporting social structures and causes. This extends both to diaspora philanthropy, which flows back to nations of origin as well as to support for local communities of residence. Finally, philanthropy and formal philanthropic institutions are becoming deeply embedded in communities throughout the world, and their leadership will only grow in the future as growth and prosperity spread to emerging and high-growth economies. Philanthropy is a worldwide tide that is lifting all boats.

It is true that globalization has created entirely new reservoirs of philanthropic resources. On the surface, this appears to be a straightforward advantage for nonprofits. But nothing that is global is straightforward. Those new and emerging resources are deeply embedded in culture. For the nonprofit, the most critical issue is culture. The philanthropy of Kenya does not necessarily think in the same ways as the philanthropy of Kansas. That is true even if the Kenyan philanthropist is located in Kansas.

This means that the nonprofit seeking to develop the capacity to reach out to one or more aspects of this globalization, whether for international or for domestic programs, must become deeply acculturated. The simple measures of ethnicity or languages on staff will not suffice. There will be no answer in merely adding token names or faces to staff lists or executive suites. Knowledge, not numbers, will be the differentiation.

Instead, the entire organization must become attuned to culture. From the board of trustees to the switchboard, entire organizations must understand how other cultures think, how they behave, and how they relate to giving. This means that a process of learning must be developed that brings anthropologists, cultural specialists, linguists, and regional experts into the nonprofit to boost understanding. Culture must be deeply embedded in personnel and processes before philanthropic partnerships can be anything but episodic and superficial. Nonprofits that seek to adapt to the globalization of philanthropy, that seek not simply to get a check but rather to deeply align with global philanthropy, must understand that it is the nonprofit side of the table, not the philanthropy side of the table, that must pause and learn what is expected and what will be required.

Only when that knowledge and understanding are deeply ingrained in an institution can strategy for alignment and support be developed that is organic to the cultural diversity inherent in globalization.

Case H: Globalization and Social Media

Author: Changing Our World, Inc.

Partner: Sightsavers

Situation

Sightsavers International, Inc. is a global charity that works to combat blindness in developing countries, restoring sight through specialist treatment and eye care, and providing medical care to prevent blindness. Sightsavers is a U.K.-based organization that was attempting to enter new markets, including the United States. Changing Our World was tapped to

(continued)

(continued)

help Sightsavers International's U.S. regional fundraising division research and plan a digital philanthropy strategy that would aid the organization in creating a model to generate a sustainable revenue stream for the United States, a model that can also be adapted for future market entry.

Stakes

Entering the U.S. market had the potential to be an enormous opportunity for Sightsavers, but many challenges needed to be addressed, the first being that the U.S. regional office lacked the necessary staff typically required in implementing, building, and maintaining a digital philanthropy program. The organization also had to consider the fact that its brand awareness in the United States was minimal and the number of international charities competing for U.S. philanthropic dollars was increasing exponentially. The organization risked losing more funds than it stood to gain.

Strengths

Keeping in mind all that was at stake, the organization's leadership was willing to dedicate significant resources in support of the regional office's vision because the United States is a leader in global development and has the deepest tradition of philanthropy. Sightsavers already had a strong organizational strategic plan in place with which a digital philanthropy strategy can align its goals and tactics. While there was great competition for philanthropic dollars, Sightsavers was poised to benefit from the fact that giving to international causes is the fastest growing subsector of U.S. giving.

Strategy

Changing Our World's digital team evaluated Sightsavers' current online presence and activities, investigated stakeholder ideas and knowledge, conducted a digital philanthropy analysis, and incorporated these findings into a strategic digital philanthropy implementation plan, including budget recommendations and short- and long-term goals.

Strategic goals were set to increase online revenue by 10 percent; enhance frequency and quality of website, social media, and e-mail content; build in-house digital philanthropy capacity; and strengthen digital philanthropy performance measurement.

Tactics and strategies were designed to help the organization increase revenue, build brand awareness, and increase engagement with its existing constituency.

Solution

See Appendix 1.

Notes

1. *Index of Global Philanthropy and Remittances, 2012* (Washington, DC: Hudson Institute Center for Global Prosperity, 2012), 8. Note that the Index unbundles foundation giving to nonprofits from private giving to nonprofits, and hence avoids double counting.
2. Ibid.
3. *Global Poverty Update 2012* (Washington, DC: World Bank, 2012), http://siteresources.worldbank.org/INTPOVCALNET/Resources/Global_Poverty_Update_2012_02-29-12.pdf.
4. *Index of Global Philanthropy and Remittances*, p. 20.
5. U. Okonkwo and D. Du, "Immigrant Assimilation and Charitable Giving," *New Directions for Philanthropic Fundraising* 48 (Summer 2005): 96.
6. F. Mottino and E. D. Miller, *Pathways for Change* (New York: Center on Philanthropy and Civil Society, City University of New York, 2005), v.
7. T. Watanabe, "Chinese Immigrants Give Back to U.S.," *Los Angeles Times*, June 15, 2008, p. 15. See also A. Ho, *Asian-American Philanthropy: Expanding Knowledge, Increasing Possibilities* (Washington, DC: The Center for Public & Nonprofit Leadership, Working Paper 4, November 2004).
8. Okonkwo and Du, p. v.
9. A. W. Hodge, "Comparing NIPA Profits with S&P 500 Profits," U.S. Department of Commerce, BEA Briefing, March 2011, p. 23.
10. S&P Indices, 2010.
11. K. B. Barefoot and R. J. Mataloni, Jr., "Operations of U.S. Multinational Companies in the United States and Abroad: Preliminary Results from the 2009 Benchmark Survey. Survey of Current Business," U.S. Department of Commerce, Bureau of Economic Analysis, November 2011, p. 39.
12. *Science and Technology Indicators 2012* (Washington, DC: National Science Foundation, 2012), 3–58.
13. D. Wessel, "Big U.S. Firms Shift Hiring Abroad," *Wall Street Journal*, April 19, 2011, p. B1.
14. *Giving in Numbers, 2010* (New York: CECP, 2010), 28.
15. S. Raymond, S. Park, and J. Simons, *The Public Finance Crisis: Can Philanthropy Shoulder the Burden?* (New York: Changing Our World, Inc., 2011), 57.
16. Index on Global Philanthropy, p. 13. The estimates from the Center for Global Prosperity differ markedly from those of the Development Assistance Committee of the Organisation for Economic Co-operation and Development because the latter relies solely on government reporting, and the former relies on its own country-by-country review of private flows.
17. S. Murray, "Fashion for Giving Starts to Catch On," *Financial Times* (Latin AmericaSocial Enterprise and Philanthropy, December 2, 2011), 2.

18. MasterCard Consumer Survey, 2010.

19. S. Murray, p. 2.

20. J. Hodgson, B. Knight, and A. Mathie, "The New Generation of Community Foundations," March 2012, p. 11. Commissioned by the Global Fund for Community Foundations with funding from the International Development Research Centre, Canada.

21. R. Berger et al., "Mexico Community Foundations: A Comprehensive Profile," Teamworks and Alternatives y Capacidades, March 2009.

22. A. Seth and M. Singhal, *India Philanthropy Report 2011* (Mumbai: Bain and Company, 2011), 2.

23. Two other terms are important. *Sadaqa* is voluntary giving over and above zakat. The Quran urges that both zakat and sadaqa be performed anonymously. The term *usher* refers to almsgiving among Christians in the region.

24. Charities Aid Foundation, World Giving Index 2011, p. 7.

25. MasterCard Consumer Survey, 2010.

CHAPTER 12

The Erosion of Place

Nearly all nonprofits are created with a sense of place. They focus on a particular neighborhood, community, city, state, or country. Or they focus on a particular problem that itself is located in a place or places. Perhaps the exception is the category of nonprofits that deal with global warming, which is not trapped in geography but certainly has consequences that are very geographic indeed.

The overwhelming majority of nonprofits in the United States are locally focused. Indeed, less than 2 percent of U.S. nonprofits categorize themselves as international in focus. Of course, this is a considerable understatement. There are 723,000 international students on U.S. campuses in any particular year and another 275,000 U.S. college students studying abroad.[1] That is nearly a million students moving across the U.S. border in any year. The fact that U.S. universities are not to be found in the "international" coding category does not make them any less global. Still, it is true that the historical lens of the nonprofit is focused on local community, and it remains so. Even universities, in thinking about their alumni and in thinking about engagement, rarely think in global terms, even though, in the last decade alone, eight million young people from all over the world have walked their campuses.

Philanthropists have traditionally oriented themselves to place as well. Indeed, a 2008 survey of high-net worth individuals conducted by Changing Our World and Campden Research, in collaboration with PNB Paribas, found that, despite their multiple homes and companies with operations in all corners of the world, their philanthropic lens was local.[2] Nearly three quarters (72.1 percent) of responders place local issues and organizations as most important to them, compared to 17 percent highlighting international issues. The tendency to be local is much deeper for American philanthropists. If the criteria are loosened somewhat, and philanthropists are asked if international concerns are either "very" or "somewhat" important, still only 15 percent of North American respondents agreed, compared to over half of Europeans and nearly a third of Asians.[3] See Exhibit 12.1.

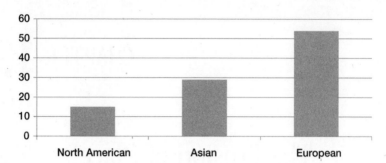

EXHIBIT 12.1 High-Net-Worth-Individual Philanthropy: International Is Somewhat or Very Important
Source: Changing Our World and Campden Research, 2009

The future, however, may be a world with much less of a sense of place. Two functions are at play here: the movement of individuals and the effects of technology.

If this is the case, then, nonprofits, especially those that see the world through a local lens, may need to adjust how they think about the problems they address, how they talk about themselves, and how they interact with what is likely to be the changing perceptions of philanthropists.

Migration

Although 2010–2011 saw an easing of migration, the past two decades have seen significant—and, for some nations, unprecedented—levels of migration, driven by economic opportunity and the technical skill needs of rapidly innovating economies. Migration into the United States has been at higher levels than at any time since the 1920s. In turn, many places that had long been relatively homogenous now have diverse populations. In the past decade, for example, the foreign-born population of New York and California, long multicultural magnets, grew by 8 percent and 11 percent, respectively. But that pales in comparison to the 48 percent growth in Tennessee, 46 percent in Arkansas, 40 percent in Kentucky, and 28 percent growth in Idaho.

But the growth in the percentage of its population that is immigrant has been highest in Europe. Spain saw a tripling in the percent of its population that is immigrant in just one decade. Exhibit 12.2 illustrates the increases. The only European nation with a decline in the percentage of its population represented by immigrants in the 2000–2009 period was Estonia.

This inflow has often had political repercussions, which have been the unfortunate pride and joy of headline writers. But it has also changed the way native populations see and experience their local communities. There are now

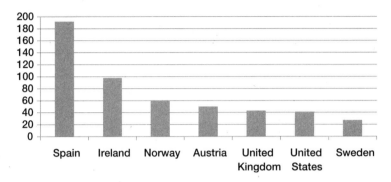

EXHIBIT 12.2 Percent Increase in Immigrant Population, 2000 to 2009

Ethiopian restaurants in Manhattan, New York, and Manhattan, Kansas. Dallas
has become the gateway to Asia.

   Yet these traditional patterns of migration are themselves changing as the
global economy changes. Today, a reverse migration is gathering speed,
equally driven by economic opportunity. Young entrepreneurs from America,
the well-educated children of immigrants, are returning to their family home-
lands of India and China and Mexico, looking for better opportunities in these
rapidly growing economies. But to that new home they also bring their
American experience, their links to their colleges and universities, their
perceptions about community. They bring with them the interests and issue
loyalties forged in their American communities and college campuses. Walks
for cancer, phonathons for schools, and 10-K runs for a cause all now will
become part of how global communities think about engagement on the
societal commons.

   This is a pattern that AnnaLee Saxenian has dubbed "brain circulation"
rather than brain drain.[4] The pattern is not one of migration and settlement, but
rather one of constant movement of talent in response to economic opportunity where professional borders are open and fluid.

   In 2010, 100,000 people of Indian descent arrived back in India.[5] Between
2002 and 2006, the ratio of Chinese students returning to China versus leaving
China tripled.[6] There is a constant ebb and flow between the United States and
Asia, for example. Silicon Valley start-ups are global from their very founding.
The relationships between new immigrants and their colleagues in their home
nations are reciprocal and constant, flowing money, expertise, and experiences constantly without concern for borders or boundaries.[7] Ethnicity and
culture are not ignored, but the sense of place is flexible and mobile. There is
as much adherence to tradition and community within the "new" location of
Silicon Valley as in the "old" home. It is not the particularities of place that
matters. Saxenian points out that this ebb and flow, this retention of culture
amidst change and transference of community irrespective of place, is all fluid

and informal, initially spawned through networks and then the integration of networks into the mainstream.[8]

And the process is not just one of mobile non-U.S. professionals. There is increasingly a native-born U.S. diaspora. Some 1.2 million U.S. individual tax returns are now filed abroad, and that number is growing at 3.5 percent per year.[9]

Victor Johnson, senior advisor for public policy at the Association of International Educators, perhaps best expressed the new realities of immigration and the erosion of place in 2009 when he described the circulation of talent and skill:

> *They (skilled people) may stay, return to their prior country of residence, move to a third country, establish homes in both the sending and receiving countries and divide their time between the two, travel back and forth constantly to engage in multinational research projects, or follow a variety of other patterns.*[10]

His presentation bore the insightful subtitle *Adjusting to What Happened in the World While We Were Making Other Plans,* a subtitle that perhaps is a harbinger for the nonprofit sector overall.

Borderless Technology

The second element in the erosion of place is technology. The pace with which technology is empowering individuals, irrespective of where they reside, to communicate, produce, create, and change is unprecedented. As noted in Exhibit 12.3, the iPad reached one million units sold in just 28 days

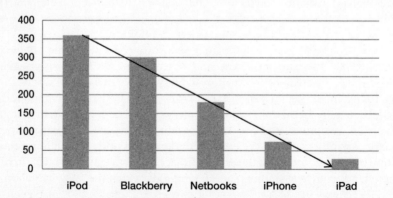

EXHIBIT 12.3 Days for Technology to Reach One Million Units Sold
Source: Morgan Stanley

(less than one month), compared with the iPod, which took 360 days (one year). And, not to press the point too hard, but the time between those two events was less than a decade. Time is collapsing into itself.

Social networking has become ubiquitous. In November 2007, social networking usage (global minutes per month) surpassed e-mail use, and less than two years later, in July 2009, the number of social networking users surpassed the number of e-mail users.[11]

It is difficult to overestimate the ways in which technology has released the individual from geographic limitations, and it is impossible in a single chapter to touch on all of the literature and commentary that described the impact of such technology. But its implications for a sense of place are profound.

There are now nearly six billion mobile handset subscribers globally, and eight trillion text messages were sent in 2011. Nearly every type of impression and experience can be unloosed from its geographic tether and sent everywhere. YouTube has in excess of two billion views per day, nearly double the prime-time audiences of all three major U.S. broadcast networks. Indeed, more video is uploaded to YouTube in 60 days than in the three major networks in 60 *years*. See Exhibit 12.4.

That video can be from any place in the world and viewed at any place in the world.

The erasing of borders by technology also powers content. As noted in Exhibit 12.5, 30 billion pieces of content are shared on Facebook per month. The pace is so constant and rapid that even the data from the companies noted

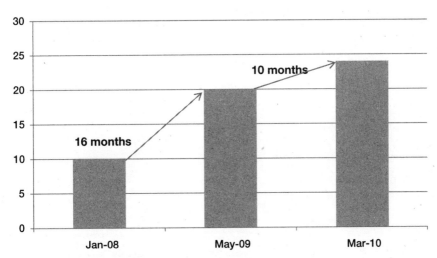

EXHIBIT 12.4 Hours of Video Uploaded to YouTube per Minute
Source: YouTube, 2012

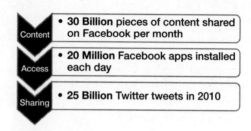

EXHIBIT 12.5 The Ubiquitous Rise of Information

in Exhibit 12.5 are outdated by the time they are cited. In 1960, 26 percent of the words read by Americans reached them through print media. Now that is less than 9 percent, and 27 percent of the words people read are accessed via the Internet.[12] Nearly half a billion people worldwide are connected through Google. There are some 60,000 new web sites added to the Internet each day, and Google estimates there are now about 15 billion pages of content accessible.

Moreover, in many parts of the world, all of this content is accessed not on a desktop computer, but by mobile device. Technology not only erases geography, but information itself is increasingly accessed on the move. Indeed, in places like Egypt and India, two thirds of people never or infrequently access the Web from a desktop. See Exhibit 12.6.

And these trends are destined not only to continue but to build momentum. Mobility and constant connectivity and access are a way of life to the young, a way of life they will carry forward into adulthood since, for many, it is the only way of life they know. Young people move between physical locations, but equally and more fluidly among virtual spaces irrespective of a concept of physical place. Place is defined as immobile, and hence a less desired condition. Even when local distances are not great, youth prefer virtual

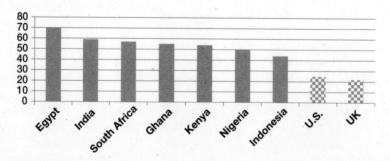

EXHIBIT 12.6 Percentage of Mobile Users Never or Infrequently Accessing the Web through a Desktop

Source: On Device Research, December 2010

mobility. A survey of young people in Denmark found that 70 percent rated the importance of access to mobile means of communication and Web access to be 8 to 10 in importance on a scale of 0 to 10.[13]

Technology gives the young not only the ability to access but also to create content without reference to place. There is no necessary workplace, no "water cooler" around which to gather. Ideas are shared instantly and fluidly, allowing a globalization of influence, of choices, and of opinions. Yet, they do, in fact, live in a domicile, eat at a table, and sleep in a bed. So, there is a reality of place. But that reality diverges from the experience of communication, work, and relationships. As Douglas Bourn has pointed out, this is the complex interplay among technology, identity, and globalization, which the millennial generation of young leaders will need to reconcile.[14]

But the pace of change will mean that doing so will be difficult. The future will empower the massive collection and distribution of data, globally and with open access. By 2020, the world will generate 35 zetabytes of data in one year, compared to 1.2 zetabytes times that in 2010. To provide perspective, one zetabyte is a 1 followed by 21 zeros. That is more than a 30-fold increase in just a decade. If you stored all the information on the Internet on DVDs, the stack would reach to the moon and back.[15] Next stop in 2020? Perhaps Pluto.

In turn, the ability to access that information will require a 10-fold increase in the number of servers worldwide and entirely new types of mobile technology to respond to the demand for constant and real-time access to information and communications.

In part, the pace of innovation is fueled by finance. Between 2005 and 2011, investment in digital enterprises increased by 50 percent, to $4 trillion.[16] But the pace of increase will not simply be fueled by technology and curiosity. It will also be powered by the realities of commerce. New technologies offer markets new ways to meet and interact with customers. This very access powers funding for access, and, in turn, urges on the pace of change. The five-year period 2011 to 2016 is projected to see nearly a doubling of marketing spending through U.S. interactive means, rising to $76 billion and representing 35 percent of all advertising expenditures in 2016.[17] And that mobile advertising allows product marketing to reach consumers who are difficult to reach in any other way in parts of the world that are growing rapidly. The data presented earlier in this chapter on mobile versus desktop Web access underscores this point. If you want to reach consumers in Asia, Africa, and the Middle East, then mobile technology is the means. See Exhibit 12.7.

When markets depend on new technology to push products, technology will be tightly harnessed to commerce, and innovation will find both ample investment dollars for development and ample advertising dollars for growth.

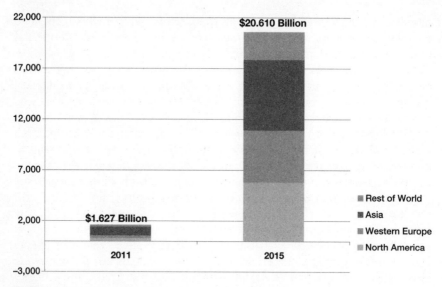

EXHIBIT 12.7 Mobile Advertising Revenue by Region
Source: Gartner Group, 2011

Summary and Implications

The erosion of the sense of place that accompanies global circulation of wealth and skilled professionals will only increase with coming generations who will define their relationships without reference to physical space. Moreover, that next generation will process information entirely differently from generations of the past. The next generation may be quicker to move among pieces of information, and therefore among organizations. Relationships and engagement will shift with interests and information. Causes will remain, but institutional loyalty, particularly loyalty premised on place, could erode.

There is also some consensus that younger brains are being rewired to adapt to new information processing needs and skills, and to think differently about information and evidence.[18] Focusing and understanding one thing deeply will be less important than quickly sorting through massive amounts of information.

And the frame of reference will not be the particularity of a specific place. It will be global, open, and digital. The Elm Street Soup Kitchen down the block will not be a physical experience for many; it will be a general thematic and will exist simultaneously with soup kitchens everywhere. Even among those passionate about hunger, it will compete for funding attention with all others.

Faced with the beginning of the arc of such changes, about which a great deal more will be said in Chapter 15, the common nonprofit reaction is to put a video on the web site and a "GIVE" button on the home page. Change? No problem. We can accommodate change and stay the same. And we can spend less than $10,000 per year in the process (which is what 82 percent of nonprofits now spend on their social networking capacity).[19]

But the scope and pace of the shifts have much more profound implications than Internet fundraising. These are fundamental changes in the way the next generation of leaders (and the next generation of wealth holders) will think. It will certainly be a matter of behavior. It may also become a matter of biology. To engage their supporters, to relate to the new generations of wealth, nonprofits will need to become quicker in their communications, totally flexible in their architecture, immediate in their time frame, instant in their reactions, and they will need to be able to change all of that on a dime as everything that was true last year changes next year.

In effect, the Elm Street Soup Kitchen has to exist in the computing "cloud" and be able to speak to the world if it is to be top of mind to coming generations of philanthropists and activists. The views of Rosabeth Moss Kanter or Harvard Business School apply as much to nonprofits as they do the great companies: "Globalization detaches companies from one specific society but at the same time requires that the companies internalize the needs of many societies."[20]

This is a tremendous challenge for all nonprofits around the world. These are not American issues. They are issues for all nonprofits nearly everywhere. It would be an overwhelming challenge if a five-year planning horizon was possible. It is doubling daunting because five years appears to be a lifetime in a process of globalization, migration, and technological change that separates perceptions and priorities from place.

Few nonprofit are ready for that reality.

Case I: Multichannel Pathways to Reach New Fundraising Markets

Author: Russ Reid

Partner: Operation Smile

(continued)

(*continued*)

Situation

Operation Smile, established in 1982, is a worldwide children's medical charity engaging medical volunteers to provide the highest-quality care to children in need. With a network of over 5,000 volunteer medical professionals, Operation Smile performs free cleft lip and cleft palate surgeries for impoverished children.

The organization came to Russ Reid in 2003 with a big vision to help more children around the world. With a traditional direct marketing program not delivering the growth they needed and an aggressive competitor stepping up its acquisition efforts, Operation Smile challenged Russ Reid to increase the organization's visibility, donor base, and net revenue through a powerful direct response television campaign.

The recession of 2008 hit most nonprofits hard. Many saw income plummet. But rather than withdraw from the marketplace, Operation Smile adopted an innovative approach to survive and grow.

Stakes

Operation Smile needed more donors, lots of them. They had field commitments to reach more children with the miracle of life-altering surgeries. Rather than facing a predictable growth curve, the recession presented the possibility of decline and disappointment.

Strengths

Operation Smile could bank on several assets: 25 years of brand recognition, a compelling and proven marketing "offer" ($240 can provide a new life for a child) and an engaged army of volunteers. They believed that if they could find a way to tell their story to more people, they could survive the recession and reach more children.

Strategy

Operation Smile decided to broaden and integrate their marketing campaigns, optimizing existing channels and infusing new communication channels into their marketing mix. They decided to present their message in the places and manner most relevant to their current donors and future supporters.

They transformed their digital marketing tools website, landing pages and display ad campaigns) to support and leverage their investment in direct mail and television.

They presented their story to supporters through an alternative "gift catalog" (both printed copy and online version). This new channel has become a significant source of both satisfaction to donors and of new revenue for Operation Smile.

Rather than overinvest in finding younger donors (who do not give as much as older donors), they focused the majority of their donor acquisition efforts on mature donors who have proven track records in giving larger donations. The result was a growing middle and major donor-giving track, which helped sustain their revenue through the recession.

They developed a "city-campaign" strategy, leveraging local media celebrities, outdoor, print, television, direct mail, face-to-face, and event marketing. Revenue from this integrated strategy widely surpassed expectations and serves a model for the benefits of integrating campaign media.

Through testing and optimization of all their direct marketing channels, they did more of what worked best and less of what didn't work as well. The result was a more efficient marketing engine.

Solution

See Appendix 1.

Notes

1. Open Doors 2011 data, Institute of International Education, 2012.
2. *Giving through the Generations* (London: Campden Research and Changing Our World, Inc., 2008), 36.
3. Ibid. p. 37.
4. A. Saxenian, *Brain Circulation: How High-Skill Immigration Makes Everyone Better Off* (Washington, DC: Brookings Institution, 2002).
5. K. Semple, "Many U.S. Immigrants' Children Seek American Dream Abroad," *New York Times,* April 16, 2012, p. A1.
6. M. Regets, "Brain Circulation: The Complex National Effects of High-Skilled Migration." Presentation to the OECD Committee for Scientific and Technology Policy (CSTP) and Steering and Funding of Research Institutions (SFRI) Workshop on the International Mobility of Researchers, Paris, France, March 28, 2007, slide 14.
7. Saxenian, *Brain Circulation.*
8. Ibid.
9. Regets, slide 22.

10. V. C. Johnson, *A Visa and Immigration Policy for the Brain-Circulation Era: Adjusting To What Happened in the World While We Were Making Other Plans* (Washington, DC: NAFSA Association of International Educators, December 2009), 5.

11. comScore global and Morgan Stanley Research. Global users are measured as monthly unique visitors, not total registered users.

12. R. E. Bohn and J. E. Short, "How Much Information? 2009 Report on American Consumers," University of California at San Diego, Global Information Industry Center, December 2009, p. 17.

13. G. Stald, Mobile Identity: Youth, Identity, and Mobile Communication Media. Youth, Identity, and Digital Media. David Buckingham (ed.) The John D. and Edna T. MacArthur Foundation Series on Digital Media and Learning. Cambridge, MA: MIT Press, 2008, 147.

14. D. Bourne, "Young People, Identity and Living in a Global Society. Politic and Practice: A Development Education Review," *Development Education Review*, August 2008, www.developmenteducationreview.com /issue7-focus4?page=3.

15. J. Gantz and D. Reinsel, "Extracting Value from Chaos." A study sponsored by EMC and conducted by IDC, June 2011, p. 3.

16. Ibid., p. 2.

17. S. VanBoskirk, "US Interactive Marketing Forecast, 2011 to 2016," Forrester Research, Inc., August 24, 2011, p. 3.

18. See results of an academic opinion survey sponsored by the Pew Research Center. J. Q. Anderson and L. Rainie, "Millennials Will Benefit *and* Suffer Due to Their Hyperconnected Lives," Pew Research Center's Internet & American Life Project, February 29, 2012.

19. "Third Annual Nonprofit Social Network Benchmark Report, 2011." Developed by NTEN, Common Knowledge, Blackbaud, Inc., 2011, p. 8.

20. R. M. Kanter, "How Great Companies Think Differently," *Harvard Business Review* (November 2011): 70.

CHAPTER **13**

Will Complexity Erode Trust?

As the nonprofit and philanthropic sector grows, and as it becomes more complex and definitions blur, three sets of problems emerge for organizations: the role of governments in meeting needs on the societal commons, awareness and understanding of what a "nonprofit" is, and the implications of both for traditional giving.

Each one of these problems is likely to increase over the next decade, and separately and together they will represent yet another element of change in the chemistry and consistency of the glue that binds the nonprofit sector to community and civil society. That change must be understood if it is to be managed. It must be grasped and molded if it is to contribute to strength rather than produce weakness. Neither hope for understanding nor wishes for a return to the simple will suffice to produce a secure future for the sector.

Taxes and the Relationship with Government

In the United States, the term *nonprofit* covers many types of organizations. Indeed, there are 33 different types of nonprofit organizations for purposes of the tax code, with varying degrees of tax-exempt status. In addition to the federal process, each state has its own registration system and reporting requirements. Hence, it is difficult to make general statements about the entire sector and its relationship to the tax base of government. However, that relationship is deep and intense. The point here is not to take a position on the right or wrong of the reality, but simply to document the dimensions of those relationships, their changing nature, and their implications.

Federal Concerns

Estimates are that the entire nonprofit sector results in an estimated cost of $50 billion per year at the federal level, both in terms of tax-free income and activities of nonprofits themselves and the taxes foregone on donations to the sector. Indeed, between 1985 and 2004, charitable expenditures rose by 107 percent, but the GDP rose by only 58 percent.[1] The combination of soaring federal budget deficits and the rising exemptions cost of charitable giving led some policy makers to rethink the traditions of deductibility.

Beginning with FY 2010 and in every budget submission since, the Barack Obama administration has included in its budget to Congress a provision to reduce the deductibility of charitable donations for high-net-worth households. Rather than being able to deduct contributions equal to a taxpayer's tax bracket (e.g., 35 percent), the tax deductibility would be capped at 28 percent. In Fiscal 2013, the budget submission recommended reducing the value of itemized deductions and other philanthropic tax preferences to 28 percent for families with incomes over $250,000 per year or single taxpayers earning over $200,000. The budget submission estimates that the action would reduce the federal deficit by $584 billion over 10 years.[2] The recommendations were not enacted by Congress in the first three years that they were submitted (as of this writing the Fiscal 2013 submission is still before Congress), but the thought that the historic exemption enjoyed by charitable contributions would be reversed, even at the highest levels, sent a shock wave through the nonprofit and philanthropic sectors.

Debate has ensued about whether or not this change would fundamentally affect the behavior of high-net-worth individuals, and the role that tax considerations actually played in philanthropic behavior. The evidence on all sides is weak. Some in the policy arena argued that the contributions of the cap to closing the federal deficit would avoid budget cuts that would hurt nonprofits, and that, in fact, there was no evidence that the extremely wealthy would reduce their giving based on a few percentage points of tax differential. Most nonprofit organizations, however, argued that reductions in deductibility and higher taxes on the wealthy (as called for by the "Buffett Rule," which recommended very high wealthy tax rates in response to the deficit) would severely cripple major gifts efforts upon which most nonprofit income depended.[3]

That debate continues,* but, whatever its outcome, the walls have been breached. The relationships among nonprofits, philanthropy, and taxes, long settled by the Revenue Act of 1913, which focused on organizational taxes, and the Revenue Act of 1917, which established an individual income tax exemption for contributions made to tax-exempt organizations,[4] are now firmly on the policy table. Initially driven by the deep federal budget deficit after the Great Recession, and the general antipathy toward wealth and tax advantage that a

---

*The "fiscal cliff" negotiations of 2012 and the continuing 2013 debate over the debt ceiling and budget cuts versus tax increases will almost certainly affect various elements of tax deductability. The charitable deduction remains on the negotiating table as of this writing.

concern over deficit reduction created, the question of who should pay for the federal budget is now an open question. The debate surrounding that question will likely continue, fed on the one hand by a slow economic recovery and a projected decades-long steep federal deficit, and, on the other, by the sheer growth and complexity of the sector. Nonprofit status and philanthropic giving are now, and will continue to be, in budget policy play.

Growth has certainly played a part in putting the sector under the budget policy lens. In the early 1980s, only 30 years ago, there were just over 300,000 public charities in America. Today, there are over 1.4 million. Most new organizations were small at inception and did not grow rapidly or robustly. The Pension Reform Act of 2006 required nonprofits with less than $25,000 in annual gross receipts, a category previously exempt from any IRS reporting, to file a simple tax form. The Act mandated that any organizations that failed to file for three consecutive years should have their tax-exempt status revoked. By June 2011, 275,000 organizations, 16 percent of the entire sector, had their tax-exempt status revoked. Nearly half of those revocations were for nonprofits founded since 1990, and 70 percent were for nonprofits founded since 1980.[5] See Exhibit 13.1.

The outcry was instantaneous, and procedures for relief and re-registration were put in place fairly immediately. But the policy precedent was clear. The growth in the sector and its visibility, complexity, and resource consequences will no longer be ignored by tax policy.

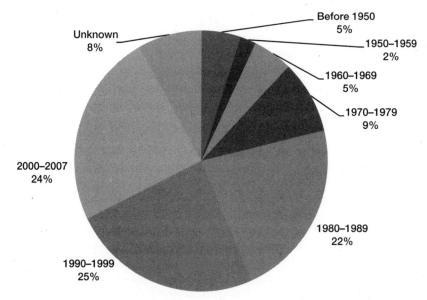

EXHIBIT 13.1 Distribution of Tax-Exempt Revocations by Founding Year
Source: Urban Institute

Although growth is a factor in federal action, over time, complexity may be a more important factor than size. The emergence of dual-purpose organizations, with one foot in commerce and one foot in social engagement, will fuel debates about taxation, as will the emergence of new ways to flow funds to such organizations. Simple solutions from the past likely will not fit complex problems (or opportunities) of the future. The concerns about definitions and responsibilities for shouldering financial burdens are legitimate. But the distinctions will be murky; consequently, the debate will be messy. Messy debates are the parents of unruly offspring, and the role of tax burden will thus become confusing, partisan, and divisive. This needs to be understood, not ignored; sinecures from the past will not necessarily represent security for the future.

State and Local Concerns

The federal debate is of recent origin, tied deeply to the Great Recession and its fiscal consequences. Local concerns over tax status, however, have been building over decades and, for many communities, are now critical policy issues. They are likely to become even more critical in the future as the costs of governing rise.

The economic benefits of nonprofit organizations at the community level is undeniable. For example, education and health care keep many local economies afloat and resilient to downturns, representing 15 percent of national employment. Nevertheless, charitable tax exemption nationwide represents $17 billion to $32 billion in property taxes foregone, or as much as 8 percent of all property taxes.[6]

Where the nonprofit sector is large within the totality of a city's economy, nevertheless, the public resource effects can be significant. In Boston, for example, nonprofits, if they were taxable entities, would represent $390 million in tax receipts, or 16.7 percent of the city's total budget.[7] Many cities have instituted voluntary payments in lieu of taxes (PILOT) policies, asking large nonprofits to voluntarily contribute resources to the city budget in recognition of the services (police, fire, sewer, water) that they consume. While such policies have been put in place in over 100 municipalities, they rarely represent more than 1 percent of total city revenues. In Boston, they total only 0.73 percent of the city budget compared to the 16.7 percent that would have been obtained through taxation.[8]

Beyond fighting nonprofit status in terms of property taxes, cities and states are choosing not to exempt nonprofits from new levies, assessments, and fees initiated to raise funds for post-recession public budgets and infrastructure improvements. Indeed, cities and counties across the country are no longer exempting charities, schools, and churches from fees for improvements to roads and storm and drainage systems that either are critical to public

service maintenance or are mandated by environmental protection regula-
tions.[9] A 2011 survey by the Johns Hopkins University Center for Civil Society
found that 63 percent of responding nonprofits were subject to various local
government fees and taxes, and the vast majority had been paying these levies
for at least three years.[10]

Despite the traditions, and the clear employment utility of nonprofits to
local economies, the distinction between nonprofit institutions and other
organizations within public budget thinking has changed. Constrained fiscal
circumstances, an aging population and therefore an increase in resistance to
tax increases dominate concerns. Moreover, the lack of alternative targets for
revenue generation (note that in only 6 of the largest 25 municipalities with
employment growth in nonprofits did that growth make up for the equivalent
decline in manufacturing jobs) means that local and state public budget and
taxation policies will inevitably turn to one of the only places left for revenue
generation—the nonprofit sector.

Once the precedents are inaugurated and the funds raised, policy will
separate from tradition and history. Nonprofits need to expect a renegotiated
relationship with government on issues of resource relationships.

The Views of the Public

The past decade has seen an erosion of trust and confidence on the part of the
American public in all manner of institutions. The Great Recession and the
exceedingly slow and uneven economic recovery, perhaps fueled by the heated
rhetoric that intersected that recovery and a presidential campaign, as well as
well-publicized scandals in public and commercial sectors, have combined to
leave most people questioning the reliability of institutions and individuals.
Indeed, by 2010, the Pew Research Center noted that only 22 percent of
Americans trust the government in Washington all or most of the time.[11]
This is nearly an all-time low in the nation's view of its public institutions.

The trends of public trust in nonprofits are matters of some debate. The
first problem, of course, is what do most people mean by a nonprofit? Again,
rising complexity of the sector and its own definitions are in play and likely to
contribute to future perplexity in the public. There is common understanding
of where Washington, D.C., is and who governs there, but there is much less
clarity around what people mean by trust in nonprofits. In part that is because
of the 33 categories of "nonprofit." After all, most political action committees
(PACs) are nonprofit, and they are in the business of flowing money to political
candidates from special-interest groups. So the public is to be forgiven for not
having a clear idea about the nonprofit business model.

In the period 2000 to 2007, public opinion on nonprofit performance
waned. By 2006, Harris Interactive found that only 1 in 10 respondents felt

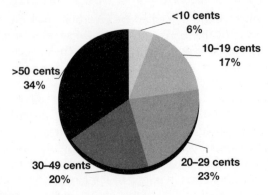

EXHIBIT 13.2 Survey Responders' Perception of Administrative Portion of Dollar Donated
Source: Ellison Research

strongly that charitable institutions are honest and ethical in their use of funds and spent money wisely.[12] A 2008 Brookings Institution survey found that 70 percent of responders felt charitable institutions wasted "a great deal" or a "fair amount" of money.[13] Also in 2008, Ellison Research found that a third of survey respondents believed that nonprofits used more than 50 percent of every dollar donated on administration, rather than less than 20 cents, which is what respondents preferred.[14] See Exhibit 13.2.

"Where does the money actually go?" was the operative question and the core of the trust problem. This is likely to become an especially difficult question as nonprofit revenue diversifies into more enterprise and entrepreneurial areas, and "gift" donations become only a part of how nonprofits think about funding their work.

Moreover, as noted in Exhibit 13.3, age brings a decline in the belief that nonprofits are "going in the right direction," a phrase that is used to allow the responder to self-define what constitutes a "right" direction. Taken alongside the aging population, described in Chapter 9 of this book, that trend suggests particularly fragile trust levels as the sector becomes more diverse and complex, and thus harder to explain and grasp in a simple way.

Of course, everything is relative. When asked about nonprofit trustworthiness relative to government, a 2010 poll by Fenton Communications indicates that nonprofits are much more in America's comfort zone. Whereas in 2010 Pew Research found that only 22 percent of Americans trust Washington all or most of the time, Fenton found that four in five Americans rate the performance of nonprofits from good to excellent.[15]

Globally, as media attention has grown, skepticism about the nonprofit sector has spread to emerging economies as well. The 2010 transparency report from the China Charity and Donations Information Center found that

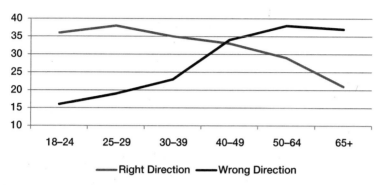

EXHIBIT 13.3 Public Opinion of Nonprofit Performance Vary by Age
Source: Harris Interactive

only 25 percent of Chinese charities were transparent in reporting their financial information, and that 90 percent of a surveyed sample of Chinese citizens felt that information disclosed by charities was inadequate.[16] Where the nonprofit sector is young, trust can be fragile. Between June and August 2011, donations to nonprofits fell by over $50 million due to a series of media reports on nonprofit scandals.

In India, the rapid expansion in the nonprofit sector (with 3.3 million registered nongovernmental organizations) has led to media coverage of high overhead, lack of uniform accounting and reporting, and misuse of funds.[17] Of the millions of Indian nonprofits, the internal watchdog, Credibility Alliance, has only about 600 members. The 2012 Bain & Company study of philanthropy in India found that over half of philanthropists cited the lack of financial accountability among nonprofits as the biggest factor in reducing their giving, although that is a decided improvement over the 70 percent who cited accountability as a factor in 2011.[18]

In Brazil, Japan, and Russia, serious nonprofit crises and scandals resulted in severe declines in trust levels in 2011. In Brazil, the decline was 31 points, in Japan 21 points, and in Russia 14 points.[19] A global survey of institutional philanthropy found that a lack of trust was a moderate to extreme challenge to the spread of philanthropy in Africa and Latin America.[20]

As in the United States, broad media coverage, engendered by the growth in and the new complexity of the sector and the expansion of giving at all levels of society, has led to rising skepticism.

These general data do not provide robust understanding of how people see nonprofits in the context of other types of organizations operating on an increasingly complex and heterogeneous societal commons. Some of the most detailed information in this regard is available for health care, where nonprofit and for-profit institutions compete virtually head-to-head for patients and

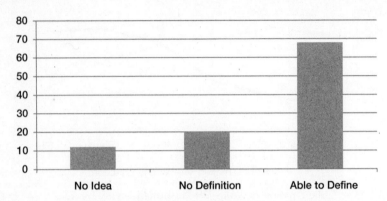

EXHIBIT 13.4 Percent Survey Responders Able to Define a Nonprofit

Source: M. Schlesinger, S. Mitchell, and B. H. Gray, "Public Expectations of Nonprofit and For-Profit Ownership in American Medicine: Clarifications and Implications," *Health Affairs* 23(6) (November 2004): 181–191.

revenues. While for-profit systems have lower average cost per stay than nonprofits, nonprofits often provide a wider range of social and uncompensated services than their for-profit counterparts.[21] What does the public think about the larger nonprofit sector?

Schlesinger, Mitchell, and Gray have completed a survey to try to answer that question. The survey also casts light on the question of who knows what. In fact, a third of respondents either had no idea what a nonprofit was or could not provide a specific definition.[22] See Exhibit 13.4.

Similarly, a 2010 survey of college students found that, while they are more likely to trust nonprofits than other types of organizations, they cannot spontaneously actually identify the organizational status of well-known institutions or brands.[23]

The confusion among types of organizations as the nonprofit sector becomes more complex extends to the distinctions between nonprofits and government where nonprofits have taken on major public service roles as private-sector providers of previously government services. Who to hold accountable, government or nonprofit, is at issue. In a survey of those who use public service agencies in Georgia, respondents regularly misidentified the service provider as government versus nonprofit, but were more likely to misidentify a nonprofit provider as governmental when they were dissatisfied with service quality.[24]

Hence, it may be that, increasingly, the public has a hard time actually differentiating the nonprofit from other institutions that are operating in communities. This is a central point made by Courtney, Kelleher, and Thiemann in their comparison of nonprofit and for-profit business models in health care; despite the clear differences in nonprofit service provision to the public, there is a potential failure of nonprofits to clearly differentiate themselves in the public view when there are so many other actors engaged in health care provision.[25]

Despite this, the Schlesinger/Mitchell/Gray survey responders did have assumptions about care. Nonprofits were viewed more favorably in terms of fairness of treatment and considerations in terms of insurance coverage. However, over half felt that the quality of medical care would be about the same for nonprofits and for-profits, and indeed 14 percent thought for-profit care would be better.

But knowledge matters hugely, and not necessarily positively. Those who could define nonprofits were *less* likely to view nonprofits as likely to offer high-quality services. And when the definition of a nonprofit was given to those who did not originally know what a nonprofit was, their view of likely quality actually declined. Furthermore, on all measures African Americans, Latinos, and Asians all had more critical assessments of nonprofits on all outcome measures. Women were especially likely to have a positive view of nonprofit health care models.[26]

If the results of this extremely well structured and detailed survey are to inform the nonprofit sector in general, the message is that communication is critical to trust, especially where there are choices in the "market" (as there increasingly will be throughout the nonprofit sector). The growth in the number of nonprofits, entrance of commercial entities into nonprofit service provision in such areas as education, health and social services, and application of business principles to nonprofit management, and the rise of hybrid organizational models in all aspects of social problem solving will make it extremely difficult to differentiate the nonprofit as an organizational type in the community. Indeed, it may bring into question the distinctiveness of the organizational form at all.

Not only is the continued evolution of organizational forms and financing on the social commons (social enterprises, social bonds, etc.) likely to fuel this trend, so will human resource trends. Nonprofit managers are now likely to have for-profit backgrounds. They are no longer simply the products of passion. They are the products of commerce. Indeed, in the 2007–2008 period, 21 percent of nonprofit management positions were filled by those entering from the for-profit sector. Indeed, half of all training age Baby Boomers (ages 44 to 50) express interest in moving into the social sector professionally.[27] The processes and systems inside nonprofits will increasingly look like the processes and systems in the marketplace. The public's opinion of "nonprofits" then may begin to look like its opinion of every other organization.

And the public's trust may follow the same path.

Summary and Implications

The concern over the burden to be borne by public finance, and the confusion about the nonprofit sector in the public view—both of which stem from deep changes in the operating environment of the nonprofit sector—will create a third challenge for nonprofits: continuing to develop the relationships that lead to robust fundraising. Trust is fundamental to those relationships—trust of the nonprofit, trust about its role in the community, and trust about its relationship to the public policy that holds the long-term responsibility for the social safety net. To the extent that the operating environment creates pressures on nonprofits that erode trust, then private philanthropy will raise its individual or collective eyebrow.

Complexity and blurred roles between markets, government, and charitable institutions will be the driving characteristic of social problem solving in the future. Being able to distinguish the nonprofit function and, importantly, distinguish its value proposition for the other organizations operating in the social problem solving space will be a key challenge for private philanthropic resource mobilization in the future.

Case J: New Strength through Simplifying Identity

Author: Interbrand

Interbrand

Partner: Feeding America

Situation

One in every eight Americans struggles with hunger—people of all ages, and from all walks of life. But hunger in America is often overlooked. It has traditionally been seen as a foreign issue—certainly not something happening in our own back yard and especially with the media putting the spotlight squarely on obesity.

In 2007, the nation's largest domestic hunger relief network was known as America's Second Harvest, the Nation's Food Bank Network. They exist to build awareness for the issue of hunger in America, and bring in donations of food, money, and volunteer support to distribute among their more than 200 local members who fight hunger on the front lines.

Stakes

But it's hard to win support for your cause when people don't know who you are and don't see the value of what you do. Leadership discovered that despite a 30+-year legacy of fighting hunger, they had only 22 percent awareness with the public. Support from their local members—the grassroots force critical to the mission—was waning due to a lack of transparency into network decision making. They weren't the first pick for corporate partners looking for a way to do good in the world. Confusion swirled around their long and complicated name.

They were facing no small challenge. Losing public, corporate, and local support would mean millions of Americans could go hungry. And because it's hard to work or go to school on an empty stomach, hunger is often a root cause of unemployment and unfinished education.

Strengths

The leadership team was no stranger to transforming a challenge into a success. They recognized the need to build a national brand that would create a greater stage for the issue of hunger and help to raise awareness and financial support at exponentially greater levels. A previously failed experience in rebranding meant that they were open to embracing a very strategic approach to building their brand. To meet these ambitions:

- All decisions would be grounded in a rigorous, data-driven fact base, to ensure action would build toward collective success.
- The decision-making process was designed to embrace the entire decentralized organization, serving as the first moment of truth inside the organization that each and every member of the organization was important to delivering on the organization's big ambitions in eradicating hunger and food insecurity.

(continued)

(continued)

Strategy

A rigorous segmentation study identified the audiences who wanted to make an impact—personally and financially—in the fight against hunger. National research validated that of four positioning approaches, "Feeding Hope" was the most compelling, harnessing the power of food to help people not just survive, but to look forward to a brighter future. The data collected during this time set the foundation for taking action, across many media channels, traditional and brand new; with many partners; with a reengaged population who could *see* the hunger issue at hand. The birth of the Feeding America brand was embraced by Michelle Obama, by new corporate partners, and by the organization at large.

Solution

See Appendix 1.

Notes

1. P. Arnsberger et al., "A History of the Tax Exempt Sector: An SOI Perspective," *Statistics of Income Bulletin* (Winter 2008): 111.
2. Fiscal 2013 Budget Submission, p. 39.
3. For a summary of arguments, see A. Naboulsi, *Analysis of the Proposed Charitable Deduction Cap: Is 28 Percent Enough?* (Phoenix, AZ: ASU Lodestar Center for Philanthropy and Nonprofit Innovation, February 6, 2012). See also J. J. Cordes, "Re-Thinking the Deduction for Charitable Contributions: Evaluating the Effects of Deficit-Reduction Proposals," *National Tax Journal* (December 2011): 1001–1024.
4. The Revenue Act of 1913 for the first time imposed a federal income tax on corporations but exempted charities. The roots of this decision are to be found in the Tariff Act of 1894 and the Revenue Act of 1909, both of which posed concerns about the need to treat organizations dedicated to the public good differently from those focused on commercial markets.
5. A. S. Blackwood and K. L. Roeger, *Revoked: A Snapshot of Organizations that Lost Their Tax-Exempt Status* (Washington, DC: Center on Nonprofits and Philanthropy, Urban Institute, August 2011), 3.
6. D. A. Kenyon and A. H. Langley, *The Property Tax Exemption for Non-profits and Revenue Implications for Cities* (Washington, DC: Urban Institute, Lincoln Institute of Land Policy, November 2011), 2.

7. Ibid., p. 4.
8. Ibid., p. 6.
9. I. J. Dugan, "Strapped Cities Hit Nonprofits with Fees," *Wall Street Journal,* December 27, 2010, p. A.1.
10. L. M. Salamon, S. L. Geller, and S. W. Sokolowski, "Taxing the Tax-Exempt Sector—A Growing Danger for Nonprofit Organizations" Johns Hopkins University Center for Civil Society Studies, Listening Post Project, Communiqué No. 21, p. 3.
11. "Distrust, Discontent, Anger and Partisan Rancor: The People and Their Government," Pew Research Center for the People and the Press, April 18, 2010.
12. Harris Interactive, "Donor Pulse Survey," April 2006.
13. P. C. Light, *How Americans View Charities: A Report on Charitable Confidence* Washington, DC: Brookings Institution, April 2008), 10.
14. "Americans Perceptions of the Financial Efficiency of Non-profit Organizations," Ellison Research, February 2008, p. 3.
15. "2010 Fenton Forecast: Leadership and Effectiveness Among Nonprofits," Fenton Communications, 2010.
16. "Donation Transparency," Editorial in *China Daily,* December 6, 2010, p. 8.
17. N. Bhowmick, "Accountability of India's Nonprofits Under Scrutiny," *Time World,* December 14, 2010, p. 3.
18. *India Philanthropy Report, 2012* (Boston: Bain & Co., 2012), 14.
19. "Trust Barometer," Edelman Consulting, 2012, p. 4.
20. P. D. Johnson, *Global Institutional Philanthropy: A Preliminary Status Report* (Boston: TPI and WINGS, 2010), 15, 43.
21. Data from the American Hospital Association and Department of Health and Human Services. An interesting analysis of the differing business models is contained in D. Courtney, R. Kelleher, and E. Thiemann, "Vital Organizations? The Viability of the Nonprofit Health Care Business Model," unpublished paper, April 30, 2012, Foresight Program, Mendoza School of Business, University of Notre Dame.
22. M. Schlesinger, S. Mitchell, and B. H. Gray, "Public Expectations of Nonprofit and For-Profit Ownership in American Medicine: Clarifications and Implications," *Health Affairs* 23(6) (November 2004): 181–191.
23. F. Handy et al., "The Discerning Consumer: Is Nonprofit Status a Factor?" *Nonprofit and Voluntary Sector Quarterly* 39(5) (October 2010): 866–883.
24. D. M. Van Slyke and C. H. Roch, "What Do They Know, and Whom Do They Hold Accountable? Citizens in the Government-Nonprofit Contracting Relationship," *Journal of Public Administration Theory* 14(2): 191–209.

25. D. Courtney, R. Kelleher, and E. Thiemann. Vital Organizations: The Viability of the Nonprofit Business Model. Forsight Program of the Mendoza School of Business, the University of Notre Dame. Mentored by Susan Raymond, Ph.D., and Brian Crimmins, Changing Our World, Inc., May 2012, www.changingourworld.com/site/PageNavigator/ow_resource_notredame.html.
26. Schlesinger, Mitchell, and Gray, pp. 699–700.
27. *Finding Leaders for America's Nonprofits* (Boston: Bridgespan Group, April 20, 2009), 2.

CHAPTER 14

Programming for the Future

The nature of change in the operating environments of nonprofits and of philanthropies is so fundamental, and is likely to continue at such a pace, that all organizations—grant makers and grant recipients—must be prepared to adjust programs constantly. The dimensions of change that have been illustrated in the previous chapters include:

- Complex problems of unclear origins and with unclear solutions.
- Totally new approaches to solutions and institutional complexes driven by Web-based communications.
- Complex problems that defy borders—local, national, or international.
- New demographics.
- New loci of poverty.
- New levels and types of unemployment in new places and at new ages.
- New types of partners not previously engaged in social problem solving and therefore new opportunities.

The nature and pace of change means that programmatic decision making must be constant and organic, with management mechanisms to continually adapt content to circumstances.

Although one cannot examine the program implications of change for every sector and every institution, this chapter will illustrate the implications of these changes for nonprofit project portfolios and funder priorities in three areas: global health, U.S. state economic challenge, and the demographics of aging. These illustrations are intended to demonstrate how changes over the past decade, and their projected continuity in the future, require adjustment in programming. That adjustment is often difficult in the nonprofit sector because neither grant makers nor grant recipients have refined systems for constantly measuring change or traditions of institutional response to fundamental changes in their "markets." Strategies and approaches for creating such measures and instituting strategies for ensuring consequent program and organizational adjustment to change are presented in Section IV, which follows.

Global Health

From the early 1970s to the present, the focus of much private philanthropy (and government bilateral and multilateral foreign assistance) in support of health has been communicable diseases, with particular emphasis on mothers and children under the age of five. This emphasis stems from the reality of the 1970s: life expectancies at birth in the developing world were between 40 and 50 years, infant mortality was nearly always over 100 babies per 1,000 live births, communicable diseases took the majority of lives and took them early, caloric intake averaged less than 2,000 calories per day, and more mothers died in childbirth than of nearly any other cause. The likes of South Korea, India, Taiwan, and Singapore were largely poor. Private charity mobilized in tandem with industrialized governments and flowed resources toward maternal and child health, communicable disease control, and reproductive health.

In part because of successes from public health and in part because of growing economies and rising literacy, that epidemiological situation has changed in much (but not all) of the world. Infant mortality has declined by 75 percent and child mortality by 80 percent. Life expectancy is within 10 years of the industrialized world. Fertility rates in many countries are now approaching replacement levels. Even maternal mortality, long an indicator that has defied solutions, has dropped by 40 percent since 1980.[1]

As a result, population structure is changing. The portion of the population in the *developing world* (itself a term on the verge of extinction as economies grow) over the age of 60 is now greater than the portion under the age of 5. Indeed, by 2020, the number of children in the developing world under the age of 5 will begin to decline in absolute terms.

The "epidemiological transition" (the shift from death from communicable diseases such as influenza and tuberculosis to noncommunicable chronic diseases such as diabetes and heart disease) is well under way. In all but Africa, even where adult and child mortality is relatively high, it is noncommunicable diseases that account for the vast majority of deaths. See Exhibit 14.1.

Moreover, that epidemiological transition has affected women far beyond a level normally recognized. Even in their reproductive ages, chronic diseases often represent a much higher portion of women's death than even the combination of maternal and HIV/AIDS causes. See Exhibit 14.2.

Moreover, when compared to women in industrialized nations, women in developing nations are dying at much higher rates and at much younger ages than their sisters in more developed economies.[2]

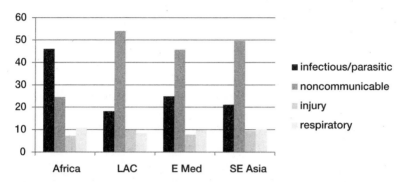

EXHIBIT 14.1 Percent Distribution of Cause of Death in High Child/High Adult Mortality Countries

Source: World Health Organization, State of the World's Health

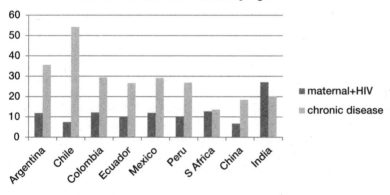

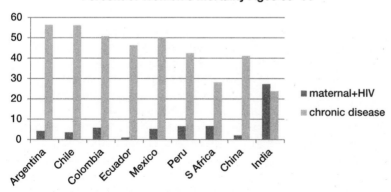

EXHIBIT 14.2 Women's Mortality by Cause

Source: World Health Organization Mortality Database

"Women's health" in global health programming has been defined as reproductive and maternal health for the past 40 years. Changing demographics, consequent changing epidemiology, and changing economics have combined to change that reality. The threats to women's health are now much more diverse than in the past.

The economic consequences of the epidemiological transition in low and middle incomes countries are stunning. The World Health Organization estimates that between 2006 and 2015, China will lose $558 billion in foregone national income due to heart disease, stroke, and diabetes. Even if cardiovascular disease rates remain stable, the process of aging will result, for example, in nearly 18 million years of productive life lost in India in 2030.[3] South Africa will see its disability payments for cardiovascular disease quadruple by 2030.[4]

That is not to say that the scourges of diseases such as malaria and tuberculosis do not still exist and take lives at young ages. They most certainly do, and therefore, prevention is a priority. But, with the exception of the very poorest nations, the majority of the developing world now must generate health systems and policies that address both the remaining traditional disease problems and a new and likely long-term wave of chronic diseases whose death rates at relatively young ages are far in excess of those in industrialized nations. The case of diabetes provides an excellent example.

Over 171 million people in the world have diabetes, and 87 percent of that disease burden is in low- and middle-income countries, a figure that will rise to over 360 million by 2030.[5] Indeed, three out of four people with diabetes live in the "developing" world.

The situation in the United States is similar to that around the world; the rising epidemic has been recent and rapid. The conditions fueling the diabetes epidemic, although certainly not responsible for the entirety of the problem, have built quickly and silently. In 1990, only 20 years ago, no state had adult obesity rates over 14 percent. Today, every state does, and in 9 states over 30 percent of the adult population is obese. In emerging economies globally, obesity and diabetes rates are growing rapidly. While 8.3 percent of the U.S. population is diabetic, so is 6 percent of Brazil and South Africa and 10.2 percent of the population of nations in the western Pacific. Indeed, by 2020, Egypt and Jordan are projected to have diabetes rates similar to the United States.

Indeed, in the past two decades, diabetes prevalence projections have consistently fallen short of the actual pace of the disease, a trend that does not bode well for any hope that resource mobilization will be able to get in front of the pace of disease growth. As noted in Exhibit 14.3, today's actual rates are much higher than future projected rates from studies published as recently as 2001.[6]

There is global action. In May 2010, 130 nations signed a United Nations resolution to hold the first-ever High-Level Summit on Non-Communicable Diseases in September 2011, which included a discussion of the global spread

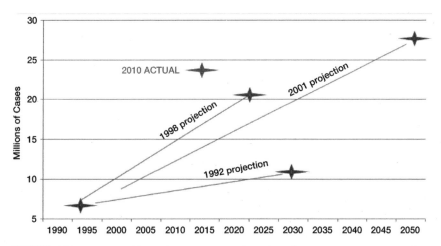

EXHIBIT 14.3 Sooner and Higher: History of Diabetes Projections Compared to Actual Incidence

of diabetes. The U.S. Fogarty International Center at the National Institutes of Health now has a program to support chronic disease work in the developing world, including diabetes. But these recent actions, though representing historical shifts, are notable for their uniqueness. Despite these clear changes in global health, the focus of philanthropic resource flows remains largely the same as in the past. The emphasis is on children under the age of five, reproductive health, and communicable diseases. An examination of Foundation Center grant records for 2003 to 2010 in the area of "global programs" showed 18 grants (fewer than three per year!) for diabetes, but 2,439 for children's issues and welfare.

In part, this is understandably a result of the complexity of addressing chronic diseases, whose roots are in many, many aspects of human behavior and economic structure. But in part it is also because decades of investment in programs, skills, and capacities in both the nonprofit and philanthropic sectors have created deep commitment to a set of historical issues. This commitment has helped to create service provision systems (e.g., in the case of HIV/AIDS treatment), which could be pivoted to address the new generation of chronic diseases. But few global health nonprofits have begun to diversify their programming through this new lens, and the vast majority of funders (and funds) continue to be solely focused on traditional problems and solutions.

The two go hand-in-hand. Where nonprofits recognize the change, a lack of funding discourages a programming response. Where funders see a change, a lack of nonprofit capacity or clearly articulated strategy turns program officers' attention toward the more familiar problems.

States, Poverty, and Philanthropy

Similarly, the changing realities of poverty on the ground often outpace or are opaque to the flows of philanthropy. This can be seen particularly where sources of philanthropy are geographically concentrated, but the changing realities are widely distributed.

An illustrative assessment of the states of New York and Illinois will make the point.

In New York State, the five boroughs of New York City are home to 52 percent of the state's foundations, but these foundations represent 63 percent of all grant making and 75 percent of the state's grant dollars. See Exhibit 14.4.

The distribution between Chicago's Cook County and the state of Illinois is similar, with Cook County accounting for 60 percent of all foundations, 72 percent of grants, and 80 percent of all grant dollars in the state.

In both New York and Illinois, the overwhelming majority of this grant spending takes place in New York and Cook counties. Historically, little grant making flows further into the state.

The Great Recession of 2007 to 2009 had unemployment effects across these two states. However, the highest rates of unemployment were often outside of the major metropolitan areas of New York City and Chicago. Indeed, in New York State by 2012, all but eight counties have higher unemployment than New York County. Nearly a third of New York's counties continued to have unemployment over 9 percent even by April 2012. Between 2010 and 2011, 83 percent of the counties outside New York City either posted no economic growth or had negative economic growth. Despite the fact that New York State by April 2012 had recovered all the jobs lost in the Great Recession, that job recovery was concentrated in New York City. Every other region, except Glens Falls, still had net job loss. Similarly in Illinois, 20 percent

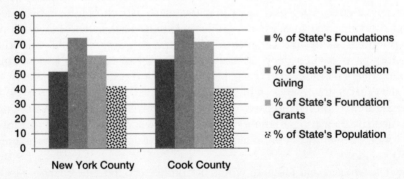

EXHIBIT 14.4 Foundation and Giving Distribution, New York County, New York, and Cook County, Illinois

Source: Foundation Search

of counties outside of Cook County had higher unemployment and higher poverty rates than Cook County by 2012.

The question then becomes: Did New York and Illinois foundations adjust their social and human services giving to reflect the differential impact of the Great Recession and/or the differential rates at which counties were emerging from the recession? Did resources from the concentration of philanthropy in New York and Cook counties flow in alignment with the recession's geographic impact across those two states?

Taking the subset of foundations that give grants for social and human services in New York and Illinois, Exhibit 14.5 demonstrates that, by and large, the answer to the question is "no."[7]

In both states, the 2006 to 2010 flow of philanthropic funds for social and human services mapped poorly onto changes in unemployment at the county level. Major geographic areas of economic downturn and slow (or no) recovery are not the areas with increases in philanthropic support from within the two states for human service provision. In Illinois, half of the counties receiving increased funding had unemployment rates that were below the state average. In New York, of the 31 counties that were at or above the statewide unemployment rate, 23 received decreased funding or no funding at all.

Of course, unemployment is not a perfect surrogate indicator for human services need, and few foundations have the ability to totally wipe their funding slate clean upon an economic crisis and pursue new work or new geographic priorities. However, at the macro level (where unemployment is a reasonable surrogate) and over a period of three years (which is a reasonable period to show adjustment) and for such a level of persistent economic distress, the divergence between the indicator and the flow of funds is striking.

It suggests that philanthropic flows, as organized at the foundation level, are not malleable to rapid or deep change in the operating environment.

The Young and the Old

America is an aging nation, and the growing elderly population represents a key economic challenge. The inexorable rise in health care costs is attributable in part to the aging of the population. The financial prospects for Social Security are deeply affected by longer life expectancies of a greater and greater number of people. As noted in Chapter 2, moreover, the Great Recession has created the specter of large swaths of low-income elderly, as early retirements and job loss have led many to take their Social Security benefits at the earliest opportunity and, therefore, lock themselves into the lowest rungs of compensation.

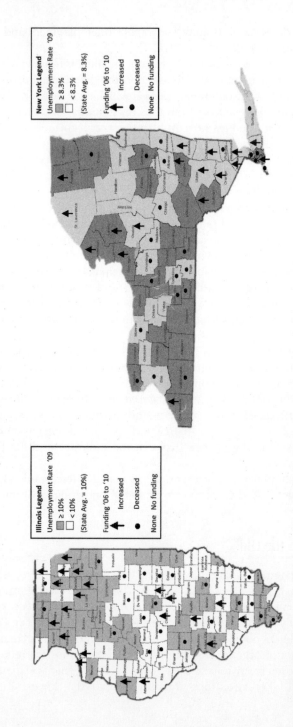

EXHIBIT 14.5 Flows of Giving for Human Services Relative to Economic Distress: New York and Illinois

Sources: Foundation Directory and BLS Local Area Unemployment Statistics

Nutrition provides an illustration of the importance of elder issues. In a 2008 study of senior hunger[8] in the United States, Meals on Wheels found that over five million elderly were food insecure—11.4 percent of the elderly population. The number is expected to increase by 75 percent by 2025 as the population ages. Elderly in nonmetropolitan areas often have higher rates of food insecurity than elderly in cities, which is not a good sign given the urban focus of the foundation data in the previous section.

How well are nonprofits and philanthropy adjusting to these changes?

In the case of philanthropy, the answer appears to be "not well." Judging by keywords chosen in portraying their grant-making areas of focus, over 8,000 foundations explicitly note their interest in issues associated with youth, compared to just 1,200 with an expressed interest in aging. Whether measured in terms of numbers of grants or dollar value of grant making, allocations of giving to issues of aging has remained essentially flat for over a decade. See Exhibit 14.6.

As Exhibit 14.7 indicates, the $290 million in grants for aging in 2010 was 7 percent as large as the $4.3 billion for grants for youth issues. The dollar value of youth grants has nearly tripled since 1998, while the dollar value of grants for the elderly population and associated issues has grown by 60 percent in the last decade. Moreover, grant support for the elderly is highly concentrated. In 2010, the top five foundations of the 50 largest givers to the cause represented 44 percent of the giving.

Similarly, the distribution of the number of grants by population group underscores that the focus of attention continues to be on youth, even as the demographic picture undergoes marked change.

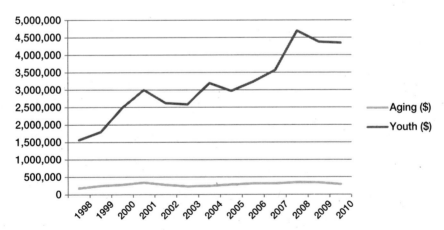

EXHIBIT 14.6 Dollar Value of Foundation Grants for Aging and for Youth, 1998 to 2010

Source: Foundation Center

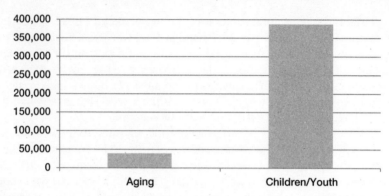

EXHIBIT 14.7 Number of Foundation Grants Aging versus Youth, 1998 to 2010
Source: Foundation Center

These tendencies are not simply a matter of foundation tradition. They are to be found both among high-net-worth individuals (HNWIs) and among young leaders in the nonprofit arena.

In a 2009 global study of HNWIs conducted by Changing Our World together with Campden Research and PNB Paribas, issues related to the elderly were rarely a philanthropic priority, irrespective of philanthropist age, experience, or geographic place of origin.[9] For no age group did issues of the elderly represent a "very important" philanthropic priority for even half the respondents. Among those younger than age 65, 20 percent or less ranked them very important at all, and even for those over the age of 65, only 42.9 percent ranked elderly issues as very important.

In a survey of young leaders in the nonprofit sector in 2011,[10] Changing Our World's Future Leaders in Philanthropy (FLiP) asked survey responders about the issues that they would prefer to work on if they had any choice of any job in the sector. Virtually no one saw working with the elderly as a first choice, and for only a third of young people were the elderly within their top three areas of work interest or passion. See Exhibit 14.8.

This is a disconcerting finding given the demographic directions of the country, doubly so given the trends noted in Chapter 2 regarding the persistent (and likely permanent) unemployment of older adults and the early use of Social Security (at low levels) as a substitute for employment among the aging population at the end of the Great Recession.

Summary and Implications

These three examples underscore a central theme in this book. "Sticking to your knitting," if taken strictly and without constant pulse taking of the

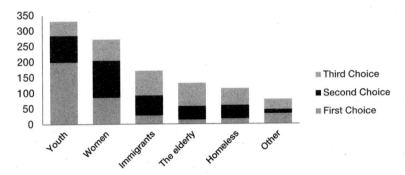

EXHIBIT 14.8 Young Nonprofit Leader Views of Youth versus Elderly Work
Source: Changing Our World, Inc. Future Leaders in Philanthropy

operating environment, is an increasingly poor programming strategy where broad and deep impact is desired in the context of fundamental economic and social change. This is as true for philanthropies as it is for nonprofits.

The changing operating environment within which nonprofits work and for which philanthropies develop funding portfolios argues for program development and management models that emphasize flexibility and adjustment. In turn, such needs demand the capacity within nonprofits and philanthropies to select and constantly monitor clear indicators of change. If funding is to flow to programs that represent the ability to demonstrate meaningful impact in problem solving—the core value proposition in post-recession philanthropy and social finance—then programs must be evidence based. As is noted in Part 4 of this book, it is evidence that will be core of philanthropy, and hence it is evidence that must be at the core of programming. And because evidence will document constant change in the dimensions of problems and opportunities, nonprofits will need to create both the monitoring mechanisms to pay attention to evidence indicators, and systems for the continual adjustment of program content and program strategy.

If they are to be successful, nonprofits will not be able to escape the need for evidence-based systems as foundations for all that they do.

These are common, straightforward matters for companies that serve markets. Change is "baked into" monitoring and product/service development and content because markets demand no less. The company that loses touch with market change—indeed, fails to anticipate change and meet it head on—will falter and fail.

But it is a harder matter for mission-driven organizations—funders or nonprofits—because it is "supply" (the mission and the programs to carry out mission), not "demand" (the surrounding environment), that is often the rationale for an organization's existence. Changing operating environments, and therefore demand for constant change in the nature and content of programs that serve that environment, are consequently often seen at threats. They are not threats. They are opportunities to grow. Indeed, in a world of rapid change, change itself provides the *only* opportunity to grow.

Case K: Communications Strategy for Shifting Demographics

Author: Grizzard Communications Group

Partner: The Salvation Army Canada, The Dignity Campaign

Situation

Operating in Canada since 1882, The Salvation Army Canada is a widely respected and recognized organization, consistently receiving generous public support. However, in recent years Canada has grown increasingly diverse ethnically and culturally. The Salvation Army was not as familiar to newer Canadians and the organization was struggling to maintain its existing constituent base, while working to attract new donors. They did have a strong portfolio of holiday direct-mail appeals that raised millions of dollars in previous years, but it was becoming increasingly difficult to maintain adequate revenue from a direct-mail-only program.

Stakes

At stake was the future of The Salvation Army's fundraising program, and consequently, the vital social services programs it supported. As The

Salvation Army approached the Christmas season, the most important fundraising season of the year, they knew a change of strategy and communication was needed. The biggest challenge was to maintain and strengthen direct-response fundraising revenue in a difficult economic environment, while competing with an increased pool of charities for a decreased number of philanthropic dollars.

Strength

The Salvation Army in Canada has for many years recognized the value of and invested in advertising. Following a successful run of "We See What Most Don't," "The Dignity Project" was launched in 2010. The Dignity Project was designed to educate the public about the reality of poverty in the twenty-first century while communicating the premise that everyone deserves basic human dignity. While many may not understand the depth of the Army's programs and services, The Salvation Army enjoys broad public awareness and support.

Strategy

The strategy was to develop an integrated communications plan to layer over the time-tested direct-mail program. Multiple media channels—with creative strategies appropriate for each—would share a consistent fund-raising message.

Giving Canadians the opportunity to meet basic human needs for food and warmth, especially for children, is The Salvation Army's most powerful fundraising offer at Christmas. A triad of words was developed and followed by a call to action that became the consistent core message for the integrated campaign. The first two words of the triad were "Food" and "Warmth"—reflecting basic human needs—and the third word was "Dignity," linking the holiday campaign to the broader nationwide branding effort.

Not only did these ads reach many in the target audience, but they also began to build awareness among people who might not donate this year but would in the future.

To achieve the desired 7x frequency a number of methods were used, including: out-of-home transit/bus shelter ads, radio traffic sponsorships, newspaper space ads, freestanding inserts (FSIs) in newspapers, and online ads at newspaper websites.

Solution

See Appendix 1.

(*continued*)

(*continued*)

Case L: New Institutions for New Demographics

Author: maslansky+partners

Partner: AARP Foundation

AARP®
FOUNDATION

Situation

When new leadership took over the AARP Foundation in the summer of
2010, they found an organization that was committed to helping American seniors. They realized, however, that there was very little awareness
of the organization, or even that AARP had a charitable affiliate. Although
the Foundationhad a strong legal advocacy department and a couple of
well-established national programs, efforts were diffused across many
independent initiatives all fending for themselves, and the organization
had trouble getting donors to distinguish between AARP the charity and
AARP the social welfare organization.

Leadership quickly recognized that making a bigger impact would
require a more strategic focus, effective integration, and a finely tuned
message that could motivate all of the key stakeholders. As a result,
leadership refocused the Foundation's energy on four key pillars—
supported by vigorous legal advocacy—but needed a strategy to get
donors and others engaged and to move the organization out from the
shadow of AARP as a social welfare and membership organization and
into its own light as a national charity focused on addressing the needs of
the struggling 50+ population.

Stakes

As the Baby Boomer generation is aging, the proportion of the U.S.
population over 50 is swelling. Additionally, the economic downturn
affects Baby Boomers disproportionately because they're losing their
jobs at a higher rate, and their cost of living—due to medications and

other medical bills—is increasing. AARP Foundation is one of the few national charitable organizations specifically intended to help those over 50 in need. As the population continues to age, the Foundation's role will only grow in importance. The need to increase their profile was real.

Strengths

Foundation leadership's initial work to focus on the four pillars of hunger, housing, isolation, and income was right on target. Donors and potential recipients alike agreed these were the crucial needs the AARP Foundation should be addressing. In addition, the name recognition of AARP, though it was currently overshadowing the Foundation, was viewed as an asset at a time when a skeptical public is likely to assume a charity they've never heard of is a scam. AARP Foundation leadership was committed to "One AARP," in which the different aspects of AARP and its affiliated entities help and benefit each other.

Strategy

In 2011, the AARP Foundation called in maslansky+partners (m+p) to help develop a compelling narrative for potential donors and recipients that would find the best ways to frame and explain the 4 pillars as worthy causes, as well as programs worthy of donations and buy-in. m+p interviewed key stakeholders to determine the barriers to acceptance. What they found drew a critical distinction: many charities work hard to help today, but the best are helping people build a better future.

Solution

See Appendix 1.

Notes

1. M. C. Hogan et al., "Maternal Mortality for 181 Countries, 1980–2008: A Systematic Analysis of Progress toward Millennium Goal 5," *Lancet* 375(9726) (May 8, 2012): 1609–1623.
2. S. Raymond, S. Leeder, and H. Greenberg, *A Race against Time: The Challenge of Cardiovascular Disease in Developing Economies* (New York: Columbia University, 2004), 34–36.
3. Ibid., p. 47.
4. Ibid., p. 51.

5. S. Wild et al., "Global Prevalence of Diabetes," *Diabetes Care* 27(5) (May 2004):1047–1053.

6. Representation developed by the author from multiple sources data presented by Elbert S. Huang, MD from the University of Chicago at the Summit on Health Disparities, April 19, 2010.

7. This represents data from 2,104 foundations in the five boroughs of New York City and 779 in Cook County and Chicago proper that were tagged as having commitments to human and social services in these two states. Data reflect data available for the 2005 to 2010 period as available. *Source:* Foundation Directory.

8. J. P. Ziliak and C. Gundersen, "Senior Hunger in the United States: Differences across States and Rural and Urban Areas." A report submitted to Meals on Wheels Association of America, Inc., 2008.

9. *Giving through the Generations: Demanding Impact, Building Unity, Securing Legacy* (London: Campden Research, Changing Our World, Inc., BNP Paribas, 2009), 39.

10. S. Raymond, S. Schiff, and K. Amore, *The Young and the Relentless: An Original Survey of the Next Generation of Philanthropy and Nonprofit Leaders* (New York: Changing Our World, Inc., 2011), 33.

CHAPTER 15

The Arc of Philanthropic Innovation

In the previous chapters of Parts II and III, the emphasis has been on documenting the fundamental changes that are taking place in the operating environment of nonprofits and in the strategies of philanthropists. Over the past decade, individual philanthropists and institutional philanthropy have responded to change, and to the complexity of problem solving, by creating new ways to move resources against problems. They have done so both to increase the levels of resources available, and to seek ways to ensure the problem solving is sustainable. Moreover, they have done so without regard to whether the resulting institutional innovation is nonprofit or for-profit. From the funding side of the table, what we now see is a world of constant adaptation to change and a constant creation of new blended opportunities.

The End of Definitions

At the end of the Cold War, Francis Fukyama wrote an essay that became a book called *The End of History and the Last Man,*[1] perhaps one of the most widely misunderstood book titles in all of publishing history. Fukyama did not mean the end of events. He meant that the end of the Cold War would create a proliferation of ways in which individuals organized themselves politically within nation states while sharing a global value for representative governance. The era of two clear and juxtaposed systems of governance—the autocratic and the free—had ended. The struggle between these two would no longer define history.

The analogy is not perfect, of course, but in a similar way, we are now at the End of Definitions in the nonprofit sector. There is no longer a juxtaposition of what is commercial and what is nonprofit. There is no longer a clear distinction between a gift and an investment, between dedication to markets and dedication to societal problem solving. Rather, we seem to have arrived at a moment in which there is growing common agreement that resource innovation will underpin progress, and that, based on that agreement, combinations of strategies from commerce and from charity will emerge and create unprecedented opportunities to move resources to problem solving.

There is, and will always be (thankfully) charitable check writing. There will always be the five-dollar bill tossed in the fireman's boot, the gift to the food bank, check for the victims of natural and manmade disaster, and the million dollars to support cosmology research. These pure gifts in response to someone else's need, or in pursuit of one's own passion, continue to be an expression of commitment to cause and a measure of fundamental human generosity in a civil society.

But those dollars are now joined by other kinds of resources flowing in many different ways, all toward social problems. Some are "gifts" in that they flow without expectation of personal repayment, but perhaps with expectation of social return. Some are not gifts in a traditional sense at all, but are akin to (or actually are) investments.

All of these resources exist together, indeed, often exist in the same program or the same organization focused on the same objective. They enable the mobilization of resources of appropriate types and at appropriate scale not simply to fund problems but to actually solve problems in sustainable ways. They allow the expansion of resource options beyond what was imagined just a few decades ago.

A Complementary Resource System

We can conceptualize these innovations as an arc of change, with charitable contributions anchoring the base of the arc, as displayed in Exhibit 15.1, yet with multiple plug-in points that enable complex resource mobilization strategies.

The arc provides nonprofits with many choices and many ways to build a resource portfolio comprised of varying types of funds and varying levels of risk.

Charity remains. And it can appropriately be the only resource point for many nonprofits. There is no merit in innovation for innovation's sake. Where pure charity is wholly adequate and appropriate, it remains the smartest option. Moreover, even where innovation along the arc is pursued, pure philanthropy often remains the resource base of many nonprofits even as they begin to diversify their resource strategies along the arc of innovation. As noted in Chapter 7, social enterprises, for example, often rely on philanthropy for long periods of time before their market-based earnings can begin to bear the weight of organizational support.

Still, in an increasing number of instances, charity itself is the starting point for a series of evolutionary stages in revenue diversification.

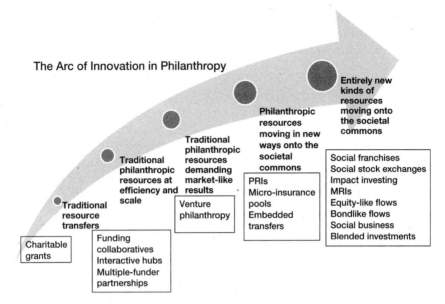

EXHIBIT 15.1 The Arc of Philanthropic Innovation

Evolution Stage One: Collaboration

The first stage of evolution up the arc is a movement to create systems and institutions that will encourage collaboration of both donors and recipients to achieve efficiency and scale. The resources are traditional—grants—but those who give seek to aggregate multiple sources of funds to get resource flows to scale. An example is the End Fund, being created with seed financing from Legatum in London and Geneva Global in the United States to attract multiple donors to a pooled fund for elimination of neglected tropical diseases in Africa.

The money involved in such pooling is still charitable philanthropy. The funds flowing in are gifts. The funds flowing out are still grants. The difference is the effort of philanthropists to reach scale efficiently through pooling in ways that they could not achieve individually, and to demand similar coordination on the part of the nonprofits that are funded. There is a central plan, a central objective, and pooled resource agreements to achieve it.

Evolution Stage Two: A Venture Perspective

The second stage of evolution moves the needle of philanthropic concern from efficiency and scale to evidence and results. At this point, philanthropy begins treating grant making as an investment in solutions, not as a source of cash for problems. Again, the monetary resource is the same—grants—but philanthropic institutions demand detailed evidence of impact and often look for clear economic results from solutions. The emphasis is on sustainability of problem solving through the creation of institutions that can generate continued resources in support of operations. Omidyar's work in venture philanthropy is an example of this next stage of evolution. The focus is not on the problem or the need; it is on the growth and sustainability of the institution addressing the need.

An additional example of applying venture capital thinking to nonprofits is the work of George Overholser at N.F.F. Capital Partners. Overholser, a former venture capital investor, was one of the first to point out the failure of the nonprofit sector to distinguish between capital and revenue. Capital builds organizations; revenues buy the services to address a problem. Overholser worked with College Summit, a nonprofit focused on helping disadvantaged children prepare for college, to develop a growth plan based on expanded capital. The resources sought were not to fund programs (to "buy" solutions) but to expand and grow the business. Investors were buying into a single goal and would accept common reporting requirements. As a result of the capital strategy matched against a clear business plan, College Summit grew from serving 3,600 students to serving over 50,000.

The creation of the Innovation Fund of the Alliance for Global Good in 2012 provides an example from the global development space. The Innovation Fund focuses on providing go-to-market grants for revenue innovation initiatives of medium-sized nonprofits (with $20 million or less in annual cash revenue) engaged in problem solving in the developing world. The money flows as grants, but the specification is that the funds will enable nonprofits to establish greater stability and an ability to address problems over longer periods of time by creating market-based yet mission-consistent[2] revenue-generating options. The focus is not on the particularity of the problem being addressed but on the ability to create revenue diversity and hence stability for the overall enterprise.

Again, the money involved was still philanthropy in the form of grants. But the structure and use of the money, and the relationship with funders, was focused on building the "business," not on funding the services.

It is at this stage that funding begins to separate from funds for projects or programs. Hence, the traditional charitable service lens must be adjusted. The venture-based philanthropist is looking not to finance a service flow, but to create sustainable institutions at scale that can address a need over long periods of time with reliability. The premium is not on helping a particular individual at a particular point in time, but rather on creating the stable capacity to address a large, persistent problem over a sufficiently long period of time and at sufficient scale to ensure that the persistence of the problem itself is reduced.

Evolution Stage Three: Integrating Philanthropy with Monetary Investment Return

The third stage of evolution takes the use of traditional philanthropic resources one step further. Grant making becomes actual investment with actual financial returns. The resources are still philanthropic, but they do not move as grants. They move as actual investments. For that reason, they involve levels of risk for funders and for nonprofits that are not present on when the transaction between funding sources and the nonprofit is based on gifts or grants.

There are myriad variations in this stage. Foundations add program-related investments to their resource transfer strategy, using both grant-making resource pools to lend rather than grant money to nonprofits. The purpose is still mission related, but the resource flow is through a mechanism that creates a financial obligation on the part of the nonprofit. The funds are not a gift; they are in the form of a loan. The loan comes with an obligation for repayment and is secured with some other asset. The nonprofit takes on risk with regard to that asset and obligations with regard to the repayment.

Social enterprises (nonprofit or not) attract investment to produce commercial products and services that have a social impact or that address social needs in the process of their creation. While many do receive grants, many also receive program investments to provide growth capital. While a social return is expected, and is often the motivation for the investment, a monetary return is demanded as well. These two elements—the social and the financial—are tied to philanthropic commitment.

The J. P. Morgan Global Health Investment Fund provides a further example. The fund is designed to introduce private investment into normally grant-funded global health projects and technologies. Investors will monitor social impact and will have the potential for a limited monetary return on their investments. Capital for the fund comes from philanthropies and philanthropists, but also from commercial investors. To mitigate risk, the Bill & Melinda Gates Foundation committed to limit investors' downside if the fund's investments are not successful.

A fourth example at this stage of evolution is pay-for-performance bonds, described in some detail in Chapter 7. Philanthropists advance capital to nonprofits for critical social problem solving under an agreement that, as problems are solved, governments will pay the nonprofit for performance on agreed terms. The resulting monetary flow will reimburse the nonprofit for expenses and return the capital to the philanthropist at some mutually agreed rate of return. A recent example is the August 2012 commitment of Goldman Sachs to invest $10 million in a pay-for-success bond to support the programs of the nonprofit MDRC in its offender recidivism programs. If MDRC reduces recidivism by 10 percent, Goldman will be repaid. If it does not, Goldman will lose as much as $2.4 million. As a corollary, the Bloomberg Family Foundation will provide the $7.2 million loan guarantee from its philanthropic resources, which, if the recidivism rate drop is met, can be used by MDRC for its other programs.

Initiatives in this third stage of the arc of innovation display a common characteristic. They take an "all-of-resource" approach to private-resource mobilization, using commercial capital and private philanthropy in integrated strategies to solve problems and, simultaneously, create monetized return to investors and clear economic return to societies.

Evolution Stage Four: New Types of Resources

The final stage of evolution completely blurs the line between "philanthropy" as traditionally defined and other types of flows to solve social problems. Stage Four represents strategies that bring onto the societal commons entirely new types and sources of finance that are not, in fact, philanthropic. However, these resources become critical elements of solving problems at a scale that was not possible with pure philanthropy.

Social franchising provides an apt example. As noted in Chapter 7, one critical problem in social enterprises is that the efforts of small-scale organizations rarely expand to reach large numbers of people or large geographic areas. Franchising promotes this scale, and therefore attracts capital to solutions. Essential drug availability through small-village efforts in remote areas in Africa, for example, would always remain cash strapped and limited in coverage. Franchising village pharmacies, however, can tie individual efforts into a service network, retain local entrepreneurial control, and be at a scale that can attract investment capital.

Mission-related investing is another example. Commercial (or nonprofit) organizations allocate a portion of their assets to investment in commercial enterprises that are consistent with their causes they may support philanthropically. This increases the total resources available for causes by bringing assets, not philanthropy, into play on the societal commons. A foundation committed to the environment, for example, may take a portion of its asset base and invest only in industries producing windmill turbines. This expands the resource base for clean energy with money that would otherwise never reach the cause through philanthropic channels.

"Social stock exchanges" provide a third example. These exchanges act as market makers for investors in social-oriented companies, nonprofit and for-profit, whereby investors can compare the nonfinancial impact of alternative organizations. These stock exchanges operate in various ways. Some act as philanthropic clearinghouses (stock market equivalents of DonorsChoose). In these, investors do not become partial owners of the organizations, but they may have a say in how or where the organizations places its program emphasis. Others are actually ways to move commercial capital into problem-solving organizations.

Some offer hybrid investment products with below-market returns in exchange for high and measurable environmental or social impact. This allows investors to compare organizations with great transparency, and allows organizations to efficiently access, and lower their cost of, capital for expansion.

Some act as actual stock markets, where shares of commercial companies that produce socially oriented goods or services are valued and traded to obtain commercial-grade capital. Variants of such stock exchanges are operating in Brazil, South Africa, Thailand, New Zealand, India, and Portugal.

Impact investing is, of course, the final example. This is not philanthropy. It is capital that invests in triple-bottom line opportunities that produce commercial-grade financial results and a social return. Many investment houses now also are forming impact investment funds and vehicles. They have the potential to bring trillions of dollars onto the societal commons, not as philanthropy but as capital. No one at any of these funds mistakes this capital for philanthropy. But, in many cases, the fact is that the investments are being made in areas of social return that, historically, would have attracted only traditional philanthropy. The social potential for these resources is many, many multiples of what would have been possible with philanthropy alone.

A Word of Caution

We are at the End of Definitions because the gift, the investment, the cash, and the capital all flow toward the same social problems. But there is a caution. It is possible to be too clever by half. Nonprofits looking at the opportunities created by the arc of innovation, and the deeper resources that innovation creates, must recognize that it is not easy to be innovative. It is not easy to manage a market-driven organization. It is not easy to merge the culture of an organization focused on gifts and one focused on markets.

There are no simple formulas for determining what approach to organizational innovation is appropriate at what point in time for what venture opportunity. There are, however, five critical questions that any nonprofit should ask itself if it seek to align with the arc of innovation.

First, why am I doing this? If the answer is "because we have to," then caution lights should be turned on. The successful organization sees opportunity for innovation as an exciting pathway for growth, not as a chore. Chores are usually and ultimately evaded not embraced.

Second, what does the external market want/need that I have to offer and/or what could be done better or more effectively with an innovation that aligns with the philanthropic arc? Again, and as will be emphasized in

Chapters 16 through 18, the first question is about the external environment. If the answer is that you do not know why innovation is better, then it is not time to innovate. It is time to do the market and constituency research that will determine the actual value proposition behind innovation.

Third, who will lead? Is there adequate expertise on your board? Indeed, is the board itself committed to such innovation? Are there sufficient skills on staff? Does the managerial C-suite have adequate and relevant experience? If the answers to these questions are no, then strengthening the nonprofit's own internal and leadership capacity is the prerequisite to aligning with the innovation of philanthropists.

Fourth, what are the risks of graft-versus-host disease? In a bone marrow or stem cell transplant, transplanted cells can sense that the recipient's body is foreign and attack its tissue and cells. The closer genetically the transplant source to the host, the less likely the result. When the host and the donor are not related, the probability of the disease is 60 percent to 80 percent. Non-profits should look carefully at the possible innovations, and think deeply about which options are closely related to their existing missions and operations. The farther away they are from the core, the more likely they are to result in organizational problems. Is the product or the service or the venture a direct extension of services or functions that are currently offered? Is there a logical connection between the innovation and the central organization and its operations? Does the potential partner share a level of knowledge about the core mission and operation that will make it an equal peer? If the answers to these or equivalent questions are no, then the risk that innovation will endanger an organization is present. The precursor need is for adjustment to the core operation to first prepare it for the graft.

Fifth, can you envision what success will look like? Philanthropists and philanthropies innovating along the arc usually know what they are looking for. They know what they want to accomplish with innovation. The nonprofit that is seeking to "dock" in one of the innovation bays along the curve must be equally clear about success. Can you articulate a goal for the innovation that can be tracked and measured? How will you know what you have succeeded? If the organization cannot articulate in one page what success will look like, preferably in some measurable way, then more thought is needed.

Whence Passion?

Interestingly, in his writings Fukyama has remarked that the end of history would be a very sad time. Where there are dichotomies, he said, people demonstrate great passion. They are capable of great acts of courage on behalf of their ideals. Where there is agreement on fundamentals, and simply the need to adjust details, that daring and idealism will be replaced by problem solving. The result can be extremely positive. But the problem solving takes place in an atmosphere of pragmatism not passion.

What will happen to the importance of passionate leadership? Philanthropy is not about the money. We may monetize the value of philanthropy because it is the easiest measure, but by doing so we misrepresent what philanthropy is. It is not about money. It is about voluntary leadership of individuals in service to a common good. It is about the health and well-being of civil society in this nation and this world, the strength and resilience of those who serve the societal commons, empowering commitment to community and deepening our understanding of the implications of change in our lives. Philanthropy is about leadership of individuals in service to community.

If we only innovate in how money moves, and do not, thereby, create new leaders committed to community, we will have failed in the core business we are in, and that is community. We may solve a problem today with a social investment or a bond or an enterprise, but, in so doing, we will not necessarily create a voice for the next problem tomorrow. It is the voices, however, the leadership of individuals, that will build resilience for tomorrow's problems.

Summary and Implications

The Arc of Innovation encourages tremendous variation in the way in which resources flow to problem solving.

Not all innovations are appropriate for all problems or all organizations. Indeed, reliance on pure charity is likely to be the best choice for many nonprofits. But some innovations for most organizations are likely to provide a better and more robust resource future.

The challenge for traditional philanthropy and for most nonprofits is how to partner with these new forms of social finance, how to find ways that grant making can leverage or incentivize other forms of social finance, other innovations, other better ways to mobilize resources for problem solving.

But this End of Definitions does complicate the lives and management of nonprofits, and, indeed, perhaps creates new competitors for their causes in the purely commercial sphere. It also complicates the lives of philanthropists and philanthropies because it encourages new ways of thinking about resource movement. Most people do not like change. Most organizations break out in hives at the thought of change.

But the Arc of Innovation is being led by younger leaders and institutions in the global financial and technology communities who have broken through traditional silos in their own industries, and are applying such creativity to their social commitments. These are people for whom change is the essence of life, not the subject of fear.

Notes

1. F. Fukyama, *The End of History and the Last Man* (New York: Freeman Press, 1992).
2. There is a distinction to be made here. The gift shop at a hospital is not a mission-consistent revenue innovation. In contrast, a woodworking shop in a halfway house for youth that makes original wooden toys is because it increases marketable skills (which is mission consistent) while creating and meeting market demand.

PART IV

Strategy for Rapid Change

C hanges in the global economy, changes in philanthropic leadership and strategy, and changed demands on nonprofits will, in effect, demand a new business model for nonprofits. Change will require a business model premised on innovation and flexibility, on the capacity to anticipate change not simply react to it. Nonprofits are going to have to think in terms of markets. Every nonprofit will need to develop clear indicators of change in its operating environment and a management system that will allow the constant monitoring of these indicators get out in front of change. This will be difficult for nonprofits that focus more on the constancy of mission than on adapting to shifting markets. The successful nonprofit will develop the ability to do both. An analytic framework in this section can provide a tool for both stability and change, and a self-administered questionnaire in Appendix 2 will assist the nonprofit manager in understanding where in the change process his or her nonprofit rests.

CHAPTER 16

Five Organizing Principles for Strategy amid Rapid Change

There is danger in adapting institutions to a changing environment, whether that constitutes change in problems or change in opportunities. It is easy to lose one's way, easy to ricochet among all manner of options, to lose hold of core goals and objectives.

Any economy is littered with companies that have chased rainbows in search of change for the sake of change, newness for the sake of racing to the front of a perceived vanguard. Rainbows are beautiful, fascinating, and inspiring. They also disappear. You may chase them, but you will never catch them.

The same is true of nonprofits and philanthropies. Standing still is falling back. Organizations that thrive must innovate. They must adapt to, and take advantage of change. But they must do so with discipline and with a keen eye to differentiating what matters from what does not, what can produce material results and what will not, which opportunities will advance a cause and which will merely divert energy. Therefore, any strategy to adapt to, and draw strength from, a changing environment must be firmly grounded in organizing principles. Those principles represent the core elements that provide a constant touchstone for strategy.

Maintain an Outward Line of Sight

One of the great differences between the nonprofit/philanthropic sector and commercial industry is the organizational line of sight.

Successful companies have an outward line of sight. Their first questions in the morning and their last questions at night are about the customer and the market. Who are the customers? How are they changing? What do they want?

What do they read, watch, think, say? Where else are they going for goods and services? Only then does the commercial entity turn its sights inward to determine how a product or service can be structured and delivered to their customers.

The beginning point for all corporate strategy is the external environment. What is happening outside the walls of the company determines how products and services are designed, managed, and sold. Companies that excel, therefore, are rarely surprised. They see change coming well enough in advance to adjust and prepare, and their own products and services are developed or adapted to this constant understanding of change.

The nonprofit, however, often places its own mission at the center of its considerations. What am I designed to do? What programs will carry out my mission? The line of sight is turned inward not outward. This can be as true of philanthropies as of nonprofits. The focus is on internal mission and mandate, not on external environment.

As a result, external changes and shifts may not be perceived at an early point. Indeed, they may not be perceived at all or until it is too late to change. This is a natural function of being mission oriented not market oriented. But in a rapidly or fundamentally changing environment, the consequent myopia will ultimately impede mission itself.

Nonprofits and philanthropies need to adjust their lines of sight to be constantly outward facing. They must learn to look to their surroundings and constituents first. They must take as a point of departure for all decisions the nature of the economic, social, and demographic environment, and the attitudes and behaviors of those whom they touch. They must learn from market analysts how to intersect an understanding of the implications of changing trends with the fundamental purpose and capacities of an organization. There is no abandonment of purpose here. Mission will remain fundamental to any nonprofit or philanthropy. But an external line of sight will help to ensure the execution of that mission is real time and flexible.

Create a Culture of Evidence

Changing generations of philanthropists, and the continued persistence of critical social problems, has made the expectation of results a central pillar of much of philanthropy today.

Of course, there is an argument to be made that this not fully a good thing. There are problems whose origins (e.g., hatred) we do not understand, and hence whose program outcomes cannot be assured. There are problems on the edges of human knowledge (e.g., the cosmos) for which research results remain a matter of theory. There are problems of such root complexity (violence) that combine biology, environment, nurture, education, economics, and a host of other factors that attributing results to any single action or grant is insupportable. There are problems that are so generational in origin and hence in solution (e.g., sedentary lifestyles) that near-term impacts will never be perceived. And, of course, there are opportunities, not problems at all (e.g., music or painting) for which results are so much a part of the human soul and the concept of humanity that speaking of impact means speaking of the meaning of beauty to human existence.

Still, there is in the philanthropic sector this constant drumbeat of results. This is not a completely unfair expectation. At some level, all organizations—whatever their financial form—should be performing well. Few would dispute that statement. The problem for the nonprofit sector is that the concept of performance has been historically been one and the same as consistency with mission. So long as I am consistent with my mission, I am performing adequately. The current expectation of performance goes far beyond this definition. Indeed, it takes mission as a given. The question of performance flows from that. How is the institution performing financially, managerially, programmatically, substantively? How are the consequences of its actions changing the status or nature of the problem it has a mission to affect?

In a changing philanthropic environment, with intense competition and higher expectations of those with resources (and of public policy and the public in general), the only way for a nonprofit to adequately position itself for success is to create an internal culture of evidence. This does not mean hiring a consultant to write a grant report. It does not mean tossing off a few statistics in an annual report.

The successful nonprofit will make evidence a fundamental part of every portion of its work, and a value proposition for every element of its organization. Evidence of performance—in terms of finances, in terms of programs, in terms of projects, in terms of efficiency—can only be produced if the value of evidence runs from the board room through the C-suite all the way through to the project manager and service provider. Evidence will be a part of every job description and an element of every decision.

Valuing evidence—of problems, of results, and of a changing environment—is a critical message and organizing principle for nonprofits and philanthropies. The wise nonprofit will determine what it will look to as indicators, and how it will institutionalize its measurement of them. If it does not, the philanthropic supporter will choose the measure he or she demands, and the nonprofit will likely not be happy with the resulting demand.

After the deepest and longest global recession since World War II, philanthropy is not interested in what the nonprofit sector needs. Every organization needs something. It is interested in what nonprofits will DO. Only a culture of evidence will constantly and consistently answer that question.

Set Reasonable and Measurable Goals

World peace is an admirable aspiration. It is just a daunting programming goal. Because they are focused on mission and vision, which are usually cast in very broad terms, many nonprofits do not think about goals in measurable terms. But a culture of evidence cannot produce documentation of progress or impact if goals are not set in ways that can be measured, and measured in reasonable periods of time.

Faced with intense competition for resources and highly complex problems, goal setting in the nonprofit sector is a daunting challenge. In the commercial sector, things are often much easier. Increasing market share by 5 percent may not be easy to accomplish, but the underlying distribution of the market, the behavior of consumers, past sales growth, and other barometers of performance are readily available over long periods of time. There are metrics in the market; the market's dynamics are well understood; and hence there is usually firm ground for choosing a business goal.

This is often not so in the social sector. We do not necessarily understand hunger or why it persists amidst plenty. We do not necessarily understand why families make budget choices that leave nutrition to the side. We do not even necessarily understand how families think about budgets to begin with. So, to set a goal for affecting hunger, with any quantitative comfort and hence any confidence about measurement of results, is a challenge. The challenge to identify a measurable goal is present for both the nonprofit who runs a food pantry and the funder who seeks to provide support toward that end.

Setting measurable goals becomes even more difficult if the subject matter is the creation of new knowledge or innovation in dance.

However, all performance assessment will need to begin with a measurable goal. Otherwise, there is nothing to assess, and a culture of evidence will raise questions that cannot be answered.

Ask, Ask, Ask: How'm I Doin'?

Once a goal has been set, constantly and honestly assess performance.

New York City's former mayor, Ed Koch, was famous for plunging into crowds of New Yorkers and asking, "How'm I doin'?" Over time, it became a media symbol of his desire to respond to the perceptions of the electorate.

Companies (or, at least, companies that last) are constantly aware of the consumer view of product or service quality in the marketplace. The consumer can always find a better, more responsive, more convenient source to meet its needs. Facing the demanding taskmaster of the market, private commerce must always be attuned to customer satisfaction.

Just as the inward line of sight of nonprofits impedes their perception of change and its impact, using that same line of sight nonprofits often fail to constantly query those they serve in terms of the adequacy of that service.

The need is two dimensional, supporters, and clients.

First, the only time many nonprofits ask their supporters what they think is when they are on brink of a major campaign to solicit large levels of funding. The message is that I only care what you think of me when I am about to reach into your wallet.

In an era of intense competition, where funders are interested in results and new philanthropists are loyal to solutions not institutions, this simply will not do. A key organizing principle for any successful nonprofit will be to constantly query its supporters on the quality of its work, the adequacy of its communications, and the continued performance of its mission. And, equally, nonprofits will need to listen honestly to the results whatever they say about any dimension of the work. Focus groups, surveys, leadership roundtables, and other techniques will need to be deployed regularly and the results made a mandatory part of institutional planning and communications.

In a world of slow economic growth, intensive competition for resources, and rapid hybridization of commercial and nonprofit organizational models, the need to regularly understand and meet supporter views and expectations is mandatory.

Second, performance in the eyes of clients or those who receive services is equally important. Often, nonprofits are so focused on carrying out their mission, again so inward in their line of sight, that what those they reach actually think of the services becomes secondary. Expectations of philanthropists, and the glare of media, make this a dangerous strategy. Most nonprofits are in the people business. Performance and a culture of evidence extend not simply to outcomes, but to what people think of the services and how they are delivered. Constituent satisfaction must be as important to nonprofits as customer satisfaction is in the marketplace.

Indeed, changes in communications technology may provide a mechanism for evaluating nonprofits by their constituents whether or not the nonprofit sector wants it. Someone somewhere will come up with a free application that will allow users to upload their assessment of the nonprofits serving them onto a Yelp-like platform that can be accessed universally in real time. And funders will listen.

For their part, philanthropies too would do well to also ask, "How am I doin'?" The audience for the question is both the nonprofits who carry out the programs and the constituents they serve. Although there will always be alternative nonprofits who will take their money if the current nonprofit is unhappy, and so there really is no "market" for the philanthropy, philanthropic leadership is about using resources to enable effectiveness. To the extent that effectiveness is compromised by the nature of process of the funding itself, or

demands regarding the constituency served by the nonprofit, then philanthropies are stunting their own leadership.

Deftness in the questioning will be necessary, of course. Philanthropies
distribute critical resources. Few organizations will bite the hand that feeds
them. But the question of performance in the "market" of grantees and their
constituents is equally important knowledge for philanthropies. For those
working globally, that question should also be asked of all partners, private
and governmental, involved in programs supported. Being well resourced but
deeply resented is hardly the stuff from which community leadership is made.

This author would argue that the question "How'm I doin'?" should
equally be asked by government agencies and by multilateral and bilateral
agencies engaged in global development resource flows. The question should
be asked of nonprofits who receive the resources, of those who are served by
the resulting programs, and, in the case of public dollar transfers, of the
government ministries affected by the transfers. Bilateral and multilateral
agencies almost never ask that question, but that is a topic for separate book.

Attend to Brand

A brand is an elusive thing. For many people, it is not definable; it is like art:
you know what you like when you see it.

But this is a world of intense competition, a more educated population, an
aging population with skepticism about nonprofits, an economy of greater
challenge, and a societal commons comprised of many types of commercial-
nonprofit hybrids. Nonprofits and philanthropies both need to understand
their brand and how it affects trust in, and the effectiveness of, their work.

A brand is not a logo. A brand is an organization's promise. Hence, it is a
serious thing. It communicates what an organization expects of itself, and what
the public can expect from it. In some cases, it will be all that people perceive,
all that potential supporters will understand, and all that its constituents know
of its deeper organization and commitment.

For nonprofits and philanthropies, thinking about brand is not a comfortable process. There is often a sense that such considerations are superficial,
focused on something petty rather than the fundamental good that an
organization is intended to accomplish.

But we are in a permanently changed world. The past two decades,
documented in previous chapters, and the results of the Great Recession have
made this so. This is a world of instant and boundless communication, of snap
judgments made on the basis of 140 characters of tweeting, not 140 pages of
research, of images that sweep by in the blink of an eye yet remain stored
electronically in perpetuity. If your brand is your promise, and your promise is
instantaneously and universally known and judged, then attending to that

promise is clearly important. Your brand is, in many ways, in the hands of the public and consumers. The external perception must be constantly tracked and understood if it is to be managed.

In turn, this means becoming comfortable with new sets of professionals, new sets of questions, and new ways of thinking. It also means establishing performance measures that are not about services or programs or content, but about changing public or constituency perceptions of symbols and words. These are not necessarily simple linear assessments that trace program A to project B to result C. We live in the world of psychology, communications, and behavior. Public perceptions are nuanced and often frustratingly complex. Nonprofits will need to become comfortable with the communications professional that can help them understand and affect these perceptions and hence, develop and protect a brand.

In the world of private resources, a promise is your bond, it is what you mean to do and commit to accomplish. Supporters will look to it for confidence, constituents will look to it for trust, and the media will look to it for consistency with behavior. And all will do so globally and instantly.

Do Not Act Alone

The last two decades have seen a proliferation of nonprofits of nearly every size and type focused on nearly every variant of nearly every societal problem. As we have seen, the post-recession resource reality is likely the long-term retrenchment of public funding at all levels and the limits to growth of private philanthropy. Taken together, this means that there is less and less rationale for nonprofits to act alone, whether they are acting relative to a common problem or whether a problem requires multiple sectors of action for its resolution. And there will not only be more and more philanthropic interest in nonprofits that collaborate to achieve efficiency and scale, but more opportunities for philanthropies themselves to pool resources to get problem solving to scale.

This core principle of collaboration must be a central organizing pillar for successful nonprofits, and successful philanthropies in the future. It will not be easy. Nonprofits and funders exist because an individual or a group of individuals has a passion to address a cause. Passions run deep and are deeply personal. Equally, boards are assembled because the passion of their members matches that of their founders. From the perspective of passion, it is easy to see how one's organization is unique in commitment and unique in action. It is harder to accept that one's organization is similar to others. Moreover, maintaining that view of uniqueness is often essential to attract support in a competitive world.

Hence, there is not only a psychological impediment to collaboration, it can also be dangerous by hobbling an argument for resources that funds the passion at its core. There is discomfort here. There is even fear. Both are understandable. Both must be overcome, for two reasons.

First, the complexity of problems requires coordinated action on multiple fronts. Disease control, world-class research, educational improvement, health care access, environmental protection—there is virtually no problem that would not be more effectively addressed if sectoral silos were dismantled. And there is virtually no opportunity that could be more effectively seized and used if it touched more than one area of life. This is as true for the funders' side of the table as it is for the nonprofit side of the table. No one philanthropy or philanthropist has sufficient resources to get a complex, multidimensional, generational problem to resolution at scale. No less than the Bill & Melinda Gates Foundation deeply understands this truth.

All of this is obvious. Indeed, it has become a bromide. But the reality of the truth of such statements is in marked contrast to nonprofit behavior. The environment provides an example. Between 1999 and 2009, there were 1,200 new nonprofits *per year* created in the United States. True, some were local and highly focused. Perhaps some were truly unique. But 1,200 new organizations per year for a decade? One has to believe that somewhere in there was the opportunity to take a new idea to an existing organization. But the reality of personal passion often trumps the common sense of collaboration.

The result leads to the second reason nonprofits must begin to act differently. In those 10 years, from 1999 to 2009, the number of environmental nonprofits increased by 78 percent. The dollar value of private giving to the environment increased by 24 percent. Even beyond arguments about efficiency and scale, the proliferation of passion is simply not resource sustainable at any level that will result in healthy, effective organizations.

Neither the nature of problems nor the nature of resources is best served by those who act alone.

Summary and Implications

All of the economic and social changes documented in previous chapters have created the need for flexible but purposeful strategy to allow nonprofits and philanthropies to monitor where change intersects their work, how to create opportunity from it, and how to adjust work to meet the changing problems it creates. But that strategy for flexibility needs to be built on five organizing principles, which serve to guide the selection of indicators and the organization of management systems that will be discussed in the next chapter. These five organizing principles are:

- Maintain an outward line of sight to ensure constant alignment with environment change.

- Create a culture of evidence to support performance.
- Constantly ask supporters, constituents and clients about their perceptions of performance and *listen* to their views.
- Attend to brand because in a totally permeable communications world, it is your promise instantly and permanently.
- Do not act alone, but seek out every opportunity for consolidation and collaboration to ensure effectiveness in the face of complex problems, efficiency and scale.

Case M: New Brand Strategy amid Economic Crisis

Author: Beanstalk

Partner: Habitat for Humanity

Situation

Since its founding in 1976, Habitat for Humanity has helped more than 2.5 million people build, repair, and renovate their own homes around the world. According to a top-ranking of nonprofit institutions, Habitat for Humanity is the number 1 brand in terms of uniqueness, relevancy, and emotional appeal.[a]

With the knowledge that 1.6 billion people lack access to adequate, affordable shelter around the world, Habitat's ability to match revenue to the rapidly growing needs of the world's poor is often challenged. For the first 25 years of its existence, Habitat was supported primarily by direct-mail contributions and, later, corporate partners, but as the need for safe

(continued)

(*continued*)

and decent shelter continues to grow and as building costs continue to rise, the organization has become more aggressive about fundraising and seeking new sources of revenue. One new source of revenue that has been under consideration is product licensing.

Could Habitat support a Habitat-branded line of retail products that would raise brand awareness and cause awareness as well as generate revenues?

Stakes

There are more than 2,000 independent Habitat for Humanity affiliates globally. Affiliates have accountability to the headquarters office but remain independently run nonprofit organizations that are each responsible for its own fundraising. Would local affiliates engage in fundraising turf wars if branded products are sold locally, potentially hindering their local fundraising efforts?

A significant amount of Habitat's unrestricted revenue comes from direct mail and modest donations (under $50); would branded products cannibalize any of those gifts and pose a direct threat to traditional fundraising at the global level?

Strengths

Global cause awareness was at an all-time high due to organizations such as (RED) and the Susan B. Komen Breast Cancer Fund. Could Habitat for Humanity tap into this growing trend and convert everyday shoppers into an army of activists, whose purchasing power could be harnessed to fuel a continuous stream of contributions? Would this be a way to attract Generation Y—known to be civic-minded, globally aware, and supporters of volunteer activism—as they themselves begin to become homeowners and consumers, to be drawn to the cause-related Habitat for Humanity licensed products and become brand emissaries? Such a program has the potential to generate significant revenues from royalty income and increased donations.

Strategy

Commercializing the brand this way would be a big step, and a detailed course of action would need to be developed taking into account the competitive landscape and market dynamics. For nonprofit organizations, funds necessary to operate the organization come from multiple sources including traditional fundraising means, although some organizations see licensing taking a more active role in impacting the bottom line. A robust licensing program would need to strengthen and protect the Habitat brand while maximizing royalty revenue for them through a well-designed and properly priced product line that has strong consumer appeal, all while ensuring that there is no encroachment on fundraising by local affiliates and that existing corporate partnerships are not threatened by competing sales.

Should licensing be a strategy to pursue? The management of Habitat for Humanity debated the pros and cons.

Solution

See Appendix 1.

---

[a] Luxury Institute's Luxury Brand Status Index for Non-Profit Institutions, 2006.

CHAPTER 17

The Utility of Fluid Discipline

The previous chapters have focused on fundamental changes in the economic, social, and demographic environment within which nonprofits and philanthropies can expect to operate in the next decade. These elements have also been examined in terms of their direct impact on nonprofit and philanthropic institutions and management.

The final question remains: so now what?

Knowing that the ground is shifting is a critical starting point. Acknowledging that it is shifting under your own particular feet, however, and that you are vulnerable to the consequences requires that courage be added to knowledge. To be sure, there are institutions that endure irrespective of a changing world. Similarly, there are changes that, for all their global import, may have little to do with any particular nonprofit or philanthropy. One does not want to chase change for the mere thrill of the chase.

But neither does one want to rue the day that the chase was abandoned and the world moved on without you.

Option 1: Run, Shoot, and Holler

The problem for managers and strategists is that, given the dimensions, complexities, and differentials of changing economies and sociodemocratics in the coming decade, there is no simple compass to guide decisions. And, indeed, there can be no final or definitive decisions. Fluidity, flexibility, and adaptability must become part of organizational culture and part of management's comfort zone.

However, there must be some structure to decision making, some mechanism against which to constantly array and analyze the evidence, described in the previous chapter, which is to guide decisions about strategy. The alternative is random and arbitrary action.

Years ago, when I was studying abroad, I was in the garden of the university on a velvet spring evening getting ready for exams. I was one of only a half dozen Americans at the time at this university, and one of those, a terrific athlete, was studying in the chair across from me. He closed his book and said he needed a break. There was a basketball court on the other side of campus, and he was going to see if he could put together a pick-up game.

About an hour later, he came back soaked with sweat. I remarked that he must have found a game. He said that he had, in fact, and that it had been great fun and great exercise. But that it also had been somewhat frustrating. He said that no matter how hard he tried to understand, the only play he could figure out that anyone knew was "run, shoot, and holler." These were his exact words. When he caught his breath, my friend at the university remarked that there was much running, much shooting, and much hollering, but no passing, no blocking, no post-ups, and no pick-and-roll. Therefore, there was not much scoring.

"Run, shoot, and holler," I have come to observe, is a common management method within organizations faced with rapid and complex change. The "run, shoot, and holler" method creates action that gives the perception of progress. There is much activity and great expenditure of energy. There is much racing around and a dizzying pursuit of every increasing new priorities, or problems, or opportunities, or thoughts, or insights, or whatever the agenda item on today's staff meeting was. Everyone is getting great organizational exercise.

Faced with a countervailing force or another alteration of condition, however, the energy results in organizational sweat, but often little sustained result. There is no strategy behind action. And action becomes wearying. Weary organizations can seldom stay the course, let alone thrive.

"Run, shoot, and holler" is great exercise, and can even be great fun. It is just poor organizational strategy in the face of complex change.

Option 2: Fluid Discipline

The alternative, what I would call "fluid discipline," is, admittedly, not quite so fun.

The alternative is premised on a system for detailed, clear, and, importantly, constant assessment of the interplay between the internal environment and the external environment. It is premised on constantly assessing the relationship between organizational assets and rapid or fundamental "market" change; building and strengthening assets to meet opportunities; and altering, paring, or shedding those that no longer deliver value, no longer match needs, or no longer capitalize on changing approaches or resources.

There is a delicate balance here, of course, that requires both discipline and fluidity. Discipline is important to continue to pursue core goals with attention to task and equal attention to efficiency and outcome. But discipline alone is not enough. It tends to generate organizational rigidity. And rigidity is not appropriate or productive in a rapidly changing world. Rather, discipline must itself be fluid, it must react to and contribute to constant change and adjustment, but within a clear and transparent system for decision making.

It was fluid discipline that my friend on the basketball court missed: the ability to be so steeped in the core choices and options—in the discipline of the game—that the fluidity of movement could take place within those core choices, forming and reforming as circumstances changed, driven toward a common goal in clear discipline and structure but with flexibility and adaptability to constant change and constantly changing opportunity.

Organizations that respond to markets are comfortable in this framework. Organizations that do not can be less so. Let us, therefore, turn to the elements that must be in place to support a disciplined process for organizational adaptation.

Exhibit 17.1 outlines five components of fluid discipline that provide the organizing elements for putting in place a capacity to constantly adjust knowledge to decision to action, even as the operating environment continues to change.

Goal Setting

No action can be informed or organized unless it is clear what is to be accomplished. Goals are not missions. They are the concrete measurable endpoints desired over a specified period of time.

The problem in settings of rapid change is that goals themselves need to be attuned to that change. Doing so requires two characteristics.

First, goals need to be conceived in ways that are measureable in the relatively short term. As we have seen, the cycles of change are now measured in much less than 10-year periods, often in cycles of 3 to 5 years. Hence, change is under way even before the ink is dry on the goal statement. The selection of goals, therefore, must be conscious of the time likely needed to achieve that goal.

This seems straightforward. It is as a matter of theory. It is not as a matter of practice. That is so because there are two series of forces with internal contradictions vying for goal-setting strategy.

With a commitment to mission and an internal line of sight, as noted in Chapter 15, there is a tendency to want to "go big," to stretch for major accomplishments in service to a passionately held mission. How can tightly formulated, precisely honed goals be married to large visions and world-changing missions?

Moreover, as noted throughout this work, the tendency of new philan-thropists to want to "fix it," to solve fundamental problems at their roots in

Structures for Fluid Discipline

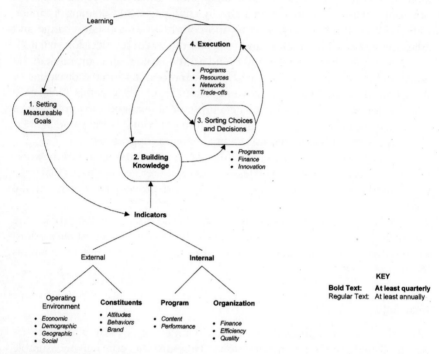

EXHIBIT 17.1 Elements of Fluid Discipline

sustainable ways also encourages organizations to articulate game-changing goals. Without a big, ambitious goal, how can an organization attract big ambitious money?

This tension between passionate mission, philanthropy's ambition, and the realities of rapid or fundamental change in tight time cycles makes goal setting in fluid but disciplined organizations complex. But it also makes goal setting one of the most important, perhaps *the* most important, function of nonprofit and philanthropic management. It is also a process that should take place and be reviewed at least annually to provide the fluidity necessary within the disciplined structure that ensures continued impact.

In addition to paying attention to the implications of tight and rapid time cycles, a measurable goal needs to be derived from, and be informed by, a set of quantitative and qualitative indicators. As noted in Exhibit 17.1, the arrow linking goals to indicators is two-way for a reason. Goals in rapidly changing environments need to be informed by data in their *selection* as well as in their monitoring. Indicators do not simply inform organizations about progress toward goals, they should actually be the basis for selecting goals to begin with.

Indicators from the external operating environment should provide the initial guidance on goal setting because they will document the nature and pace of change in relevant elements such as demography. Longitudinal data will also provide evidence of the underlying rate of change in the problem itself. For example, if heart disease in a community is already declining by 3 percent per year, then a goal of a 10 percent decline in the coming three years is not much of a goal. However, if the preexisting 3 percent decline now faces a rapidly aging population with a different health profile of vulnerability, then 10 percent is an aggressive goal. One cannot choose a goal rationally absent the data.

External indicators are critical inputs to goals setting from the beginning, not just in tracking goal progress.

Similarly, internal indicators also provide critical input to goal setting. Evidence of the internal capability (program, human systems, leaders' influence) to affect a problem provides guidance in selecting a goal. Both constituents and funders care about execution. Whatever the operating environment evidence about the nature and time cycles that argue for a realistic yet material goal, if there is no evidence that existing or even a reasonable expansion of capacity will reach that goal, then goal-setting is moot.

These goal-setting interrelationships with evidence must not be ad hoc or informal. The process must be disciplined and regularized. It must be deeply tied into the ability to generate evidence. And so we turn to possibly the most important part of the structures that create fluid discipline, the ability to generate real-time knowledge and future projections in the midst of change.

Knowledge and Indicators

The source of fluidity is knowledge. All organizations, commercial, nonprofit and philanthropic, need real-time knowledge to inform goals and guide decision making. As noted in Chapter 16, commercial organizations generate knowledge constantly. It is the sole way to understand markets and to anticipate market changes.

For nonprofits, knowledge generation can be a more episodic effort tied to a particular function. Knowledge is pursued and absorbed when internal changes are being considered (a new program idea) or is developed to support a desired initiative (a capital campaign). But such knowledge is generated and used in pursuit of specific ends, not to provide a constant backdrop of intelligence about an organization's operating environment and its "markets" (clients, constituents, members, or the like). This can be equally true of philanthropies, whose program commitments, expertise and priorities can be long-standing and whose grantees are often also long-standing. Seeing, understanding, and accommodating fundamental changes in issues or problems is not automatic unless it is consciously built into the grant-making system.

In that emerging gray area between commerce and nonprofits occupied by social enterprise and its variants, the role of market knowledge is more akin to commerce because the goods and services produced must meet the needs and expectations of clients or customers. But, for now, these are exceptions in the nonprofit sector.

In a flat and interconnected world, where knowledge moves at the speed of electrons, the problem, of course, is what knowledge? One cannot pay attention to everything and get anywhere. A clear set of indicators is needed. Those indicators must have three critical characteristics.

1. They must provide relevant intelligence. The indicators, and the changes that occur therein, must clearly be tied to the kinds of goals and decisions that need to be made over time. Curiosity is a fine and admirable thing. Indeed, curiosity has a place in the "futures" insights of top management, and senior managers should always be asking hypothetical "what if" questions to test the margins of their understanding. But the focus of a disciplined, regularized indicators system must be on a limited highly decisionable set of road signs that provide guidance on the nature of market change and its alignment with goals and programs. They must highlight, guide, and inform decisions.

2. Indicators must cover periods of time that are both accurate to the information and material to decision making. There is no single solution here. For some problems or issues (e.g., infectious disease), changes can be rapid. For others (e.g., global warming), changing can be generational. Indicators must accommodate the appropriate cycle of change if they are to provide relevant intelligence to decision makers.

3. Indicators must lend themselves to being gathered consistently and efficiently. An indicator system that, by virtue of its complexity and/or inconsistency, is not used quickly becomes a pointless exercise that is quickly (and justifiably) abandoned. Simplicity is the heart of elegance.

All three of these characteristics must be embedded in two categories of indicators, those focused on the external operating environment (the equivalent of the commercial market) and those focused on internal operations.

EXTERNAL INDICATORS   There are two categories of external indicators to be built. Both are important because each represents pulse taking from a different lens and hence contributes to fluid decision making within a disciplined system of adaptation to change.

Operating Environment   The first watches change in the operating environment. Indicators here address the types of changes to the relevant economic structures or flows, demographics, geographic dimensions of programs, or social structures that are relevant to an organizations programs, constituency, and leadership. The importance of these indicators has been discussed throughout Sections II and III of this work. The fundamental changes in process, and likely to occur in the future, along economic and societal dimensions must be tracked as they relate to any organization's programs or goals if that organization is to stay ahead of the curve of rapid change.

Again, the specifics of these indicators must be driven by organization mission and program content. Chapter 18 suggests some subcategories of indicators for consideration.

In addition, the time over which these indicators should be tracked will be determined by their internal "clock" of change. For the most part, however, the indicator tracking system should be established so that data are examined at least annually and fed into a knowledge acquisition and dissemination system that informs both goal adjustment discussions and choices and decisions.

Constituents   The second category represents indicators focused on constituents. These may be program recipients, users of goods or services, donors, volunteers, or networks of leaders. These indicators need to track attitudes (e.g., do people see the issue differently now?), needs (is this program seen as a priority?), preferences (would you like to have that in pink rather than green?), and quality (perhaps even a Yelp-like ability to rate service). How people of all types, from all nodes of connection to the nonprofit, see that institution and its functions and services is a critical piece of information that builds knowledge. It is not just important to programs and services, it is important to the continuity and strength of leadership, both financial and voluntary.

Philanthropies also need to be concerned about changing attitudes and behaviors in the communities or constituents served by those that they fund. Changes in what communities think and what they value, what they see as their own priorities and their own preferences, must be critical input into the goals of funders as well as their decisions about what and how to fund.

The second category of indicators should also tap changes in behavior. How is the broader constituency changing its use of media? How is it changing its engagement with the nonprofit sector in general? What other nonprofit services is the constituency using?

The final element of attitude knowledge is brand, a topic discussed at some length in Chapter 16. In some ways, this is a bridge indicator, linking external constituent and market perceptions with internal systems, messages, and management. Few nonprofits, and fewer philanthropies, actually develop and pay close attention to indicators of brand performance and strategies for maintaining brand. Yet, if a brand is your promise, then how that brand is seen and what it conveys about the organization is critical knowledge.

Commercial organizations are vigilant about brand. That vigilance is a skill that is less well developed in the nonprofit sector, but one that, with instantaneous communication and unfiltered commentary about institutions and initiatives flowing globally, will become essential.

All of this knowledge is critical to helping an institution intersect change. The question for nonprofits now is not speed; how fast can we move? Rather, the critical question to be answered in rapid change is trajectory. What is the angle of change needed to intercept changes that are already underway in our constituency, our leaders and our volunteers?

And because that change is likely already under way and continually evolving, external indicators focused on constituents should be reexamined at least quarterly.

INTERNAL INDICATORS Similarly, there are two sets of internal indicators that must generate data to constantly inform the knowledge base that feeds both goals and decisions. Here, many nonprofits are more comfortable because their focus on execution of mission creates a natural synergy with the examination of internal systems. But a set of internal indicators that produces the fluidity needed to adapt to change is of a different nature. There can be no indicator silos.

Programs and Services The first set of indicators must be focused on programs or services. There are two elements here. First, how does content align with what is being learned from external indicators about environmental change and constituency attitudes? Internal programmatic indicators cannot stand apart from the external environment. They must be constantly related to what is being learned about external change. Objectively, how are programs performing relative to their anticipated outcomes? But, equally, how are they performing relative to changing issues, constituencies, attitudes, and behaviors? Performance systems inside nonprofits often (but, unfortunately, not always) measure the former. They rarely measure the latter. But in a world of extreme competition for philanthropic resources among an increasing number of organizations, the inability to relate performance to attitudes and preferences will erode loyalty of both donors and or constituents.

The same is true on the philanthropic side of the table. Grant makers are often focused on grantee performance relative to their stated objectives. Indeed, many large foundations have brought grant performance evaluation directly into the C-suite. However, few break through that internal silo of performance assessment and link it back to external indicators about community preferences, behavior changes, or surrounding economic or demographic change.

There is an important distinction to be made about performance on the funder side of the table. Philanthropy is not simply about money. It is, at its core, an expression of private voluntary leadership commitment to the common good. Grant performance is usually denominated relative to the dollars given and stated objectives. Philanthropic performance on the other hand—the degree to which philanthropy and the programs it funds actually creates and incentivizes leadership in the pursuit of the common good—is quite another matter. Yet if we truly want to craft indicators of performance for philanthropies, the creation of leaders who sustain common effort is certainly a place to start. This is, obviously, a much more difficult matter than counting grant dollars. But it would certainly provide meaningful guidance about long-term effects of those dollars in a changing social and economic environment.

The Organization   The contents of the second set of internal indicators, with one exception, are more mechanical. Nearly all organizations have developed financial indicators to assess performance and produce knowledge for decision making. Many (but not all) also increasingly worry about efficiency, all the more so after the Great Recession and the continued erosion of public and private sources of support for nonprofit programs.

Program quality is less frequently assessed, tied up as it is both with the need for clear definitions, internal indicators of objective quality, and links to deep understanding of the changing nature of constituency expectations and experiences. Education and health care have long been comfortable in this space. Professional critical review certainly provides this service in the arts and culture (although artists may disagree!). Other sectors, such as international relief and development, international affairs, advocacy, and some areas of social services less so. Again, however, the demand of philanthropy for results and the keen competition for resources, which will almost certainly begin to turn on issues of quality, means that internal indicators are essential.

The added complexity is that quality needs to be tracked on two levels. First, and most obviously, program or service quality is at the heart of being true to mission. However difficult technical measurement may be, this issue is deeply within the comfort zone of most nonprofits and philanthropies.

The second level is much less considered—the quality of the performance of the organization overall. This includes its management and communications systems, its human resources systems, its staff development functions, and its overall culture. Yet organizational performance is critical to stability in a changing world, especially where there is competition for financial resources, but also for the human resources, especially the up-and-coming young human resources, that will be the future. In 2010, Changing Our World conducted an international survey of young nonprofit professionals through Future Leaders in Philanthropy, its young leaders program. As noted previously in Chapter 10, responders rated organizational effectiveness, leadership, and professional development functions as problematic.[1] Indeed, only 10 percent were very satisfied with their organization's effectiveness and only 25 percent were very satisfied with their leaders. With the aging of the top management of the nonprofit sector, demonstrating organizational performance will play a key role in attracting and keeping tomorrow's leaders.

KNOWLEDGE MANAGEMENT   Volumes have been written about how to organize for knowledge management in complex organizations. There is no point in repeating that work here. There are, however, two central points to be made with regard to the nonprofit sector and its effort to create knowledge-based fluid decision making.

First, if the creation and management of an indicator system is not clearly designated as someone's responsibility, it will be no one's responsibility. And, therefore, it will not get done, or, if done once, it will lie dormant. Indicator management, knowledge development from indicators, and knowledge distribution must be placed firmly in the responsibility and accountability portfolio of someone, and that someone must be in the C-suite. There must be both the perception and the reality of top management support. The degree to which managers take the indicator process seriously, and its effect on the necessary fluidity within the discipline of change-based decision making will determine the degree to which the indicator process will be taken seriously institution-wide. Clear responsibility and accountability for crafting the indicators and producing and disseminating the knowledge is essential.

Second, there must be room to question the emperor's sartorial selections. If the indicators show a divergence between goals and operating environment directions, if the indicators show constituent changes in attitude, if the internal assessment shows delamination of programs from external demographics, there must be room for those findings to be articulated and discussed. If the emperor is, in fact, naked, it would be wise to recognize and remedy that fact. All the more so if you are the emperor.

In commerce, the market and investors play that role. There are many companies whose myopia to market changes and internal dysfunction led to eroded value to consumers and hence eroded share value to investors. In the nonprofit sector, there is no market. To some extent, philanthropists play that role; certainly, that is increasingly so among venture philanthropists. But, in the midst of fundamental change in their environment and in the ways in which philanthropic resources flow to problem solving, it will be up to the nonprofit to ensure that cautious news, or bad news, or the sounds of a blaring klaxon are expressed and heard throughout the organization.

Choices and Decisions

The articulation of goals, and their constant assessment in light of external and internal evidence, will create the need to make choices and decisions about directions and content on a regular (at least annual) basis. This is not simply a matter of the annual budget review, or how to distribute existing or desired resources across cost centers (which are often also power centers). The problem with knowledge, the problem with evidence, is that it carries weight. As litigators are fond of saying, the facts are recalcitrant.

Establishing and taking seriously an indicators system that tracks change has consequences. It will present choices and force decisions. Evidence about the fluidity of change will empower the discipline of decision making. Just as evidence will contradict the validity of a "run, shoot, and holler" approach to change, so it will cry out for an alternative to that approach. It will cry out for— it will demand—constant and clear evidence-based decision making.

Those choices and decisions will be on at least three levels.

First, they could (but more likely, will) affect programs and program content. Sections II and III outlined the directions of fundamental changes in global economic, demographic, and social issue content and structure. With those changes will come an alteration in the nature of societal needs and the nature of opportunities to address those needs. Establishing a specific capacity to take the specific pulse of these general trends in the specific parameters of any nonprofit or philanthropy will produce evidence that will likely argue for alteration in the content and process by which the organization pursues its mission. Nonprofits and philanthropies build up specific expertise, often deeply rooted over time. Creating a culture of evidence, described in Chapter 16, will provide the critical context for ensuring that programs do not simply tolerate the indicator results, but actively embrace them as the means to constantly adjust programs, products, and services.

But, even so, given the realities of human preference for the known rather than the unknown, and human tendency to prefer control over fluidity, it is likely that these decisions will be difficult until they are routine.

Second, they could (but, more likely, will) change networks, relationships, and approaches both to programs and to the core mission of the institution. Indicators may provide evidence of new constellations of institutions addressing relevant problems, new types of leaders emerging, new geographies, and new cultures bounding the problems or opportunities tied to organizational mission. Philanthropies that have long seen themselves as purely domestic in their interests may find that those interests no longer are contained by the Atlantic and Pacific oceans. Indeed, those interests may be better informed by experiences in Peru than in Peoria. The choice will be to hold to geography or maximize mission. A nonprofit long considered the leader in problem solving in its mission area may find that all manner of entrepreneurial approaches have created a new constellation of institutions coming from entirely different perspectives whose parallel leadership is critical but toward whom the nonprofit has no board leadership bridge. Becoming fluid in relationships and in approaches will require choices and decisions that may reach deeply into mission as well as into traditional ways of doing things and traditional pools of leaders.

Again, it is knowing that will create these choices. Knowledge, that pesky annoyance, and evidence, that hard taskmaster, will demand a reaction. There will be a need for management and decision making skills at the core of nonprofits, within top management, boards, and senior program managers. There will be a need for discipline in taking knowledge up into its organizational implications. But there may also be a need for courage.

Third, they could (but, more likely, will) change the sources, nature, and expectations of those providing resources. Changing structures of wealth and changing community ethnicity will create new philanthropic leaders whose desires and expectations may be totally unknown. New dimensions, new needs, and new opportunities will open the door for new approaches to resource mobilization. As we saw in Chapter 15, these new approaches are expanding rapidly. Evidence will not only document changing problems; it will identify changing opportunities, and hence open the way for adjustments to resource mobilization strategies. Fluid adjustment to indicators can create organizational strength not just organizational pain.

Learning

In some ways the hardest discipline is that of learning. This can be the biggest organizational and management challenge in institutions attempting to adapt to rapid and constant change. There is no "there, there." The need for constant examination of indicators, constant pulse taking of how adjustments are performing, and constant rethinking of both goals and indicators on the basis of experience is critical to keeping pace.

This is difficult for any organization. It is backbreaking for all but the largest nonprofits with the resources to invest in learning systems. Take the simplest of examples, the speed with which digital communications is changing. Struggling to keep up, most nonprofits are attending to web sites and ensuring that online donations can be processed. Social media presence for most is basic. Yet right under our feet the entire digital function is changing so that all media interact, all interrelate and talk to one another. And digital strategy becomes not simply image and fundraising, it becomes one and the same as engagement. Conversations take place digitally; people learn and react in real time; users create content. Large organizations—commercial, nonprofit, and philanthropic—can have whole staffs of professionals focused on this function. For medium-sized and small organizations, it means the need to totally reengineer budgets to ensure resources availability.

And for everyone, it means that tomorrow the newest technology or the newest use or the most innovation combination will arrive unannounced. And the entire process will begin anew.

Not to mention figuring out what was learned from the last go-round.

Learning, and then using learning to adjust strategy, action, goals, and indicators, is the biggest challenge for nonprofits. The critical elements for the medium and small nonprofit and the medium-sized philanthropy are threefold.

First, keep it simple. Just as a limited number of meaningful indicators is necessary, so is a limited objective for learning. Focus on critical "need to know" areas (are we better reaching the changing set of families in need?), not all of the would-like-to-know areas (what is the median age of the male family members?). The latter areas of knowledge are important, but grow into them gradually. Do not try to learn everything at once.

Second, track costs as well as lessons. Knowing "what works" is important. Know how much it cost is also important. Change program approaches effectively so that a rising immigrant population, for example, has effective access to services responds to a changing environment. But it cannot be scaled up unless marginal costs of doing so are known. Learning must not just be technical—it must be financial. This is especially important for small and medium-sized organizations where adaptation to change will require serious budget shifting rather than simply resource addition. In nonprofits and philanthropies, too often "learning" becomes a matter of technical communication to and by program officers and managers. Programs are siloed from finance. Finance should be forgiven, then, for insisting on budgets that do not accommodate the best practices required to serve changing environments.

Learning about "what works" must break through programmatic boundaries and generate knowledge and evidence regarding financial implications if resources are to follow.

Third, learning should be subjected to outside inquiry. We all have a tendency to embrace good news and see not-so-good news in its best light. This is not helpful in a rapidly changing world. Whatever is learned should be objectively accurate in its core but also in the margins of its implications. Fresh eyes can see where vested eyes may not. It is for this reason that universities regularly invite inside their walls boards of visitors from other academic or academically relevant institutions. These boards are invited in to examine performance evidence and institutional learning results and provide university leaders with a broader view.

Every nonprofit and philanthropy serious about learning from its effort to adjust to change should create and use a "board of visitors" concept, forming a group of three to four outside and totally dispassionate individuals every three years to examine evidence about performance and lessons learned, and provide program, finance, and management officials with reactions and insights. This is a time-intensive process every few years, to be sure, but it is not an expensive proposition. It can serve as a reality check, and also be an efficient way for organization's to tap knowledge of change in their operating environments that may not have been part of the indicator and evidence gathering process. In this way, an external board of visitors can not only validate (or question) learnings, but also keep the entire indicator review process open and fresh.

Summary and Implications

Rapid, fundamental, and constant change both in the operating environment and in the organizational and financial forms populating the global societal commons argues for the constant discipline of indicator- and evidence-based organizational and program strategy, and the fluidity of constant adjustment of those indicators to reflect the pace of change.

As noted in Chapter 16, the core requirement for that strategy is for the nonprofit and the philanthropy to develop a line of sight that values and acts on evidence of external change as much as an internal line of sight that values mission. The development of external and internal indicators, and the flow of evidence from those indicators both to goal-setting and to program content and management, must be a constant process. It must also be an inclusive process across all elements of the organization, including the finance office, to ensure that resource decisions are as informed by evidence of change and of effectiveness in the face of change as are programs and organizational management.

The question, of course, is whether most organizations in the sector have the quantitative skills to set and track indicators, and the management skills to create and administer fluid responses to the discipline of the resulting evidence. There are no data to inform that response. But there is reason to hope. As noted in Sections II and III, business schools now require social engagement courses of their students, promising a new generation of board members that is both knowledgeable about social causes and whose skills can align with nonprofit needs.

Second, there are now many, many nonprofit management programs in the nation's universities, and a growing number in universities around the world. True, these programs need, in this author's opinion, a much, much stronger quantitative and economic core. This is a near universal weakness. But the platform is there, and the capacity can be built.

Finally, one of the unexpected benefits of the Great Recession has been a flow into the nonprofit sector of young leaders from the for-profit world. In the 2009 young leaders survey by Changing Our World referenced earlier, nearly a quarter (23 percent) of responders had entered their current nonprofit work directly from previous positions in private commerce. These young leaders bring experience with using a market-optic as a fundamental part of defining organizational strategy, as well as a comfort with constantly adjusting to a disciplined and continuous assessment of the directions of that market.

Mastery of the discipline of evidence and the fluidity of constant adjustment to evidence may be the hallmark of successful nonprofit and philanthropic management in the coming decade.

Case N: Measuring Subtle Change in Diverse Organizations

Author: Changing Our World, Inc.

Partner: ConAgra Foods Foundation

Situation

Child hunger in the United States is a major societal problem with more than one in five children[a] at risk of not knowing where their next meal will come from; it is estimated to cost the country at least $28 billion per year.[b] Child hunger, a largely invisible issue, exists in every county in the country. Hunger disproportionally affects African American and Hispanic households with 25.1 percent and 26.2 percent, respectively, experiencing food insecurity, compared to the national average of 14.5 percent in 2010.[c]

Understanding the power of food to nourish lives, the ConAgra Foods Foundation has dedicated the last 20 years to identifying and scaling programs that increase children's access to hunger relief and nutrition

(*continued*)

(continued)

education programs. Yet, hunger continues to affect nearly 17 million children. With the magnitude of the issue, knowing the Foundation's impact on child food insecurity is challenging.

Stakes

Child hunger has both short and long-term effects on the health, growth, and development of children.

The Federal Nutrition Assistance Programs—school lunch, breakfast, and more—are the first line of defense, but there are gaps in access rates. Nonprofits are on the front line to address immediate needs, and provide support for a particular time and place. The dual challenge of under-utilized assistance programs and the need for long-term solutions makes it important to continuously examine the foundation's strategic invest-ments, and break down the impacts to a combination of measurable activities and outputs.

Strength

ConAgra Foods Foundation has established strategic partnerships with leading anti-hunger organizations and experts. It has built a portfolio of relationships that provides the company with a network of institutions that can work simultaneously to influence, guide, and seize opportunities that help the field better understand the challenges and barriers of child hunger as well as advance best practices. The Foundation has also sponsored multiple research reports, technical assistance efforts, and special initiatives to further strategic investment decisions. Working in this manner has afforded the foundation the ability to define milestones that determine a pathway (or proxy) toward the ultimate goal of helping children have increased access to meals and nutrition education.

Strategy

Drawing from Feeding America's *Hunger in America* 2010 report, a new study, *When the Pantry Is Bare: Emergency Food Assistance and His-panic Children,* funded by the ConAgra Foods Foundation, found that one out of every three Latino children in America receive emergency food assistance from the Feeding America network of food banks. *When the Pantry Is Bare* also found that Latino households are significantly less likely to utilize the Supplemental Nutrition Assistance Program (SNAP), the cornerstone of the federal nutrition safety net. The foundation saw these findings as an opportunity to take action and enhance their success toward long-term goals.

Solution

See Appendix 1.

---

[a] USDA ERS, "2011 Food Security Report," www.ers.usda.gov/Briefing/FoodSecurity/Stats_Graphs.htm.
[b] Joel Berg, "Feeding Opportunity," Center for American Progress, May 24, 2010, www.americanprogress.org/issues/poverty/report/2010/05/24/7743/feeding-opportunity/
[c] USDA ERS, "2011 Food Security Report."

Note

1. S. Raymond, S. Schiff, and K. Amore, *The Young and the Relentless: An Original Survey of the Next Generation of Philanthropy and Nonprofit Leaders* (New York: Changing Our World, Inc. and Future Leaders in Philanthropy, 2010), 21–28.

CHAPTER 18

Indicators and Evidence: A Suggested Place to Begin

E very organization exists within an ecology of indicators that, taken together, point to its future. As noted in Chapter 17, some change quickly, some slowly; some are simple to identify, some represent surrogate measures of deeper change; some speak to the heart of mission, some to the arms and legs of capacity to carry out mission. What is needed is a way to organize this cacophony of potential evidence into a manageable system, and then a way to select the appropriate indicators to measure and follow.

Appendix 2 of this book contains a self-administered questionnaire for nonprofit and philanthropic managers. It is intended to assist managers who do not have a disciplined indicator system in thinking about what they do and do not know about their environment, the directions and the rapidity of its change, as well as what they do and do not know about their internal program and organizational and brand performance. The hope is that this tool will aid both in understanding what is known but also, and importantly, in helping to narrow the possible list of what could be known to a manageable set of indicators with material meaning to constantly inform goals and directions.

The discussion that follows is intended to explicate the categories and content of indicators that might be part of a system of evidence. The lists are obviously not definitive; they are intended to suggest ways in which indicators might be organized such that they are manageable in number yet revealing in their implications.

It is important to recognize that, although the illustrative indicators are presented here in two separate categories, external and internal, the resultant evidence is constantly flowing across those boundaries. External constituent perceptions inform programs, and knowledge of program use or performance is constantly matched against, for example, changing measures of external demographics. The use of evidence within decision making is continuously iterative across measures and over time.

Categories

As noted in Chapter 17, there are two broad categories of indicators: those that inform about changes in the external environment and those that track changes internally.

External Operating Environment

ECONOMIC   Few nonprofits have economists in their C-suites, and so, beyond an occasional glance at the business section of the local newspaper and an eye toward the Dow, there is little effort to actively track relevant economic indicators or project their implications for fundraising, grant making, or programs. Whether these are tracked at the national or local level, and at the local level whether by district or zip code, of course, depends on the focus of the organization. There are, of course, many, many elements that could be tracked. Exhibit 18.1 is suggested as a way to begin thinking about important road signs for economic change.

EXHIBIT 18.1 Dimensions of Economic Indicators

Indicator Category	Illustrative Indicators	Rationale
Employment	Change in unemployment rates, both U3 and U6, the latter measuring such areas as involuntary part-time employment	Unemployment rate changes correlate highly with private giving as well as with household income, but changes are tracked monthly and so provide a more frequent surrogate for income
	Unemployment change by gender, age, and ethnicity	Differential impacts likely over time relevant for key constituencies and categories of supporters
	Unemployment by industrial sector	Differential impacts that reveal arc of change in industrial makeup of economy
Households	Median incomes and changes	Indicates household well-being
	Poverty rates (total and child)	Distribution of need and economic dependency

	Wealth distribution by quintile	Increasing or decreasing wealth concentration; changes in positioning of middle class
	Real estate prices/turnover	Asset health of households
Business	Business formation rates by industrial category	Indicates economic dynamism and changing nature of economic structure
	25 largest employers as percent workforce	Business concentration
	Job formation by skill or profession	Further indication of changing economic structure
	Number of social enterprises formed	Status of innovation in the enterprise intersect
Public Finance	Budget deficits and reductions (overall or within program-specific areas or interest)	Critical knowledge for nonprofits with more than 30% public funding and for philanthropies that support them
	Tax receipts	Indicator of upcoming revenue problems
	National budget transfers locally	Tracks future potential local growth or cutbacks

DEMOGRAPHICS   Nonprofits and philanthropies are largely in the business of serving humans. This is not always directly true, of course. Basic scientific research institutions serve people in the long term, but their immediate line of sight is the research itself. Nevertheless and more broadly in the sector, changes in the nature of constituents—be they clients, service users, or donors/supporters—represent critical intelligence for both program and funding goals. Exhibit 18.2 contains illustrations of indicators that might be part of an evidence-tracking system. They only begin to suggest categories (e.g., violence data is clearly important for some, or youth development data for others, or home-bound data for still others), but the intent is to provoke thinking about categories, specific indicators, and, very importantly, the rationale for including the indicator in a manageable evidence set.

ATTITUDES AND BEHAVIORS   Understanding what people think and how they behave is critical to anticipating change. Obviously, this set of indicators intersects with the previous two in portraying the operating environment. Economic expectations, for example, can drive markets much more powerfully than economic production realities because expectations and attitudes control purse strings. As noted in Chapter 17, corporate marketing departments spend enormous amounts of time and resources on understanding this

EXHIBIT 18.2 Dimensions of Demographic and Social Indicators

Indicator Category	Illustrative Indicators	Rationale
Age and Ethnicity	Population distribution by age group	Possible growing divergence from programs or from traditional support groups
	Age group by ethnicity	New languages, cultures, and expectations to be accommodated
Gender	Gender distribution by age	Differing constituencies by age, and gender differences in aging
Origins	Foreign-born population and places of origin	Implications for communications strategies, service needs, giving cultures
Dependency	Percentage of population under age 5 and over age 65	Changes in service demand and household disposable income
Education	Degree holding by degree level	Changes in household prospects
	Employment rates by education level	Changes in income prospects of constituency over time
Geographic Distribution	Changes in population distribution, ethnicity, and age groups by geographic sub-area	Transportation issues, service location issues, constituent proximity issues

dimension of their environment. Nonprofits and philanthropies tend to do so only when there is a particular project or program or initiative at a particular point in time that requires reaching out.

A disciplined approach to knowledge and strategy adjustment, however, requires more than just episodic pulse taking. It requires regular effort. Nonprofits and philanthropies need to know what those they serve think, what surrounding communities think, and what their supporters think, and equally how they behave relative to critical elements of strategy. And they need to project changes into the future to determine how to intersect existing rates and dimensions of change.

Exhibit 18.3 illustrates the dimensions of regularly gathered indicators that will help nonprofits and philanthropies understand their constituencies and changes in their attitudes and behaviors, and thus feed that knowledge into their program, communications, and funding strategies. Obviously, all of the

EXHIBIT 18.3 Dimensions of Attitude and Behavior Indicators

Indicator Category	Illustrative Indicators	Rationale
Use	Frequency of service use or organizational interaction	Changes in how close people are to the organization; changes in demand patterns
	Frequency of personal interaction with individuals in the organization	Degree to which satisfaction (below) is grounded in exposure
Knowledge	User knowledge of programs and services	Depth of alignment with need
	Supporter knowledge of programs and performance	Likelihood of continued empathy
Satisfaction	User satisfaction with services or products; satisfaction with personal interaction	Quality performance
	Supporter satisfaction with communication and individual treatment	Likelihood of continued support
Communications	Use of social media or other electronic means of communication	Changes in strategies for communication
	Views of adequacy of communications received	Effectiveness of outreach
Loyalties	User knowledge of and use of alternative providers or nonprofits	Changes in the organizational market
	Supporter most important social or charitable sectors	Stability of loyalty to organization's issues; new issues to address
	Supporter community volunteer behavior	Propensity to engage
	Supporter participation as nonprofit board member or other leader	Competing loyalties
Hopes and Fears	User aspirations for the coming period (year) and major fears	Understand alignment with core of user concerns
	Supporter personal hopes and fears	Red flags from changing levels of concern that could affect personal support behavior
	Supporter hopes for the organization	Red flags where hopes diverge from plans

(continued)

EXHIBIT 18.3 (*Continued*)

Indicator Category	Illustrative Indicators	Rationale
Brand Performance	Satisfaction data from attitudes	Brand is a bridge between internal intent and public perception
	Comparison of terms used to describe the organization and its mission, and the words used to describe satisfaction or dissatisfaction	Is the organization keeping its promise?
	Social media measures of mentions, positives, and negatives	Instant communications requires careful attention to social media and brand maintenance requires organizations to not just listen to what is said, but to be an active part of the discussion in real time

indicators would need to be collected with attention to cross-cutting variables of age, gender, and ethnicity, at a minimum.

Internal Environment

It is obviously much more difficult to suggest indicators for monitoring changes in an organization's internal environment because the structure of nonprofits is so different. A local social service agency is much different from an Ivy League university is much different from a hospital is much different from, for example, a parish. The critical element is regularity of indicator data collection. Alignment and performance are not five-year strategic planning matters, although they are often treated that way. They are matters of at least annual review, and in some cases (e.g., finance) at least monthly and quarterly review. When it comes to internal performance—programmatic, financial, or managerial—there is no such thing as a good surprise. With the external environment changing fundamentally and often quickly, the ability to be fluid in adjustment will require that internal systems stay well-oiled and flexible. Arthritic joints internally will impede flexibility externally.

Exhibit 18.4 contains a few suggestions of the categories and measures that might be included in an indicator system for internal performance.

It is important to note that these are *not* indicators for the performance evaluation of any particular program or project; this is an increasingly critical

EXHIBIT 18.4 Dimensions of Internal Indicators

Indicator Category	Illustrative Indictors	Rationale
Program Alignment	Demographics and economic profile of program or service users	Compare to external changes to assess alignment of use or access
	Program substance compared to constituency hopes/fears	Ability to see current or approaching divergence from constituency
Program Performance	Numbers served/reached Geographic scope served/reached	Comparison to growth rates or geographic distribution of relevant population
Leadership Alignment	Demographic characteristics relative to operating environment change	Ethnic, geographic, age, or gender disparities that are material to performance
Efficiency	Costs per user reached or per product or service produced	Estimation of marginal cost of reaching users or producing services relative to changing nature of users or services
	Costs per supporter generated by type of supporter	As nature of supporters changes (ethnicity, geography, wealth, etc.), ability to predict impact on cost structure to reach that change
Financial Structure	Distribution of revenue by type of source	Ability to assess likelihood of matching resource mobilization effort against changing capacity of public and private sources to provide support relative to the external public and private economic indicators
	Distribution of revenue by geographic locus	Alignment with changing loci of programs, users, or supporters
	Numbers and types of innovative revenue diversification precedents occurring in the relevant sector	Taking advantage of innovation opportunity requires recognizing where it is taking place and projecting how innovation might be applied to financial structure

element of work in light of funder expectations for impact discussed in several parts of this book. Rather, these are indicators that will provide evidence of the degree to which the organization and its work is moving in concern with, or sufficiently well to intersect, changes in the external environment.

As such, they are critical to a disciplined approach to projecting and predicting the effects of external change on the program and cost structure internally. However they are structured, these categories or types of internal indicators are fundamental management tools in a changing environment.

Possible Partners in Implementation

For small and medium-sized nonprofits and philanthropies, it is difficult to know *how* to begin, even in the illustrative indicators provide guidance on *where* to begin. Where will all but the largest organizations get the human resources to construct the indicators, let alone regularly update them?

There are three possible partners to consider.

First, this author believes that community foundations can play a fundamental part in solving this dilemma. This is especially true for systems of external indicators. Community foundations can develop and maintain indicator systems for demographics, economics, and social dimensions, as well as distribute data regularly to nonprofits throughout their catchment area. They can also carry out regular community attitude surveys regarding the nonprofit sector that will provide guidance on changing level so knowledge and trust. Furthermore, they can maintain expertise internally that will also help small and medium-sized organizations develop their own internal measurement systems, as well as provide guidance on how to create manageable survey tools that will help nonprofits regularly tap the attitudes of their constituents about needs and quality.

Second, and with the notable exception of many very rural areas, it is the rare nonprofit that does not have a college or university within an hour's drive. Students or interns can help access data and populate indicator systems. Graduate students in business, social sciences, political science, or psychology can develop indicator systems and maintain them over time. These are not expensive resources for the nonprofit. And the nonprofit itself is actually providing a service in partnering with academic institutions. In this extraordinarily slow economic recovery, the job prospects for graduates without work experience are dark indeed. The ability to show two or three years of consistent experience with evidence-based assessment systems can substantially strengthen the resumes of young graduates. The benefits in partnership with academic institutions will flow both ways, to the nonprofit seeking to develop, maintain, and interpret an indicator system and to the undergraduate and graduate students working on the system.

Third, and again as a function of the difficult economy, volunteer agencies or even churches are an important source of potential partners. As noted in Chapter 3, the deep reservoirs of unemployment, and the unprecedented length of unemployment, mean that many, many very qualified professionals who are older Americans have poor prospects for work. It is easier to get a job if you have a job than to get a job if you do not. Nonprofits should look to this older workforce for expertise, and bring those individuals in perhaps not as volunteers but as "technical experts." They compensation will not need to be large; the value offered is not monetary. It is to restore to the resume of the individual a position and a description of a responsibility that will enable him or her to more productively look for employment from the position of being employed. In turn, the nonprofit benefits from mature experience in developing tools for assessing both external and internal evidence.

For many nonprofits, at least one of these partnership strategies may provide the capacities for indicator system development that may not otherwise be possible with limited budgets. Getting started may require creativity and out-of-the-box thinking about available assets. But in nearly every community, those assets are present.

Summary and Implications

In order to approach rapid and fundamental change with discipline, nonprofits and philanthropies must regularly and consistently take the pulse of their environment and the alignment between that environment and their internal operations. The purpose is not simply (in fact, is hardly at all) to understand the moment. It is to be able to project the future, to see where and how the trajectory of change externally is moving away from the programs, or content, or mission, or leadership, or financing structure of an organization.

This is an important distinction. Fluid discipline is not about coping with today. By the time that adjustment is made, today is gone. Being constantly too late is not a productive approach for those who aspire to success.

Rather, fluid discipline provides the ability to anticipate and predict, to skate, as Wayne Gretzky is famous for saying, not to where the puck is, but to where it will be. Anticipation of the trajectory of change, and adjustment of the angle of intersection to meet that change, is the key to thriving in a rapidly changing world.

Faced with rapid and fundamental change, many organizations believe that speed is the key. Change fast. Go fast. Adjust on the fly, if need be, but just *move*. Movement is indeed important, but speed without the correct trajectory will miss the arc of change every time. It is the discipline of evidence produced by constant attention to indicators that will yield the correct calculus to ensure that nonprofits and philanthropies thrive in a changing world.

APPENDIX 1

Case Solutions

The following are the "solutions" associated with the case materials contained throughout this book. These solutions represent new ways of working with communications, brand, markets, and evidence to strengthen nonprofits in a changed world.

Case A: Plunging Resources and Community-Wide Crisis

AUTHOR: ANN DAVIDSON, MANAGING DIRECTOR, VOX GLOBAL

PARTNER: CRISIS ASSISTANCE MINISTRY   The strategy worked. The emergency triage program put into action at Crisis Assistance Ministry allowed them to see over 100 percent more clients per month, nearly 30,000 families in crisis during 2009 and 2010. Amazingly, leaders came through with a Critical Need Response Fund, personally raising and channeling $3 million in philanthropic funds to this and other social service safety net groups.

By early 2012, as the economy began to rebound, Crisis Assistance Ministry had survived its most challenging financial scenario and emerged with its reputation for meeting community need strongly in place and its own financial house in order.

Today, they are working to apply the lessons learned from collaboration with other social service agencies to ensure that going forward they address individual needs more holistically and manage the anticipated reductions in government funding for social services. "We took it as a once-in-a-lifetime opportunity to build an innovative, sustainable solution," Hardison told an editor for the *Huffington Post*.

253

Case B: Private Resource Strategies for the Long Haul

AUTHOR: MASLANSKY+PARTNERS

PARTNER: NATIONAL HEAD START ASSOCIATION   Head Start and maslansky+
partners (m+p) found a new conversation about education that appealed to
values that ran deeper than political affiliation. People are divided on "public
spending for education." But they're united on "investing in our youth." A "war
on poverty" is partisan, but "access to opportunity for all" is a rallying cry. Head
Start moved its language to the middle, and in doing so changed from a liberal
cause to an essential American opportunity. The result? A program that had
been squarely in Tea Party sights received nearly a billion-dollar budget
increase in 2011.

In 2012, Executive Director Yasmina Vinci presented m+p with the
National Head Start Association's Corporate Champion Award in recognition
for identifying the language that changed the conversation about Head Start in
ways that resonated with both supporters and skeptics alike. This reframing
made clear the value that Head Start delivers to constituencies, both conser-
vative and liberal, and ultimately helped maintain the program's funding
levels. HHS Secretary Kathleen Sibelius, several members of Congress,
and even President Obama has adopted language from the lexicon m+p
developed for Head Start.

Case C: Private Fundraising Strategy in a Newly Open Society

AUTHOR: GRIZZARD COMMUNICATIONS GROUP

PARTNER: THE SALVATION ARMY   The two-day think-tank meeting inspired a
Russian revolution for fundraising in the former communist nation.

The Russian territorial commander Colonel Ken Johnson reported in
December 2011:

> *The Federation continues to move our fundraising agenda forward.
> Several identified goals have been accomplished and are underway. We
> have started our first Advisory Board in the Georgia Division. Almost
> immediately we received donations as a result of one of the board
> member's activity. It is a small but growing group. They have also
> been able to start a modified Advisory Board in Yalta, Ukraine, which
> has great potential. The goal is still to start one in Kiev and St. Petersburg.*
>
> *The first goal was to develop a Christmas fundraising strategy. They
> now have kettles operating in Georgia, Romania, and Russia. Angel trees*

are to be strategically placed to not only help with recognition but donations as well.

The Federation developed a PR manual update, had it translated and distributed to all five divisions. This was followed up with training, and a PR Secretary was appointed.

A week in December has been established as Salvation Army week. This creates a target period for the officers when they can put extra emphasis for community involvement and fundraising.

To be expected, there are many obstacles to overcome. International Headquarters has been unable to change the link for credit card banks, so banks are still unable to process donations. This is an ongoing process.

The group has made contact with the United Way of Moscow, with plans to approach them with application for full membership.

As the strategy continues to unfold, the initiative, led by a few integral international leaders, was instrumental in expanding the Salvation Army's mission of hope and help.

Case D: Global Company Seeks Global Engagement

AUTHOR: KETCHUM

PARTNER: ROOM TO READ   To date, more than 30 Ketchum offices and affiliates have participated in the Room to Read pro bono partnership in locations as diverse as Dubai, London, Sydney, San Francisco, and New York. Nearly 500 employees have contributed their time to the cause, and the numbers increase year after year. The primary support includes strategic communications counsel and program implementation. In addition, Ketchum colleagues have collectively established a library in Nepal, published 5,000 local language children's books in Laos, and supported the holistic education of 82 girls in Zambia. The agency also makes a donation to the organization in honor of clients every year for the holidays.

Staff members at all levels are encouraged to participate. As one example, Ketchum West developed an internship project that focused on delivering a fundraising program and toolkit for the Room to Read chapter network. Ketchum's CEO has been a member of the Room to Read advisory board since 2008 and regularly contributes his time and expertise to the organization. Ketchum also has engaged employees at every level and extended opportunities to staff members beyond the traditional PR function. In addition to its global media team, members of Ketchum Research and Analytics. Ketchum Digital, Ketchum Sports and Entertainment, and other specialty areas have participated in the global effort. As Ketchum continues to expand its global footprint, the agency is committed to extending its reach to support Room to Read in the places it does business and beyond.

Case E: Public Resources and Private Outreach

AUTHOR: KALEIDOSCOPE YOUTH AND FAMILY MARKETING

PARTNER: U.S. CONSUMER PRODUCT SAFETY COMMISSION[1]   Together, Kaleidoscope Youth Marketing and Stratacomm supported CPSC and helped accomplish the goal of increasing the NSN database to 5,000 members. Leveraging strategic recruitment efforts through grassroots outreach, working with community-based organizations, and relationship building with national organizations, the Kaleidoscope and Stratacomm team ultimately built the NSN to 7,268 members (a net increase of 4,520, or 101 percent over goal). Stratacomm and Kaleidoscope utilized their experience and expertise in public relations, youth and family marketing, influencer relations, media relations, and grassroots marketing to swiftly and efficiently elevate the NSN and drive recruitment.

Highlights of the campaign include:

- *Creative and messaging development*. Stratacomm and Kaleidoscope developed new marketing creative materials and key messages that would resonate with community leaders and serve as a "call to duty."
- *Grassroots recruitment*. Kaleidoscope leveraged direct access to millions of families through grassroots, community-based organizations to drive direct recruitment and awareness. Kaleidoscope engaged leaders within day cares and preschools, faith-based organizations, afterschool programs, teachers and school staff, community recreation centers, YMCAs, and Boys & Girls Clubs via an aggressive phone outreach of over 6,000 calls, 50,000 direct-mail pieces sent to organizations, and e-mail and social media delivered via their current community affiliations.
- *Partnerships*. Stratacomm identified, prioritized, and initiated outreach to strategic third-party partners to assist with the promotion of the NSN recruitment campaign. These were both new and existing partnerships that needed to be established or reenergized. Partnerships include Safe Kids, National Safety Council, Boys & Girls Clubs of America, American College of Nurses and Midwives, National Association of County and City Health Officials, and the Afterschool Alliance.

---

[1]CPSC cannot endorse a contractor, its writings, or its claims.

Case F: New Leaders, New Passion, Persistent Problems

AUTHOR: WOLFF OLINS

PARTNER: i2 INSTITUTE FOR IMAGINATION AND INGENUITY   Wolff Olins partnered with Dr. Sindi to create the i2 Institute for Imagination and Ingenuity,
and worked in collaboration on all aspects of the brand, including naming,
visual identity, writing, web site development, communications, the global
launch presentation for the 2011 PopTech conference in Camden, Maine, and
event communications and guidance for the official launch in Jeddah in the fall
of 2012. The i2 brand gives Dr. Sindi a powerful and consistent way to
introduce, and ultimately realize, her vision in the world.

Since announcing i2 in 2011, the institute has received overwhelmingly
positive feedback. i2 has been heeding the strong responses and voices of the
youth, while Dr. Sindi has been meeting with potential investors around the
world, from private and corporate donors to the Saudi government, as well as
institutional and educational partners, some of whom, like Wolff Olins, will sit
on i2's board of directors. An action plan has been created, and a business plan
has been developed with help from i2's partner network. Applications for i2's
future innovators will open up in November 2012.

Like Dr. Sindi, we see the need for opportunity, innovation, and new
industry throughout the world and are excited about our ongoing partnership
to realize i2's ecosystem of innovation.

Case G: Strength to Strength: Partnership to Boost Engagement

AUTHOR: THE MARKETING ARM

PARTNER: U.S. OLYMPIC COMMITTEE   Partnering with Team USA and NBC,
AT&T launched the official Team USA Olympic Soundtrack, featuring exclusive, "never-before-heard," inspirational tracks from 16 of the nation's hottest
artists, including 3 Doors Down, Lady Antebellum, Goo Goo Dolls, and Sheryl
Crow. This soundtrack musically chronicled Team USA's Olympic journey and
highlighted their hopes, struggles, determination, and triumph.

One new song from the AT&T soundtrack premiered each night during
primetime coverage (on NBC and Telemundo) accompanied by a video
montage of the day's key highlights from Team USA. At the end of each
segment, consumers were driven to download the songs, ringtones, and
answer tones via AT&T products and services. The artists, labels, publishers,
AT&T, and all download partners donated all proceeds from downloads
during the games to Team USA.

The AT&T Team USA Soundtrack program generated $1 million in proceeds for the U.S. Olympic Team.

Case H: Globalization and Social Media

AUTHOR: CHANGING OUR WORLD, INC.

PARTNER: SIGHTSAVERS   At the recommendation of Changing Our World, Sightsavers executed two interactive campaigns.

- October 2011: World Sight Day Awareness & Advocacy Campaign: *Share Our Vision: Be a Sightsaver.* This integrated digital and print campaign grew the organization's U.S. Facebook presence by 200 percent, raised 9 percent of calendar-year revenue in 10 days, and increased the organization's e-mail file by 3,000.
- November 2011 to January 2012: *Financial Times* Seasonal Appeal Campaign.

Sightsavers was selected as the *Financial Times (FT)* charity of choice for their 2011/2012 Seasonal Appeal, which involves *FT* coverage of a chosen charity's work in print and online to raise funds for and awareness of its work. With an average daily global audience of 2.1 million and more than 5 million registered users of FT.com, the *Financial Times* provided a global platform to build Sightsavers' brand awareness and increase engagement with the *FT*'s strong U.S. audience. Changing Our World designed a digital strategy to optimize Sightsavers' web site and social media platforms in preparation for the campaign, including a Twitter strategy for *Financial Times* journalists to advocate on behalf of Sightsavers. The appeal has raised more than $5 million in matched giving.

Case I: Multichannel Pathways to Reach New Fundraising Markets

AUTHOR: RUSS REID

PARTNER: OPERATION SMILE   Russ Reid helped Operation Smile refine one of the most tangible offers in the nonprofit world. For as little as $240, a child's life can be completely transformed by a surgery, and there were images to prove it.

Russ Reid TV crews went to Vietnam and Venezuela to capture the stories of transformation and create a direct-response television program designed to dramatically increase mass exposure and acquire valuable donors.

With two 30-minute TV shows, Operation Smile and Russ Reid seized the opportunity to test and fine-tune the offer, make strategic media buys, develop powerful creative, enter untapped markets, set up solid positioning of the show, and even refine call center scripting.

While TV, phone, and digital continued to be a success in acquiring valuable supporters, Russ Reid and Operation Smile partnered in crafting a Direct Mail program to integrate with the new TV focus. Implementing a thorough Direct Mail acquisition strategy, the donor file was extended outside of TV and the complete surgery offer. Russ Reid led vigorous tests on creative, list sources, co-ops, modeling, and segmentation.

The result? Direct Mail acquisition results increased 59 percent over the previous four years.

Multichannel acquisition efforts did not stop there. To continue to grow Operation Smile's donor file, Russ Reid developed a citywide campaign to challenge communities to take action by joining local leaders who were already involved with Operation Smile. Launching the first campaign in Salt Lake City, Russ Reid crafted a layered media approach featuring long- and short-form television, radio spots and traffic sponsorships, online banners, bus and light rail signs, billboards and direct mail, with a combined total of an estimated 15.5 million impressions.

The campaign goal was to raise enough funds to provide 1,000 smiles, and the Salt Lake City community delivered. Supporting major gift efforts as well, the campaign even moved one man to pledge 1,000 smiles himself and commit to raise funds for an additional 1,000 smiles.

With diverse acquisition efforts bringing in high-value donors, Operation Smile asked Russ Reid to apply similar messaging and targeting strategies to cultivate their growing file.

Through Russ Reid's comprehensive reporting and analytics, the cultivation file was segmented and targeted to optimize donor communication and increase response. Using best practices that Russ Reid developed, Operation Smile improved the creative and positioning of the offer in existing appeals while also creating new appeals.

The analytical team identified an untapped segment of middle donors. Russ Reid and Operation Smile crafted a middle donor appeal with a unique offer to support the building of a Care Center in Ethiopia. Response to this offer was strong, and prompted the launch of an ongoing middle donor cultivation stream that has successfully increased net revenue and donor engagement.

As the cultivation file matured, Russ Reid's Donor File Analysis identified lapsing and prelapsing segments of valuable donors. In collaboration with Russ Reid, Operation Smile implemented a multitouch point strategy to offset attrition and reactivate supporters. The results of this strategy were encouraging; donors were reactivated with higher average gifts, becoming more beneficial to the organization.

As opportunities arose, Operation Smile and Russ Reid were quick to identify, craft, and test additional offers. As Operation Smile moved to help in the aftermath of the Haiti 2010 earthquake, Operation Smile's Emergency

Response offer was created—expanding the organization's capabilities and increasing support of their mission.

Armed with a track record of success, Operation Smile and Russ Reid launched a new brand initiative to better communicate Operation Smile to our audiences. In keeping with the newly refreshed and focused brand, Operation Smile joined forces with Russ Reid to redesign the Operation Smile web site with a concentration on fundraising. The new web site was a great success, significantly increasing the organization's income.

In keeping with the newly refreshed and focused brand, Operation Smile joined forces with Russ Reid to redesign the Operation Smile web site with a concentration on fundraising. The new web site was a great success, significantly increasing the organization's income.

Looking to take advantage of holiday shopping behavior, Russ Reid and Operation Smile launched an Operation Smile Holiday Gift Catalog. The catalog diversified the cultivation lineup and allowed donors to give a Christmas gift of hope and transformation in the name of friends and family. The new Holiday Giving Catalog was promoted through the media by Operation Smile's A-list celebrities, and was a success with their current donor base.

With the increase in online shopping, Russ Reid refreshed the catalog's e-commerce site to streamline the catalog giving experience and increase online gifts.

Together, Operation Smile and Russ Reid have placed a focus on growth and a strong strategic partnership.

Since 2003, Operation Smile has evolved into a sophisticated, multi-channel and holistic marketing organization that has achieved year over year double-digit donor and revenue growth with a healthy return on investment (ROI). Through alignment of multiple channels and consistent messaging across layered media efforts, Operation Smile has:

- Increased average gift size by 51 percent.
- Increased annual giving per donor by 93 percent.
- Increased the number of active donors by 324 percent.
- Increased direct response revenue by 719 percent.
- Most importantly, forever changed the lives of more than 200,000 girls and boys with transformative surgery.

Case J: New Strength through Simplifying Identity

AUTHOR: INTERBRAND

PARTNER: FEEDING AMERICA To make their story simple and accessible, we developed three essential assets that helped signal their promise and clarify their purpose:

- *The name Feeding America.* For the first time, all members could quickly convey the mission, the value of the network, and the power of food to be a positive catalyst in enriching people's lives.
- *The logo and visual identity.* The clean, bold wordmark represents a living, growing national community connected in a single purpose. Use of orange builds on the power of the color most associated with the hunger movement, to reinforce their dedication to the mission. Green symbolizes the rebirth, regeneration, and growth that the organization fosters in communities. It represents their belief in a better tomorrow, which filters up through every level of the organization.
- *A messaging framework tying national purpose to local outcomes.* People who care deeply about the cause want to *see* relief for their neighbors. Relief can be delivered to more people through the efficiency of a collaborative network. We built a messaging framework that tells both sides of this story—supported by data points drawn from their fact base.

More important, we helped them create the two fundamental shifts that they identified as fundamental to success—working together, making informed decisions. The process itself was as vital as the product of our partnership.

After the launch of the new brand, revenue doubled in one year, enabling the organization to deliver $50 million in grants in 2008—more than ever in their history. They grew from a $25 million dollar organization in 2007 to a $1.2 billion organization today. They now help feed more than 37 million people in America each year.

In the words of Feeding America President and CEO Vicki Escarra, "You have made a tremendous impact on our organization and we thank you so sincerely for bringing such passion and expertise and partnership. I am convinced that your work will be a catalyst for profound change in the antihunger movement."

That's the power of a brand being used simply, for good.

Case K: Communications Strategy for Shifting Demographics

GRIZZARD COMMUNICATIONS GROUP

PARTNER: THE SALVATION ARMY CANADA Results to the campaign showed that an integrated strategy was the solution The Salvation Army Canada had been seeking.

- Increase in new donor revenue: 16 percent
- Increase in new donors: 7.5 percent
- Increase in average gift: 22 percent

- Increase in website visitors: 27 percent
- Increase in online donations: 15 percent

This campaign proved that adding an integrated marketing strategy to an existing direct mail program can dramatically boost results—especially where it matters most, the acquisition of new donors. For decades, The Salvation Army had relied on direct-response fundraising as a critical lifeline of support. Adding an integrated strategy across multiple channels has added new life to their direct-mail program, proving that direct marketing continues to be a powerful way to acquire new donors and raise funds.

To review all media and solutions, see http://64.79.166.50/lab/TSA/2012/06-Canada-Case-Study/lp.

Case L: New Institutions for New Demographics

AUTHOR: MASLANSKY+PARTNERS

PARTNER: AARP FOUNDATION   The research also revealed an increasingly cynical population turned off by utopian goals. The AARP Foundation has long talked internally of "a country free of poverty." But outside, as one Memphis donor summed it up, "Poverty has been here since man has. There's no way to eradicate it." The foundation shifted to helping those over 50 *gain stability*, and to *preventing* rather than eradicating problems. The shift in both paradigm and vocabulary focused on *serving* those over 50 to one suffused with *providing opportunity*. This signaled to donors and recipients that the foundation is focused on improvement and hope, not merely the present. Since the new leadership tenure began in 2010, donations to the foundation are up 46 percent, with a 30 percent increase since 2011, when the new language began to be employed in support of the new strategic direction of the organization.

Case M: New Brand Strategy amid Economic Crisis

AUTHOR: BEANSTALK

PARTNER: HABITAT FOR HUMANITY   Balancing the need for revenue against strained resources and a lack of internal expertise in licensing, Habitat's first step, before making a final decision, was to seek counsel from outside experts. Habitat engaged New York-based Beanstalk, a global brand licensing agency. Knowing that there would have to be internal trade-offs to support licensing opportunities and that revenue would have to be significant to offset potential risks resulting from the complexity of Habitat's grassroots structure, its management and its consultant agreed that launching a successful licensing program would work best if it were initiated in a big way, as a major initiative across multiple product categories, and with a big partner. A comprehensive licensing and product design strategy was developed and the concept of a range of Habitat-licensed products was presented to one of the world's largest retailers. Unfortunately, the downturn in the economy in 2008 coincided with this effort and the response was "good idea, but not now." And, as a result of this response, Habitat reined in its efforts.

Habitat remains receptive to licensing its brand and working with outside partners, but it has now deferred further efforts pending an upturn in the global financial outlook when it believes that its efforts would have a greater probability of success with retailers and consumers.

Case N: Measuring Subtle Change in Diverse Organizations

AUTHOR: CHANGING OUR WORLD, INC.

PARTNER: CONAGRA FOODS FOUNDATION   In October 2011, ConAgra Foods Foundation and Feeding America partnered to leverage the study's key data and pilot an initiative to increase awareness of and participation in SNAP among Latino households. Since inception, the *Latino SNAP Outreach Project* has attained marked results through its food bank partners in Arizona, California, Florida, New York, and Texas. As of September 2012, the project has established 642 new access points, trained 285 people to conduct SNAP outreach and/or application assistance to Latino households, prescreened 16,110 households for SNAP and submitted 8,033 SNAP applications by trained food bank outreach workers or volunteers. The Foundation is using the momentum of the *Latino SNAP Outreach* project to explore potential efforts that will target eligible low-income families in the African-American community to increase enrollment in the Federal Nutrition Assistance Programs.

Self-Assessment Questionnaire

	Yes 3 points	Somewhat 2 points	No 0 points
Your External Environment			
General Systems			
Do you have a formal system for tracking external indicators?	☐	☐	☐
Do you track external indicators quantitatively?	☐	☐	☐
Do you compare these external indicators at least quarterly?	☐	☐	☐
Is a specific person responsible for managing tracking?	☐	☐	☐
Do you get reports on that tracking at least quarterly?	☐	☐	☐
Is your board engaged in external indicator selection?	☐	☐	☐
Do you report external indicators to the board at least annually?	☐	☐	☐
Subtotal			

16–21 points = Excellent
10–16 points = Good Effort but Needs Work
0–9 points = Vulnerable to Change

Indicator Content			
Does the indicator set include measures relevant to the economy?			
Employment	☐	☐	☐
Industrial composition and health	☐	☐	☐

	Yes 3 points	Somewhat 2 points	No 0 points
Business investment	☐	☐	☐
Government finance	☐	☐	☐
Do you yourself know the local unemployment rate?	☐	☐	☐
Can you list the 10 largest employers in your area?	☐	☐	☐
Does the indicator set include measures of social environment?			
Demographics	☐	☐	☐
Poverty	☐	☐	☐
Income distribution	☐	☐	☐
Do you yourself know the percent of area population foreign born?	☐	☐	☐
Do you track indicators related to your particular cause (e.g., education, diabetes, etc.)	☐	☐	☐
Do you track indicators that measure the relative progress or position of your competitors or peers?	☐	☐	☐
Subtotal			

30–36 points = Excellent
20–29 points = Good Effort but Needs Work
0–19 points = Vulnerable to Change

Attitudes and Behaviors

	Yes 3 points	Somewhat 2 points	No 0 points
Have you surveyed client/constituent attitudes in the last year?	☐	☐	☐
Do you survey client/constituent attitudes at least quarterly?	☐	☐	☐
Do you compare survey results regularly over time?	☐	☐	☐
Is survey data a part of your decision making at least annually?	☐	☐	☐
Do you track comments about your organization on social media?	☐	☐	☐
Do you engage in those social media dialogues in real time?	☐	☐	☐
Subtotal			

14–18 points = Excellent
10–13 points = Good Effort but Needs Work
0–9 points = Vulnerable to Change

	Yes 3 points	Somewhat 2 points	No 0 points
Your Internal Environment			
Do you have program performance indicators?	☐	☐	☐
Do you review those indicators at least quarterly?	☐	☐	☐
Do you reexamine goals in light of indicator results at least annually?	☐	☐	☐
Do you match external indicators to internal program indicators at least annually?	☐	☐	☐
Do you update communication strategies using internal performance indicators at least annually?	☐	☐	☐
Do you measure organizational efficiency?	☐	☐	☐
Do you measure revenue by diversity of sources?	☐	☐	☐
Is there a single point of accountability for measuring and communicating internal indicator results?	☐	☐	☐
Do you report internal indicators to the board at least annually?	☐	☐	☐
Subtotal			

22–26 points = Excellent

12–21 points = Good Effort but Needs Work

0–11 points = Vulnerable to Change

About the Author

Dr. Susan Raymond is director of research and analytics for Changing Our World, Inc. Dr. Raymond is responsible for designing and conducting business operating environment research for both nonprofits and foundations, as well as developing business plans and program evaluations for new and existing institutions.

Dr. Raymond has extensive experience in research, analysis, and planning. Prior to joining Changing Our World in 1999, Susan held positions with the New York Academy of Sciences, where she founded the public policy program, The World Bank, Center for Public Resources, and U.S. Agency for International Development. In February of 2011, Women United in Philanthropy honored her with the Women in Excellence and Achievement Award.

Dr. Raymond is a member of the Advisory Board of the Center for Global Prosperity in Washington, D.C., a Faculty Lecturer at Columbia University, and a member of the Advisory Boards of The Global Index of Philanthropic Freedom and America's Unofficial Ambassadors. In 2012, the Director of the National Science Foundation appointed her to the Board of the Civilian Research and Development Foundation.

Dr. Raymond earned her BA Phi Beta Kappa from Macalester College and her MA and PhD from The Johns Hopkins University School of Advanced International Studies in a joint program with the School of Hygiene and Public Health. She has worked on philanthropy and economic development projects throughout Africa, the Middle East, and Eastern Europe, as well as in Russia and Asia.

Index